Eagle Eyes

The Development of Aerial Reconnaissance
In the United States

**Other Books
by
Jeannette Remak**

To Slip the Surly Bonds

Jeannette Remak and Joseph Ventolo, Jr.

Black Lightning
A-12 Declassified
XB-70 Valkyrie Ride to Valhalla
XB-70 the Return to Valhalla

Eagle Eyes

The Development of Aerial Reconnaissance
In the United States

Jeannette Remak

SPEAKING VOLUMES, LLC
NAPLES, FLORIDA
2019

Eagle Eyes

Copyright © 2019 by Jeannette Remak - Phoenix Aviation Research

Edited by Lt. Colonel (Ret.) Art Powell

All rights reserved. No part of this book may be reproduced or transmitted in any form or by any means without written permission.

Speaking Volumes is committed to publishing works of quality and integrity. We are proud to offer this book to our readers; however, the information, the words are the author's alone.

ISBN: 978-1-64540-091-2

This book is dedicated to

President George H.W. Bush—who's leadership helped to win the Cold War.
And to all the
Silent Warriors
who gave their lives to keep this country safe
during
WWI, WWII, Korea, Vietnam, the Cold War.
From the terrorist attacks of the
1993 World Trade Center Bombing
The USS COLE
and
9/11 WTC Attack, The Pentagon Attack, Flight 93 Shanksville, Pennsylvania,
and all involved with
Afghanistan, Iraq and the Mid-East today
and
on into the future.
We honor all those that
serve to protect the United States
in the silent world of collecting intelligence,
past, present and future.
&
Colonel Donn Byrnes (USAF) who has since flown west,
Thank you for being there the short time we had to
work on this book together.
God Bless the United States of America

Acknowledgments

The author would like to thank the following for all their support, input and knowledge and patience in the writing of this book:

Joseph Ventolo Jr. of Phoenix Aviation Research; Marti Ventolo-Phoenix Aviation Research; Mary Anne Ruggiero-Phoenix Aviation Research, The late Colonel Donn Byrnes, for all his knowledge and help with this book, while he was with us; Kevin Batterman, T.D. Barnes and Roadrunners Internationale for their service, their courage and the access to their histories; Frank Murray, USAF and CIA pilot of the A-12 Blackbird-Roadrunner Internationale Archivist, Mike Relja—SR-71 Blackbird Crew Chief, Ray Scalise-Fire Control Officer on the YF-12 Blackbird-USAF, The National Museum of the U.S. Air Force ™; The United States Navy Archives; The United States Air Force Archives; The Department of Defense Archives; The Boeing Corporation and Mike Lombardi, their archivist for all their help; The Lockheed Corporation; Central Intelligence Agency for their FOIA archives; DARPA-FOIA office for all their help; Eastman Kodak Corporation, The Library of Congress; Kevin Westling-SR-71 Crew Chief.

Special thanks to my editor Lt. Colonel (Ret.) Art Powell, thank you for your wise and formative editing, I couldn't have done this without your help. Many thanks and much appreciation.

If I have forgotten anyone, I do apologize. It was completely unintentional.

The author would also like to thank my little wingman, Shanghai, my Pekingese, for all his support and efforts in keeping his Mommy sane while writing this book.

And always…St. Jude, thank you for helping me when I needed it the most.

Table of Contents

Foreword 1
Introduction 3
Chapter One 8
Chapter Two 30
Chapter Three 52
Chapter Four 69
Chapter Five 78
Chapter Six 99
Chapter Seven 127
Chapter Eight 148
Chapter Nine 171
Chapter Ten 181
Chapter Eleven 200
Chapter Twelve 217
Chapter Thirteen 265
Chapter Fourteen 336
Chapter Fifteen 382
Epilogue 386
Bibliography 388

Foreword

"SPIES IN THE SKIES ARE DESPISED"

I would like to think I coined that phrase but probably not. Spying, in all forms, have prevented and started conflicts throughout the world. In battles, "he who controls the high ground" has a distinct advantage over his adversary by being able to foresee what his adversary is about to do or is planning to do. During the Civil War, both sides used tethered balloons to spy on each other. In World War I, fighter planes were converted to observation planes using cameras to take adversarial photos. Many of those aircraft were shot down. During World War II, fighter planes were stripped of all armament to make them faster and used to take photos of enemy installations, but still many were lost to ground fire. After World War II, we as a nation, entered into a "Cold War". Planes were now jet propelled and rocket propelled ground to air missiles were used to destroy them, as these jet planes hunted for intelligence. A dedicated spy plane was needed and one that could fly at altitudes greater than the ground to air missiles could achieve. Lockheed Skunk Works came up with the U-2, which met this requirement but it was slow. Nevertheless, it was used to spy on our adversaries and their ground to air missiles could not reach the altitude the plane flew at, so it spied with impunity. However, the ground to air missiles were modified to reach the altitude at which the U-2 flew, and took one of the U-2s out of the sky. The A-12 and the SR-71 were the next to come up to help the spying situation and with their speed of Mach 3 and their high altitude, nothing touched them . . . ever! They flew and delivered the photographs needed so urgently by U.S. intelligence.

As time went on, satellites took over spying and the A-12 and the SR-71 were retired. The U-2 was eventually brought back to life as the TR-1 and is still used, but does not fly directly over adversarial territory, but alongside their borders. Using advanced radars and cameras, they provide us with much needed "on the spot" information. The age of the unmanned spy planes remotely controlled by pilots thousands of miles, as well as small control units for in the field military usage is upon us. In the mill, are planes that will travel at hypersonic speed (Mach 5 and above). The future of spying does look good.

Ray Scalise
(Fire Control Officer (FCO) for the YF-12 Blackbird. First of the "second seaters" to fly the Blackbird at Mach 3 (certificate #7)

Introduction

The Art of Reconnaissance

What is the definition of reconnaissance? The Encarta dictionary says *"The exploration or examination of an area, especially to gather information about the strength and positioning of enemy forces. A preliminary inspection of a given area to obtain data concerning geographic, hydrographic or similar information prior to a detailed or a full survey."*

There has never been a time in civilized history that spies haven't been needed and used to compile military knowledge of the enemy position. In early times, the use of a local fisherman, a seller in a marketplace bazaar, or even a member of the royal family could be used to gain information on what the other side was doing regarding the next military campaign.

Back in the world of Ancient Egypt and Rome, all the battles fought depended on what information could be gotten from tortured prisoners or spies in disguise sent out to see what they could find. As times became more technically developed, inventions to help the spy and the need for knowing just what was happening on the other side of the track was just as necessary as air to breathe. Sun Tzu, the consummate Oriental warrior wrote in "The Art of War" that money was no object when it came to laying out the funds to create a spy system to serve the feudal lord. "To remain in ignorance simply because one grudges one hundred ounces of silver is the height of stupidity." Truer words couldn't be said, not even today. Sun Tzu even broke down the different levels of spies: the local spy, moles, double agents, doomed spies and the surviving spies. Spies are the battle commander's most precious tool. This would change only in the respect that as inventions came into play, the role of the spy would change to one of a technological nature.

In the later centuries, the need to know just what your adversary was thinking or doing had become a government pastime. Peace treaties and wars were based on it. Aerial Reconnaissance made its debut as far back as 14th century China, and the attempt to attach a man to a large kite "to attempt to overfly the enemy". Time, tide and technology began to look closer at getting into the air and having a bird's eye look around at the enemy. In the 1700's, the Montgolfier brothers began their experiments with hot air balloons. June 4, 1783 was historic as the Montgolfier brothers flew their balloons in a public demonstration. It was made of sackcloth with three thin layers of paper inside and was very successful. It wouldn't be long before the use of the balloon, as a reconnaissance tool would happen.

By the 19th century, balloons were used in the United States Civil War to oversee the battle formations and pass information down to the commanders. WWI arrived and with it brought the airplane that evolved into a weapon and aerial reconnaissance platform. Albeit, pilots may have had to buy their own cameras and film and they had a trial and error means of perfecting this new approach to photo taking but perfect it they did. The first successful photo reconnaissance flight was made on January 1915 of the La Basses Canal in France and it showed the French military the new offensive German trenches that were being built. The contribution of that photo-reconnaissance added to the success of the Allied attack on January 6, 1915. However, by 1918, photo-reconnaissance stagnated. The Royal Air Force of Britain did use aerial reconnaissance to map the countries of Iraq and India. The United States had tried to develop an interest in it. Yet, when it entered WWI in April 1917, the U.S. Army only had a handful of obsolete aircraft and some poorly trained pilots to fly them. There was one mission that tested the use of American aerial reconnaissance. It had to do with the tracking of that Mexican desperado, Pancho Villa in 1916. The mission was not successful and showed just how needy the U.S. aerial reconnaissance service was.

However, airplanes weren't the only means of flying. The Germans soon developed the next stage in aerial reconnaissance, dirigibles. The German Navy version was the Zeppelin, along with the German Army's "Schutte Lang" airships. The United States also experimented with airships. The U.S. Navy's "Macon" was a rigid airship used for scouting. It also served as an "aircraft carrier" by launching and recovering the Sparrowhawk biplane. Macon's sister "Akron" was a helium filled dirigible; she could also launch and recover the Sparrowhawk biplane. Both Macon and Akron were lost in storms at sea.

Fragility was the main issue with the use of the airships. The beginning of WWII brought with it a pronouncement. Not long before the outset of World War II, General Oberst Freiherr Werner Von Fritsch, commander and chief of the German army in the early years of Nazi regime said almost prophetically *"The next war will be won by the military organization with the most effective photo reconnaissance."* Truer words couldn't have been said. In 1938-9 Germany had the lead in the field regarding picture taking from the air. The Dornier DO 17 and Junkers Ju 88 did the job for the Germans.

Many aircraft during WWII were doing double duty as both bombers and reconnaissance platforms. The B-17 and later the B-29 were known for this. The Korean War of the 1950's showed the lack of U.S. aerial reconnaissance and the effect it had. This hole in intelligence allowed North Korea to gain a greater hold on territory with the aid of the Communist Chinese before the United States even found out. The need for being able to see and interpret from the sky was now becoming mandatory for winning the day. As technology improved and rockets came into being in WWII with the German V-2 rocket. The U.S. developed rockets and a new concept which created satellites, the proverbial eyes in the sky.

President Dwight D. Eisenhower was pleased with the satellite plan and supported the process of getting the satellites up into space. With the help of Werner von Braun, late of the Third Reich to take over building rockets for the U.S. The U.S. later reached out and held the moon in her hands in the 1960s with the Apollo program.

The products of the Apollo technology allowed the U.S. to create more sophisticated satellites. The DISCOVERER/CORONA satellites better known as KEYHOLE flew and served until the late 1980s with tremendous success. While the satellites were flying, the CIA also entered the game of aerial reconnaissance. The Lockheed U-2 high altitude, subsonic spy plane relied on its altitude to keep from getting shot down. However, on May 1, 1960, to the chagrin of President Eisenhower, Francis Gary Powers was shot down in a flight over the USSR. The Blackbird was also a Kelly Johnson/Lockheed-Skunk Works creation. She was to become the fastest aircraft ever built. Flying at high altitudes of close to 90,000 ft and at speeds of Mach 3, the A-12 kept missiles off her tail. She was never touched and remains the fastest aircraft known today. Politics ended the OXCART/A-12 program, No one knew about the OXCART for over 40 years, which showed how deeply the program had been buried in the CIA archives. It wasn't until the 1990s, as the A-12s were released from storage and sent to museums, that curators and aviation buffs alike began to question just what was this aircraft about. Many thought it was the SR-71, however it wasn't until aviation researchers started the declassification process on Project OXCART that we really found out what a magnificent creature the A-12 actually was.

From the A-12 came the next Blackbird, the SR-71. The SR-71 was an offshoot of the A-12 Blackbird. This two-seater aircraft was a bit slower than the A-12, but did carry a vast array of sensors for aerial reconnaissance. It was the USAF version of the deeply classified A-12. The 1960s and 1970s world of aerial reconnaissance was both revealing and creative as far as technology went. The best was yet to come. The late 1980s and 1990s brought a much different type of reconnaissance animal, the UAV. UAV translates into Unmanned Aerial Vehicle or pilotless cockpit aircraft, in short, a drone. No longer was a pilot needed in the aircraft. Now he flew remotely by video from a mobile van or room, miles away from the heat of battle. That was a major step in technology. No longer would a pilot have to risk his life flying over enemy territory with the possibility of being shot down. This was a huge development and it did change the state of aerial reconnaissance.

Today, aerial reconnaissance has developed into not only pictures but also picking targets. The UAV Predator drone has lived up to its name and now carries Hellfire missiles for picking off prime targets, be it buildings or terrorists, all from directions given from miles away. How has this unique advantage of the UAV changed the face of aerial reconnaissance and is it a good change? What is lost by not having a pilot with eyes in the sky? In this book, we will explore the many different types of aerial reconnaissance and how they evolved, and we will look at the question: Is it necessary to have a pilot's eyes in the cockpit overseeing some situations, or will satellites and UAVs rule the day?

The U-2 decked out in air superiority grey scanning the enemy
(USAF)

Chapter One

Chinese painting: Kite flying during the Qingming Festival.
Note the party of people on the kite directly in the center of the painting
(Author collection)

The Start of Aerial Intelligence Gathering

The beginnings of flight gave nations the chance to view from the air what was happening behind enemy lines. It was a monumental step in the planning of strategic and tactical battles, allowed for nations to view the order of battle[1] of an enemy from the air where they couldn't be touched and became the solid base for the art of intelligence gathering. Reconnaissance is the sauce, but intelligence is the meat that nations thrive on. Every nation revolves around the need for this information or intelligence. In the simplest sense, knowledge about the current trends, actions,

---

[1] Order of Battle—Shows the formal order or military command, structure, position of personnel and what type of equipment, how many pieces and the formation of troops on the battlefield

civilian or military may affect a country's outlook on the world. Such information identifies, describes and defines the situation and supports making the decisions needed. Intelligence is the description. It is a product that results from collection, analysis of photographs or images and the interpretation of those materials

In today's world of twenty-four-hour cable TV news, there isn't much that is missed. With cell phone cameras in hand, many enterprising reporters go to the most dangerous places on earth during wars to cover the news and get it back to their stations. We are now able to see within hours how Syria murdered so many children, women and men, by the use of chemical weapons and watch the rebels fight for their country live and in color on TV, is truly a miracle of technology. It's also a method of reconnaissance, while many would not consider it so. It's the ability to see the enemy real time that makes the point. Intelligence of any sort is gold to the party that needs to know. The feudal lords, as far back as 14th century China, tried using a man tied to a kite to further the ability to know what his warring brethren was doing, not successfully we might add. However, it was a view of things to come.

In Sun Tzu's "Art of War", the statements are solid tactical, military common sense. In the last chapter of the book "The Use of Spies" details the five different versions of spies and what they are supposed to accomplish:

    a. Local Spies—employing the inhabitants of an enemy's territory.
    b. Moles—making use of the officials of the enemy.
    c. Double Agents—getting hold of enemy spies and turning them to your purpose
    d. Doomed Spies—doing certain things openly for the purpose of deception and allowing our spies to know and report to the

enemy. Of course, this meant certain death when they were caught.

e. Surviving Spies—those who bring home the news from the enemy camp.

Now, add all this to the ability to see from above what your enemy is up to. You could almost knock out four of the five positions listed above. That's quite a heady thought for a commander on the ground. Where there is a will, there was a way and that is precisely how aerial reconnaissance came into being along with the art of photography. Both went hand in hand to create the one, vital tool in the realm of warfare…aerial reconnaissance.

The Role of the Military in the Process of National Security

The discussion of the military and how it uses the tools of reconnaissance in the view of a nation's security is vital to understanding the reconnaissance/intelligence factor.

During the Civil War, President Lincoln relied on the military, and actually created national policy due to the Military's influence in 1863. Military influence in national policy formation was also evident during the occupation of the Philippines, right after the Spanish American war. During World War I, General John J. Pershing was given a wide berth in dealing directly with the allies and in establishing a requirement on the government at home. Shortly after World War I, both Generals March and Pershing, proposed plans to Congress for maintaining an Army that was basically stronger than the existing pre-World War I establishment. These plans were considered before they were rejected.

These few examples above just identify the accepted role, before World War II, that the military should play a role in the formation of a national security policy. Only when the threat of war is made, did the armed forces have responsibility for executing the policy. The basic absence of any threats to the nation, apart from the Civil War (at the time) left the military with only the routine problem of defense, internal protection of the interior and planning a passive support of an isolationist foreign policy. Neither the structure of the government or the essentials of a military mission compelled sustained involvement of the military's national policy. As time wore on and the needs of the country changed, so did the need for reconnaissance and intelligence to work hand in hand. One fed the other and each was urgently important to protecting the nation.

Drawing of the Montgolfier bros. and their first balloon flight
(Author Collection copyright free)

Photography, The Horse Before the Cart

Thanks to the Montgolfier Brothers, in France, back in September of 1783, the hot air balloon became a fact of life. With the creation of the balloon sometime later, Andre' Giroud de Villette made the first flight and realized just what the potential of flight could be. While de Villette was on the right track thinking aerial reconnaissance could be used for military purposes, it took a lot longer before it actually came to pass. In 1794, aerial reconnaissance had its real start for the French Army when on June 2, 1794 Colonel Jean-Marie Coutelle, the commander of the French "air force" per say, made his first balloon flight to observe the enemies battlefield actions on the progress to the northeast city of Maubeuge. It made the difference and allowed the French to win that battle. The other part of the equation was photography and that too, was a distance away.

A daguerreotype by Daguerre of the Midwest river and riverboats
(NY Public Library)

Eagle Eyes

Louis Jacques Daguerre was responsible for bringing the imaging process to the world. Daguerreotypes were the first image processing method created in 1835. Actually, it was an accidental unearthing of the process when he left an exposed plate of chemicals in his cabinet and forgot about it. A few days later, he found that a latent image had actually developed on the plate. Daguerre figured out that the image presented itself due to the presence of mercury vapor that was leeching out of a broken thermometer left in the cabinet. This proved that a latent image could be made and exposure time could be cut down from eight hours to thirty minutes. This was a huge breakthrough. By August 19, 1839, Daguerre made public the process in front of the French Academy of Sciences and sealed the first process of holding an image onto a plate. The process later developed by the use of the "Sheffield Plate" which used a fusion of cold rolled cladden. This is a process that heated and rolled out silver foil along with a copper support. The surface of the Daguerreotype behaves much like a mirror and is extremely fragile which was a huge disadvantage in displaying the product. The image had to be placed into a glass case to keep it safe. The process was slow and tedious and couldn't be used to document any type of movement of an image. As the process developed, lenses that had been developed for the "camera obscura"[2] were slow. Using silver iodide and "fuming" the silver plate with iodine vapor now created the plates used for the latent image. This did allow for a better exposure, yet the time was still very slow.

This process was good for taking images of buildings or portraits.

Photography improved by 1841 by the development of larger aperture lenses, which allowed in more light and the exposure plates being used were now being treated with bromine, chlorine and light sensitive crystals

---

[2] Camera Obscura-is a darkened box that used a convex lens or aperture to project the image of an object onto a screen or slide. The first camera used in the world.

of silver iodide, silver bromide and silver chloride. The exposure time was shortened even more.

The advertisement for the first Kodak camera
(Eastman Kodak Bettman/Corbis)

Kodak—The Start of Everyday Photography

As time moved on and the photography processes changed, cameras and glass plates got smaller and more effective. The process really began to move upward when George Eastman stepped into the picture.

Eastman was born in Waterville, New York. His family wasn't rich and he was a high school dropout. He was left to support two sisters and his mother who was widowed. Eastman started work in an office at the age of 14 as the ALL-AROUND office boy and later moved on to an insurance company. Eastman's talent for turning things around for the better was obvious by the time he hit his early twenties. At the age of 24, he purchased a wet plate photographic set. If you could imagine the size of this camera, by today's standards, it would be equal to a microwave oven and that wasn't all that went with the package. He had all the paraphernalia to create his own wet film plates. There were bottles of chemicals, glass plates and just tons of other equipment. Eastman took one look at all of this and made the decision to try to make this whole process easier and more portable. The first thing he did was to create a company that sold dry film plates to the public. This really was a revolutionary idea and simplified photography for all to enjoy. That was one step that was taken out of the equation and that put money in Eastman's pocket.

As time went on, Eastman continued to create and refine the photographic process. He was determined to make photography something the everyday person could use and enjoy without all the hassle. He did just that. In 1885, his advertisements announced that "shortly there will be introduced a new sensitive film which it is believed will prove an economical and convenient substitute for glass dry plates in both outdoor and studio work." The idea of using a roll holder for the film, grabbed on and Eastman was on his way to creating a dynasty.

However, there were a few glitches to the new process, the paper was not suitable as a carrier for the film emulsion. The paper grain was likely to be duplicated in the photo image, which was not conducive to clear photographic reproduction. Eastman came up with another idea.

Eastman's plan to coat the paper with a layer of plain, soluble gelatin, and then with a layer of impenetrable light-sensitive gelatin was the magic bullet. After image exposure and development of the film, the gelatin bearing the image would be stripped from the paper then transferred to a sheet of clear gelatin, and varnished with collodion—a cellulose solution that would take shape as a tough, flexible film surface.

While Eastman went on to perfect this transparent roll film process and the roll holder, he changed the entire sway of his work and established the base on which his fame in photography would be built on. His mother helped him to create the KODAK logo. The logo came from his mother's idea to use an anagram set. The concept was to keep the name simple and strong and make it so unique that it could never be discerned as anything else. Eastman loved the letter "K". In his words, "It seemed a strong, decisive sort of letter." The same went for the distinctive red and yellow colors in the Kodak logo which was developed in the 1930s.

Eastman was on the way to creating one of the most identifiable companies in the world. Eastman said, "When we started out with our scheme of film photography, we expected that everybody who used glass plates would take up films. However, we found that the number, which did so was relatively small. In order to make a large business we would have to reach the general public." Eastman was determined to do just that. He said, *"You press the button, we do the rest."* That was the milestone that Eastman placed on the map. He unveiled the Kodak camera in 1888. It took only a year and the jingle became one of the best known phrases in American advertising. The Kodak camera and film company became one of the largest grossing companies in the world. It had supported the American military from WWII right into current day operations, working with digital imaging and satellites. Eastman's designs made the use of photography an everyday item. Anyone could use it, that included pilots who were flying aircraft.

The balloon *Enterprise* flown by Lowe during the Civil War
(University of So. Carolina)

The First Aerial Reconnaissance Platform

In April of 1861, the United States was in the beginnings of a very painful Civil War. Literally, eight days into the fighting, Professor Thaddeus Lowe of Cincinnati, Ohio attempted to cross the Atlantic Ocean in his hot air balloon. His test flight originated from Cincinnati, Ohio. The *"Enterprise"* balloon was inflated on April 19th. According to Lowe, who did not have time to change clothes, he rushed to his balloon followed by Murat Halstead and a Mr. Palmer who was the owner of the newspaper called "The Commercial." While the final preparations were being made, Mr. Halstead threw a number of still damp newspapers into the balloon basket that announced Lowe would depart that morning. Halstead was eager to show how quickly he could get the "news" out with "The Commercial." However, due to some air currents and miscalculations, he actually ended up in Union, South Carolina, some five hundred miles from his Ohio starting point.

Initially, Lowe wanted to make it to Washington D.C. and then try to cross the Atlantic, but it wasn't to be. Lowe ended up with his hot air balloon, *Enterprise*, in the South, right in the middle of the Civil War.

Lowe tried to find out what State he was in, but got no notice from the people on the ground as he called down to them in earnest from his balloon. Lowe finally put down on the Kelton Plantation in Union, South Carolina. In his best formal dress to greet the expected hordes of admirers, Lowe brought the *Enterprise* to rest on the South Carolinian earth. Yet, there were no hordes of admirers only some very frightened local folks who hid behind their log cabins in terror, yelling "take that hellish contrivance elsewhere."

After Lowe secured *Enterprise* to the ground, the locals carrying muskets, threatening destruction to that "devil" that could travel through the air, met him. Yet, there was one fearless woman in the crowd who helped Lowe to secure the balloon and helped Lowe through the local crowd. She was about six feet tall and assured all those present that there was no danger in the balloon or in Lowe himself. She basically called all the men gathered at the balloon landing cowards, since the rest of the brave men had left to fight for the war. Lowe finally got to town, where a hotelkeeper did recognize him from a trip he took up north recently. As the local newspaper editor wrote on Lowe's story. Lowe proved the truth of his tale by presenting the newspapers that he had brought with him. The townspeople were still not convinced by Lowe's story and were yelling to Lowe that they would like to "tar and feather the Yankee!"

Lowe was finally taken to meet the town mayor and it was here that he was treated like the hero he was. The mayor arranged for a "golden passport" that would allow Lowe to travel through the rest of Confederate territory without incident.

After all of the commotion was over, Lowe took off again in faithful *Enterprise* and headed for Washington D.C. He wanted to offer his services in aeronautics to the Union Army where he felt he could make a significant difference. In order to show what he was worth, Lowe arranged for a demonstration to prove to President Lincoln that aeronautics truly was a usable asset to an army. Lowe set up the balloon with wireless equipment. He brought *Enterprise* up to 500 feet altitude and sent President Lincoln a telegraph right there on the National Mall from the balloon. Lincoln was so impressed he created the "U.S. Army Civilian Balloon Corp." in June of 1861[3].

Lowe did do reconnaissance flights for the Union Army at the very important Battle of Bull Run, the Battle of Seven Pines, Chancherville, Gaines Mills and Fredericksburg, along with other battles during the Civil War. Lowe continued to serve in the Union Army and created what would someday be the concept of a modern air force. He retired from his position in 1863, leaving the legacy of what could be seen from the air as valuable to any army fighting a battle. Aerial Reconnaissance had its foot in the proverbial door.

---

[3] Hoehling, Mary Duprey: Thaddeus Lowe, America's one-man Air Corps; pp107-108, Messner 1958

Jeannette Remak

Telegraph message sent to President Lincoln
from Lowe in the Enterprise Balloon (NARA)

The Wright Brothers flight in 1903 at Kill Devil Hills
(Nat'l Museum of the USAF ™)

The Wright Brothers Enter the Picture . . . Literally

While balloons opened up a new world in which the military could now find out what the enemy was doing in detail, the Wright Brothers, Wilbur and Orville, had already found the realm of flight in their first aircraft.

The brothers' base camp at Kill Devil Hills, North Carolina was the fortress of their dreams of flight. The brothers went through weeks of delays and problems caused by everything from the wrong wind direction to broken propeller shafts during their engine tests. The prop shafts were swapped out for new ones and that only cost them two trips back to Dayton, Ohio and more time on the ground. However, December 13, 1903's flight attempt wasn't made because it was a Sunday and the brothers were religious about keeping the Lord's Day. On December 14, 1903, Wilbur won the coin toss and made a three-second flight in the Wright Flyer but stalled after takeoff, which resulted in some damage to the aircraft. However, the weather that day was perfect. There were more problems with the Wright Flyer. Wilber cabled home to his sister Katharine saying, *". . . only partial success. The power is ample, and but for a trifling error due to lack of experience with this machine and this method of starting, the machine would undoubtedly have flown beautifully."* More fixes were made to the aircraft and finally on December 17, 1903 on a freezing cold day, four flights were made successfully. Orville described the flight; *"Wilbur started the fourth and last flight at just about 12 o'clock. The first few hundred feet were up and down, as before, but by the time three hundred feet had been covered, the machine was under much better control. The course for the next four or five hundred feet had but little undulation. However, when out about eight hundred feet the machine began pitching again, and, in one of its darts downward, struck the ground. The distance over the ground was measured to be 852 feet; the time of the flight was 59 seconds. The frame supporting the front rudder was badly broken, but the main part of the machine was not injured at all. We estimated that the machine could be put in condition for flight again in about a day or two."*

History had been made and the Wright Brothers brought the aircraft into reality. As the Wright Brothers moved on with the Flyer, they started touring various U.S. states and even overseas. In 1909, Wilbur Wright actually took photos while flying over Cento Celli, Italy, using one of the first motion picture cameras. The sad part of the story is that the United States Military was very slow to decide to take on the new Wright Brothers aircraft even though the brothers were pitching it hard. However, many of the military leaders in Europe were not wasting any time in trying to mold this new tool into a working system for its purposes. On Oct 23rd, 191.

An Italian military captain by the name of Captain Carlo Piazza took off in his French Bleriot aircraft to check up on the Turkish gun placements in the Italian –Turkish skirmish that was going on. He tried a couple of times but failed and came down to land. He decided to take the camera and mount it to the belly of his Bleriot aircraft with the lens pointed downward to the ground. It proved to be a great success. However, the process itself was left to idle. No one really took enough of an interest in the concept. That was going to change rapidly.

A World War I Graflex camera
(U. S. Army)

World War I and the Beginning of True Military Aerial Reconnaissance

Europe was in a very tense situation before the start of WWI. Many feel that the assassination of Archduke Franz Ferdinand and his wife on June 28, 1914 was the true start of everything falling apart. However, some of it had to do with treaties that were in play at the time. Austria/Hungary was looking to work with Germany on a promise that would allow a war to commence between Serbia and possibly Russia. Austria/Hungary, however, wasn't planning on Russia, which was Serbia's ally to jump into the fight. Austria/ Hungary was looking to get back some of the land that it lost in the Balkans. The catch was Serbia seemed to agree with the "request", but it did have a few questions regarding some provisions. These provisions didn't go over and pushed Austria/Hungary to get into fighting mode. As a series of small national treaties soon collapsed, the small "war" with Serbia that Austria/Hungary planned, ultimately turned into the "Great War" known as "World War I."

As this war broke out in Europe, it would soon draw in the United States as well. At the start of World War I, it didn't take long for the British, French and Germans to get the message that those who had "eyes in the skies" meant wins in battles on the ground. The British were one of the first countries to jump on the aerial reconnaissance wagon by planting some twenty-four aerial reconnaissance aircraft in German skies during the French invasion. In preparing for war, the European armies had expected to use balloons for observation along with dirigibles and some aircraft for scouting missions. By 1912, the British made the decision to take all their dirigibles and turn them to the Navy while the Army worked with the airplanes and the balloon kites. The War was only a few weeks old when aircraft were soon to become the commodity to have.

One of the true heroes of early aviation and its soon to be partner photography, was Sergeant A.V. Laws of the British Royal Engineers and the Royal Flying Corps. He took the first photographs from a dirigible called "Beta". These photographs actually were overlapping images, and to many, this was the birth of military aerial reconnaissance. If anything, it was one of the first attempts to map terrain from aerial photographs.

The camera lenses of the day weren't exactly the precise works of art we see today. The lenses back then were known to distort images on the edges of the photograph, so only center sections of the photos were of any use. The idea of taking photos at different intervals actually gave a continuous strip of images that could be put together to make one long image. It was a great idea. However, because these early lenses did not have the depth of field necessary, many of the images could not be relied on for precise height or depth. Much like the old fashioned stereopticon[4] the images that Laws took could be viewed as three-dimensional by overlapping the images. This was a good system for mapping, but it wasn't going to be what was needed in trying to catch the enemy's secrets. Sgt. Laws continued working on the process and while doing so, he uncovered many secrets and new methods of catching images from the air. Part of the problem was that technology had not yet caught up with the thinking. Lenses of the type Laws felt would be needed weren't even available yet. There were only two firms that were making lenses at the time and that was Goertz-Anschutz and Dallmeyer, both companies were in Germany, and Kodak in the United States. While they were the only two companies working in Europe, France was trying to make a start, however, they weren't interested in helping anyone but themselves.

There was also the problem of what type of camera to use. There was the Kodak box camera, which was strictly an amateur's camera. Even so, while the men that flew were busy taking photos of themselves standing in front of their aircraft on the ground, some were trying to find a way to adapt it to the aircraft so that they could take photos from altitude. Experiments with these box cameras ran rampant. There was so much to think of. There were the angles from the sun that would produce problems on the oblique photos which were shot from the side. The only use they had was that it gave the ground troops some mapping information, but nothing that would help as far as finding out what the enemy was doing.

---

[4] The Stereopticon, which was actually an offshoot of the "Magic Lantern" of the later 1700 early 1800s, actually held a concave mirror at the back and a light source in the front and would allow a hand painted image or later on a photographic plate to be displayed through a lens in the front and the image would appear on a wall or screen.

Vertical photos were finally considered to be of use when it came to any form of mapmaking. As the time and testing went on, the Germans, decided that the oblique angle would serve them, after fixing them to work as a vertical image with special instruments. The vertical camera looked like the way to go and it was used extensively.

More Aerial Observations

The aerial reconnaissance methods that the British were bringing into the war showed great value. By September, the Royal Flying Corp found a gap between the German armies and the exposed right flank of the advancing troops, which set up the "Battle of the Marne" and averted an early German victory. Both the French and German pilots were super active. The French flyers had put more than 10,000 reconnaissance missions behind them in the first months of the war. It didn't take long for the French to grab hold of the reins of the aerial reconnaissance trade and turn it into grief for the Germans. The Germans were also getting something out of this new tool of war. Field Marshall Eric Ludendorff was quoted as saying "Better shooting by means of aerial observations." With the despicable trench warfare in the winter of 1914 and the German spring offensive of 1918, the use of aircraft for observation developed into a more usable variant of being able to see just what was going on in the trenches and realign troop concentrations to support a battle. Between 1914 and 1918, another dramatic breakthrough happened. Sgt. Laws of the RAF, with tireless work and testing, made it obvious that things really needed to be revamped. There were so many problems. The aircraft would shake terribly, the mounts used to hold the camera were not stable enough. Everything was tried to stabilize the camera, but it was something that was not going to rectify itself until technology caught up.

British Aerial Reconnaissance

The British were the first to step up with the Royal Flying Air Corp. In August of 1914, their use of aircraft to do the work of aerial reconnaissance brought the most accurate reports of the German troop movement.

On August 22, 1914, Captain Leo Charlton and Lieutenant V.N. Wadham of the British Royal Air Force, were the ones to report that General Alexander von Kluck's German army was about to surround the British Expeditionary Forces contrary to all the other intelligence that was received. The aerial reconnaissance proved out to be very fruitful. Prior to the use of photography, sketches were being made of critical sites from aircraft above the ground and not always accurately. The British high command did listen to their pilots and started a quick retreat out of the area which saved thousands of British lives.

Approximately a week later, the French used aerial reconnaissance to find that the Germans had moved eastward towards Paris. While the intelligence officers didn't quite buy it, General Joseph Gallieni, Chief of Command for Paris forces and a huge fan of aviation also listened to his pilots. Orders were sent to the French troops to move against the German line that was already exposed. The first Battle of Marne took place and the French pushed the Germans away from the borders of Paris.

More reports from aerial reconnaissance came in from Poland. The reconnaissance presented that the Russian Army had helped the Germans and Austrians to stop the advance at the Battle of Tannenberg. It ended pushing the armies fighting on both sides to new defensive positions and into the trenches. By 1915, the first of the aerial reconnaissance cameras came on the scene. It was designed by Lt. Colonel Jonathan Moore Cuthbert Brabazon (British title-First Baron of Brabazon) of the British forces and built by the Thornton Pickard Ltd. Company.

Of course, if one side was using aircraft, it was only common sense that the other side of the battle line was using them, too. It wasn't an easy job, as there were many logistical problems in trying to fly and observe. There were two people in the aircraft, one as pilot and the other as the cameraman or observer. There were problems with both men trying to communicate with each other. Many times, there was no place to land safely and packages were dropped from the aircraft to waiting hands on the ground. It wasn't until 1915 that the telegraph was added so that the observer could send Morse code signal to the ground.

The war was locked into place, actually into the trenches, the most hateful part of this war. The pilots and their observers were developing their basic roles in how to do reconnaissance. It was a learning curve to be sure. Sometimes, aerial observers reported on their own army, which led to confusion. Of course, there were also times when actions on the ground were misinterpreted in the air. Yet, even with the terror of antiaircraft guns shooting from below and dog fights in the air, the reconnaissance flights continued.

Eagle Eyes

The First Aero Squadron in the Punitive Expedition 1915
(National Archives)

Chapter Two

The United States Enters World War I

The First Aero Squadron

On April 6, 1917, the United States officially entered World War I, sending some two million U.S. soldiers into the fight with their British, French and Russian allies. That wasn't all that they sent. While the United States was slow on the learning curve in developing aerial reconnaissance in its own right, it did have a start. However, the U.S. Army lacked any form of air intelligence organization.

On July 18, 1914 Congress created the Aviation Section of the United States Army. It was called the *"United States Army Signal Corp."* It was going to cover anything that had to do with intelligence. That meant using and developing aircraft, use of dirigibles, balloons and any other means of collecting intelligence. The Air Service as it was known, was to provide coverage for the Army infantry section by informing them of battle situations and order of battle for the enemy. While it looked good on paper, it did crawl along to finally attaining some form of reality. World War I just pushed it into gear. While there was some action prior to WWI to test aircraft in battle situations, the Air Service did have a mission.

In April of 1915, the First Aero Squadron was sent down to the border of Texas and New Mexico to seek out the infamous Pancho Villa[5]. Villa was conducting raids between the borders of New Mexico and Texas. On March 12, 1916, following a March 9th raid by Villa and his

---

[5] Pancho Villa was a Mexican revolutionary general prominent in the Mexican revolution of November 1910

men, the First Aero Squadron was given their marching orders to move down to Columbus, New Mexico and began to assemble their aircraft that had been shipped from Ft. Sam Houston in Texas. The missions flown were to determine the location of Villa's trenches around the town of Matamoras and to watch the area surrounding it. The plan was for the detachment was to locate Villa's gun trenches.

In March of 1916, Captain Benjamin Foulois, the commander of the First Aero Squadron, had grown his detachment to the level strength of one hundred twenty enlisted men and sixteen officers. Called a "punitive expedition", Brigadier John J. Pershing led the group. Pershing knew that there were many problems, the first starting with the aircraft that they were using the Curtis JN-3, which were actually JN-2s that were refitted. There were eight JN-3s in the squadron. With only one civilian mechanic, some eighty enlisted men and eleven officers the squadron had only half of what it needed to do the job properly. On March 19, 1916, orders were sent from the Commander at Nuevo Casas Grande, Mexico that the squadron had to be ready for duty. The aircraft all left at approximately 5:15P.M. One aircraft had to turn back due to engine problems. It wasn't long before darkness set in, separating the rest of the team, with each of them landing at different locations. It also didn't take long to find out that the aircraft were not capable for the job. On March 20th one crew found out that there were not able to clear the Sierra Madre foothills. Another reconnaissance flight turned back because of engine failure. Another crash-landed while on duty. On it went, as the JN-3s failed, crashed or just sat on the field, stalled and useless.

The mission was limited because the aircraft were just not up to the heat and dust in the desert and far too fragile to carry any payload or climb a mountain. In short, the expedition was a disaster and General John J. Pershing knew it. The United States needed to look at the lessons learned by this expedition and step up its aerial service quickly. World War I was not going to wait for them.

The Aircraft and the Camera

Germany had become the first of the countries to adopt a specialized aerial camera for its balloons in 1913. The Germans were already ahead of the game when it came to thinking about aerial reconnaissance as a distinct tool of war.

The Royal Air Corp, of course, had the brilliance of Sgt. Laws who had devised a camera with a six-inch focal length that would give them a 4"x5" photo. His camera could produce a usable photo at six thousand feet in altitude. By the end of 1915, the Royal Air Corp was capable of producing a camera that could give them a 7"x9" negative. However, pilots needed to get higher to get away from enemy fire and the higher they went, produced a bigger problem for picture taking and that went for anyone exploring the use of photography in aircraft. The next step would be to start training the people that would interpret these images. That would be an art form in itself.

Back in the United States, at the Army Air Service, there was a complement of sixty aviators. Not a one of them had ever flown any of the modern aircraft the Allies were using, and definitely had no instrumentation experience. The United States owned some two hundred aircraft that were all useless. While Congress had given some $54 million to create 13 squadrons for the war effort, it was a drop in the bucket compared to what was really needed. President Woodrow Wilson received a telegraph from Premier Alexandre Ribot of France explaining that the United States didn't comprehend the immensity of the war's scale. Ribot told Wilson that they needed an American Air Force of at least 4,500 aircraft, plus 5,000 aviators to man the planes and 50,000 mechanics to service the aircraft. Ribot felt that they needed this by at least 1918 in order to win the day. On June 24, 1917, Congress gave the military $640 million to build some 354 squadrons. It was the largest amount ever given out by Congress for anything. To support this, Wilson created the Aircraft Production Board to build the needed planes. However, the U.S. didn't have anything remotely resembling factories necessary to do this. There were a few shops available, but no work force trained to handle building the aircraft. There was also the question of materiel to make the aircraft. Spruce was the main wood used. To attempt to produce enough to support this huge mandate of aircraft was a nightmare. President Wilson again stepped in and created a Bureau of Aircraft Production in 1918 with John Ryan, a civilian, who was the president of Anaconda Copper. Ryan was put in command, with a separate division for the Military run by Major General William Kenly. Yet, the offices were not joined and since there was no one person responsible for both offices, it wasn't until four months later that Wilson appointed Ryan the Director of the Air Service and added another position to the post as second assistant to the Secretary of War, in an attempt to bring cohesion to the two departments. Even though Wilson tried to bring the aircraft production up to speed, it was falling short of every goal it needed to meet.

On April 6. 1917, the United States declared war on Germany. Major General Peyton C. Marsh who was the wartime chief of staff recalled that when the U.S. went to war, the Army intelligence organization had exactly two clerks and one civilian manning the desk.

On May 23, 1917, it was decided that the General Staff's War College division would open a military intelligence section in February of 1918. This became a separate military section was known as MID (Military Intelligence Division). By August of 1918, the Army approved of the unit by raising it to one of the forty coordinate divisions of the General Staff, which ran under the assistant Chief of Staff of Intelligence or G-2. The MID became the operating agency which supported the policy making of the G-2. By the end of the war the MID consisted of some two hundred eighty-two officers, twenty-nine non-commissioned officers and nine hundred forty-eight civilians. For a short time, the Air Force legend, then Major Henry (Hap) Arnold, was in charge of the MID.

Images of the various ways that photos were taken in WWI and later put together as a photo mosaic for photo interpretation
(Courtesy of the USAF)

Goddard and the U.S. Cameras

General Billy Mitchell was already a hero to all in the Army Air Corp. He met with Lieutenant George Goddard at Goddard's home base at Carlstrom Airfield in Arcadia, Florida. Goddard had been working on the aerial reconnaissance theory, along with building and reworking the cameras that were being used to make them more adaptable for use in the aircraft. The K-1 Folmer-Schwing aerial camera and mount had just been installed on an aircraft by Goddard. Mitchell had brought a special guest with him to meet Goddard, that person was Edward Steichen[6], the famed photographer. Mitchell was pleased with what he found and all that he had heard about the lieutenant and his experiments with cameras and aircraft. It didn't take long for Goddard to find himself out of Florida and into McCook Field at Dayton, Ohio in charge of aerial research for the Air Service Engineering division. It wasn't all heaven for Goddard though. He wanted to be a pilot in the worst way and found himself far away from that goal and now tied to the camera and aircraft. It would take time, but eventually he would gain his wings. Since the United States was already involved in WWI, they were trying desperately to find a way to gain some aerial reconnaissance experience quickly. The Air Service started classes on how to use aerial photography in the field. They were trained on the Folmer–Schwing camera, that took 4"x5" negatives and held a twelve-image magazine. The camera contained a pistol grip and could take oblique photos from an open cockpit. The French and English helped out the training classes by showing thousands of images that they had taken from their aircraft which really brought the idea home. However, the images were good, but how did you train someone to interpret the information that those photographs held and make it useful to the troops? How did you figure out what they were telling you about the enemy? That would be the next step: training the photographic interpreters.

While training and fighting were going on, the Eastman Kodak Company was now running the research and development of camera construction up in Rochester, New York. Dr. Kenneth Mees was an Eastman Kodak scientist considered by many to be the best in the world. He had developed Panchromatic film[7] and was the first to come up with the

---

[6]Edward Steichen was a photographer, painter and curator of paintings and photographs. He often worked with Alfred Steigliz another famous 20th century photographer.
[7] Black and while film emulsion that is sensitive to all wavelengths of visible light.

concept of roll film for the aerial cameras, making life in the cockpit much easier.

The camera used during the war was the Folmer-Schwing, which was designated the K-1. It had a twenty-inch focal length and could take a magazine which held a roll of film good for some seventy-five exposures. This camera became the backbone of the U.S. military and other U.S. services. There was also the T-1 Bagley camera. There is a story behind the scenes here. As usual, and even so today, there was a "failure to communicate" between the various government services. It was nothing new in 1917 and even after the First World War, it lasted right up into today's communication efforts. The Corp of Engineers at McCook field hadn't bothered to give the news to the Air Service (which they abhorred) because they felt the Air Service was encroaching on their territory that happened to be mapmaking. The only way the Air Service managed to get a T-1 camera occurred when it was left behind in a spare aircraft that they had retained. It didn't take Lieutenant Goddard too long to find out about the camera and its range of ability. The T-1 was able to take a vertical photo while also taking a left and right oblique image at the same time. There were already devices that could clear the deformations that appeared in the oblique images. Goddard went to work and developed a mount and fixed the shutter problems that the camera had. It was after the war, in the 1920s, money was hard to find for anything. The Air Service was low on the list for receiving funds, having done their job. However, since they did have a lot of DH-4 De-Haviland aircraft left over and a couple of good camera systems, they looked at mapmaking. Billy Mitchell was already striving to build the Air Service and its reputation. He wanted to have the Air Service as a separate unit. Mitchell used the opportunity to show just what the Air Service could do when in June of 1921, he attempted to sink a battleship with bombs. Of course, Goddard was there to document the whole thing on film. There was a happy moment for Goddard, who finally after many hours in the DH-4s, managed to get his sorely wanted wings allowing him pilot status.

The U.S. Contribution to World War I

The U.S. Infantry that arrived in France during WWI experienced the reality of the hateful trench warfare up close. The flyers would soon see it from the air. The War was fought in these muddy, squalid trenches by the infantrymen. These were the soldiers that airmen would have to protect with their reconnaissance/observation flights. All of the War's massive amount of equipment, guns and supplies were poured into these trenches sometimes daily, sometimes not at all. In June of 1917, Major Raynal Bolling was sent to probe what the conditions were on the western front. The best idea according to Bolling, was to offer the United States raw materials to the Allies. Doing this would allow the Allies to build the aircraft in Europe as they needed. It would save time, however, it wasn't well received by the American public. The U.S. would build all the engines, trainer aircraft and the British De Havilland DH-4 bombers. The money would also buy aircraft for France, Britain and Italy. Yet, American industrial strength was not as bad as it seemed. The U.S. did manage to produce some 11,574 aircraft and 15,572 Liberty engines along with a University and flying schools.

One of the arriving airmen from the states was then Major William "Billy" Mitchell. Mitchell had made a study of the Allied methods and made a recommendation to both air forces. He felt one should support the ground troops and the other launch attacks against the German infrastructure. Some Americans had gotten combat experience with the French Lafayette Escadrille, a famous unit, and transferred back to help the U.S. Forces. They helped to train the new aviators just arriving from the States. With this new training, it wasn't until the American ground troops were ready for the fight that the U.S. squadrons joined up with the

American troops. They flew many different Allied aircraft like the Nieuport 17 fighter, the Breguet bomber and the British DH-4 bomber. By March of 1918, all units were ready to begin operations.

Even though the U.S. was very slow in creating the needed aircraft and materials, the second it was available, the U.S. Commanders put them to work. There were airmen working in infantry contact patrols which would help to find some of the detached units and get them the aid that they needed, reporting their positions to their commanders. The 50th Aero Squadron's hunt for the "lost battalion" in Meuse-Argonne during the battle went on from September to October 1918. It is the best known of all the missions. Two pilots, Lt. Harold "Dad" Goettler and Lt. Erwin R. Bleckleywere killed trying to draw German fire away so that they could attempt to find out if the "lost battalion" was in the area. What they did helped to narrow down where the battalion was. They were posthumously awarded the Medal of Honor, of which there were only four given out for WWI. The other two went to Eddie Rickenbacker and Frank Luke for their roles in aerial combat.

The missions were very tough. In order to find out the order of battle for the enemy, aircraft were usually flying at low altitude, until they were finally shot at. They did bring home the goods necessary to help the Allied troops gain control.

As Armistice Day thankfully arrived on November 11, 1918, the U.S. Air Service had sent forty-five squadrons to war and they were under the command of Major Billy Mitchell, which equaled about ten percent of the Allied forces. While the United States had a slow start into the art of aerial reconnaissance, it proved its mettle under fire. The aircraft also proved itself and the days of using the element of surprise on the enemy were officially over. There were now "Eagle Eyes" in the skies and because of those "eyes" the realm of war had changed forever.

How Aerial Reconnaissance Continued to Develop in the U.S.

By the end of WWI and into the 1920s things began to change rapidly for the Air Service. The Army rebuilt itself with the "Reorganization Act of 1920." The new legislation brought General Pershing to the U.S. Army Headquarters in Washington D.C. as Chief of Staff in 1921. There were now four different divisions in Air Intelligence:

a. Personnel G-1
b. Military Intelligence – G-2
c. Operations and training – G-3
d. Supply / War plans – G-4

The new officers in charge of these departments ranked equal with each other as Brigadier Generals with the exception of G-2, which was usually a Colonel. His duties for the Assistant Chief of Staff for Intelligence (G-2) consisted of duties for support of the War Plans Division (WPD) in strategic planning to provide the War Department intelligence for field commanders at the outbreak of a war. The post war reduction of the original MID (Military Intelligence Division), were cut to twenty-five officers and fifty-two civilians by 1924. It would remain at that level till 1940.

With the Air Corp Act of 1926, additional representation for matters of aviation were provided. A new G-2 Air section was cultivated to the more important grade that was responsible for policy and anything pertaining to the use of Air Corp personnel in both combat intelligence and aerial photos and mapping, codes, communication which occurred between the air and ground and on the advice of special studies. The first head of the section was Major Joseph T. McNarney. In the "Air Corp

Act of 1930", the G-2 intelligence branch absorbed the then separate air branch.

In January of 1931, Major General Mason M. Patrick became the Chief of Air Service Personnel and approved a plan to phase out the information section of the Air Service and transfer its personnel and printing equipment to Washington D.C. to join a new group, the " Director of Air Service."

The Curtiss JN-4 "Jenny" used in the training
U.S. Army Pilots before they left to fly for France.
(Photo by Brian Karli at Amarillo Texas in 1918/Holcomb's Aerodrome)

The Photo System Develops Further

The new mission for the Air Service in between wars would be map making. The Army Corp of Engineers, Coast Guard and the Geodatic survey and Geological Survey Services of the U.S. were clamoring for updated material. The momentum started to build and new equipment was designed to aid the photograph and the art of photogrammetry[8]. The

---

[8] Making measurements or scale drawings from photographs using aerial photography in the construction of maps.

U.S. agencies were pleased with the results and demanded more from the Air Service.

This type of flying did call for a very precise piloting skill because it was to always stay at the same altitude and the aircraft had to be level at all times. A pilot had to follow some very calculated flight lines and go off the calculated line directly over the point on the ground. This had to be compensated for if there were a tail wind or a cross wind, so the aircraft had to pass right over the needed areas along the flight line. It wasn't easy by any stretch. In the backseat, the "observer," as he was called, would revolve the camera in the opposite direction so that the pictures he took would be in as straight a line as could be determined. This was no easy trick to pull off in the DH-4 De Havilland biplanes.

In the viewfinder, the observer would have to decide if the angle to move the camera was correct and lined up on the markers in the viewer. The observer would take each image so that one overlapped the other by at least some 60% allowing for a stereoscopic effect. It also allowed the map makers to use the less imprecise center areas in the photo mosaics[9] that would be made to make the map as the final product.

At the end of each flight, the pilot turned 180 degrees and flew an equivalent flight in the opposite direction. He would have to fight to keep the aircraft on the right course so that the photographs would now side lap some 25%. There were machines that would compensate for any corrections needed and allowed for some great maps to be made. By the early 1920s, there were six photo detachments in the Air Service and many pilots and other airmen wanted a chance at the new art form. The DH-4 was used for some ten years since the Army had a thousand aircraft in storage. It was literally a throwaway aircraft, if one got damaged or

---

[9] Photo mosaic-photo made up from hundreds of smaller photos

something broke, they tossed it and brought out another. However, cameras were precious commodities.

Lieutenant Goddard had risen in the ranks and been transferred to Washington D.C. as the Chief Photographic Officer for the Air Service. Back at Kodak, the K-1 had become the K-2 with all the new fixes in it. Both the K-2 and the T-1 were the heart and soul of the Air Service Photographic Detail. However, something else was about to be added to the mix. Goddard, now in Washington met with Sherman Fairchild who was the son of Congressman George Fairchild of New York. General Billy Mitchell brought the two of them together, Fairchild was sort of an inventor who tinkered with cameras. He had designed a camera that could change the pace of aerial photography. The camera was driven electrically instead of hand wound as they were then. The shutter was between the lenses which would give a sharper definition and the magazine for the film would keep spacing between images equal. Fairchild had also created an "intervalometer" which was preset so that photos could be taken at any interval needed.

Mitchell seeing all of this, managed to get two thousand precious dollars approved for an experimental version. In two years, the K-3 was rolled out as the standard camera for the Air Service and any other government agency that needed or required cameras. It turned aerial mapping on its head.

The New Art of Night Photography

Dayton, Ohio found itself in the midst of its first unidentified flying object (UFO) sighting, one night in the Fall of 1924. It only took a second but the engineers for the Air Service over at McCook Field were testing some new equipment. This equipment would change the face of aerial photography forever. It would allow for night photography.

Eagle Eyes

On November 20, 1925, there was an intense bright flash which sent the citizens of Rochester, New York, running mad. The telephones almost crashed with all the calls that were coming through to report the sighting. Some headed to church thinking the end was upon them, others hid in basements, even the City had its nightmare thinking its central heating system had blown up. There weren't any little green men wandering around and it wasn't the end of the world as many feared, it was just the Air Service[10] at it again. Over at Rochester field, Lt. George Goddard had just landed in a Martin bomber. With his crew in tow, they drove to the labs of Kodak to develop a sheet of film that they had just taken from that same Martin bomber, scaring the bejesus out of the City of Rochester's public. That next afternoon, a beautiful nighttime photo appeared of City of Rochester dressed in her evening's finest. It was clear and bright and sharp. That photo changed the ability of the military to actually photograph the enemy at night and that was a huge breakthrough. Because of the Fairchild camera's ability to use an electric shutter, the problem of night photography was partially solved. The biggest problem now would be how to light the ground so as to get a good image.

Goddard and his team came up with one idea that consisted of a small glider made from wood that was loaded with flash powder and could carry about forty pounds of it. It would be towed behind the mother aircraft carrying the camera. McCook Field's engineers built one that had a five-foot wingspan and they attached it to the DH-4 that was used for photography. The idea was to have the glider a safe distance back and to send an electric charge through the towrope that would set the powder off. The second signal would travel to the shutter and open it. After the first tryout, Goddard knew that this wasn't going to be cheap

---

[10] The Air Service "United States Army Air Service from 1918 until 1947 when it became the US Air Force

since every time they lit off the glider, it would blow up and another one would be needed. Goddard tried another idea. Making rudimentary bombs with some help from a local fireworks company, they attached a long rope to the bomb and the pull that ignited the bomb opened the shutter taking the image. The biggest problem was how to get the shutter and the light source to match so that both went into action at the same time. Dropping the bomb via parachute got something of a better result. The problem was turned over to the U.S. Army's Ordnance department. The glider idea was kicked out after a few more tests, one being an almost disaster with the glider twisting and turning in flight until the cable broke and it went exploded.

Since the Air Service had already been working on solving the problem of how to sync up the shutter and the flash, they had another idea. The Air Service carried a portable lab and they worked on the technique of trying to develop the photographs in the air and dropping them down to "potential users" on the ground. A number of times the acid used to develop the film spilled and literally ate through the fuselage. However, by 1925 photographers were able to take a photo in the air and develop it within 10 minutes. That was miraculous.

More Changes in the Photography World

As technology changed and grew there were many other forms the photograph was taking. AT&T, the American Telephone and Telegraph Company, had come up with a way to transmit a photo image through its telephone lines, in short the literal first fax machine. Goddard heard about this and set up to do a demonstration by taking a photo, developing it within seven minutes and dropping it to a transmitting station on the ground. The whole thing took some 29 minutes from the time that the photo was taken, till it was received in New York, Chicago and San Francisco. The transmitting equipment had a drum inside, much like an old mimeograph machine, which contained a photoelectric cell. As the light hit the cell, the electrical current started to generate. Goddard used the new Fairchild K-3 camera shutter, that opened electronically and the photoflash that created light. The photoelectric cell was what Goddard was looking for to solve his problem of syncing the shutter to the flash. Goddard brought the problem to the Westinghouse Research and Development Center in Pittsburgh where one of the foremost engineers in the field, Vladamir Kosmich Zworykin would come up with a photoflash amplifier. It would take a year to complete.

In the meantime, over at McCook Field, the crews continued building a fourteen-foot wooden bomb to keep working on the flash. They packed this glider with over eighty pounds of magnesium powder. The mathematics to hold that flash would last approximately 1/100th of a second, and would give enough of a flash to catch the City of Rochester again. Since there wasn't a conclusion as to how to solve the shutter synchronization, Goddard decided to leave it open at full. As with Alexander Graham Bell and the telephone, it took this planned accident of leaving the shutter open to solve the problem. In some seven months Dr. Zworykin delivered the T-shape photo electric cell to McCook Field. The engineers installed it in the DH-4 and had a flight over downtown Dayton, Ohio planned as the first test. The results were spectacular! It looked as if the photo had been taken in broad daylight. Goddard wrote in his personal memoirs; *"No more would I have to drop bombs attached to parachutes or tow a glider full of powder. All the pilot had to do was to release a flash bomb and when it exploded, the light at the peak of the flash, working through the photoelectric cell, would trip the camera shutter and in doing so unwind the next exposure automatically."*

What happened in this test literally changed the world of aerial reconnaissance. Goddard's setup was used for the next thirty years and in another world war. Goddard's creation allowed for all kinds of nighttime uses for photography and photo mapping. By the 1930s, it had gone so far that Wright Field, was now working with color photography. Even though in the 1920s, the use of color photography was a thought, that's about all it was. It wasn't until 1935 when Eastman Kodak invented the famed film, Kodachrome that would be used for aerial reconnaissance.

The Start of U.S. Intelligence Gathering

As the war progressed, it was obvious that the service was going to need more trained officers with a specialized study of what aerial reconnaissance and intelligence gathering was really about. When the Air Intelligence Section in Washington D.C, was reorganized, its mandate was to collect foreign aeronautical data, engine performance, aircraft characteristics and anything of a technical nature. The office which was renamed the "Information Section" would then distribute the information to the Army aviation units. After the United States declared war on Germany, it actually made the job of collecting intelligence a lot easier. If the United States remained on the sidelines, trying to get information from European air forces and nations would have been twice as difficult. When the United States joined its allies on April 1917, the British, French, Russian and Italian agencies came to headquarters in Washington D.C. to bring all its technical information on both friendly and enemy air forces in hopes of getting some greatly needed United States materiel help.

President Woodrow Wilson then transferred the aviation section from the Signal Corp to the new Air Service that was developed in May 1918. At that point, the General Staff authorized the Air Service to send some twenty officers to Europe to help keep them informed of the next development for the Air Service (AEF).

With the organization of the service in this manner, General John Pershing arrived to help organize this section. Pershing kept to the existing dogma that a "theater commander was responsible for combat intelligence in his area of operations." Pershing established the Intelligence Section and classified it as a second section G-2 that was termed: GHQ AEF. The GHQ intelligence section included the MID G-2A with its lower level functions that included Air Intelligence G-2, A-7. At the Headquarters AEF in Paris, France, the different sections G-2 A-7 labored on the interrogation of captured enemy airmen, along with bombing target information and enemy air activity. The G-2 A-7 group also supervised branch intelligence officers (BIO), which were attached to each Army headquarters and army observations, along with bombing squads, which were operating independently at the front lines. General Pershing wrote: Before our entering into the wars, European experience had shown that military operations can be carried out successfully and without unnecessary loss only in the light of complete and reliable information of the enemy. The invention of the airplane provided another means by which to obtain this information."

Pershing also noted that: "Warfare with the battle line separated by short distances only makes possible the early acquirement of information. While there were many means of getting information, with us the simple methods such as observation from the air and ground, the exploitation of prisoners, documents have proved more effective than the less direct means." All the WWI experience contributed to a perspective that would end up defining air intelligence as the use of the aircraft to collect information usable by ground commanders. This all grew from the facts that most of the work of the Air Service units (with only seven months in combat) was tied to ground operations in both observation or artillery spotting, or possibly in direct combat support via strafing runs and the bombing of enemy positions. In the report of the Chief of G-2 A-7

(Office of Air Intelligence) and GHQ AEF showed that most of the work done by this office involved information not directly related to observation or support. It really dealt with the collection, evaluation, and allocation of information that was needed to conduct air operations separate from support.

The Air "Order of Battle"[11] that was obtained and updated constantly was information on the "enemy air and balloon units, enemy airdromes and the organization of every air service for inclusion into the daily summary of air information."

In seeing the effects that the leaders had on the Air Unit, the G-2 A-7 kept a "file" on leading German airmen, with a view to determining what might be expected of any new unit, which were the most prominent issues brought to bear. Every month, the G-2 A-7 office put out a map of the airdromes that showed the location, size of the hangers, shed, estimated capacity and troops present. A good deal of the information came from photos and reports; changes in enemy dispositions were released in daily summaries of air information. The Air Service Reorganization required that all the new information be maintained in a library, and the Air Service declared that " It be essential that copies of all reports, manuals, pamphlets, and publications of a tactical technical or engineering nature received by the Air Service be furnished so that the library may be kept up to date. "

In November of 1918, the AEF developed a target file on systems such as railroad stations, switching yards, manufacturing plants, supply dumps and barracks of the German army.

---

[11] Order of Battle—Shows the formal order or military command, structure, position of personnel and what type of equipment, how many pieces and the formation of troops on the battlefield

The first information chief Major Horace Hickman divided the office into sections:

A. Collection
B. Dissemination
C. Library

This also allowed a special division to be responsible for the preparation of the Congressional correspondence and distribution of information to the press. Hickman also believed that the information group should also be the "central publishing office for the Air Service." It didn't matter if it were rigging charts, handbooks, folders, technical bulletins, curriculum, technical reports or organizational diagrams." It all had to come from one place, the Central Publishing Office.

There were many in the Service that weren't happy with Hickman's decision. They felt that the "Information Group" was "attempting altogether too much and a good part of the work being undertaken was of little or no value to the service in general." That wasn't the end of the story, however. The Information Group also specified that all of the assistant military attaches for the Air Service stationed in Paris, Rome, London, the Hague, should be made aware of all the aeronautical developments in the U.S. and all other countries. In January of 1920, the Air Service prepared a questionnaire for the London and Paris groups, which specified technical information that they wanted for electrical equipment, instruments, parachutes, radio and aerial photography. The London team, which had to return with the information, found it wasn't such a simple matter to secure technical information. The British Air Ministry was dead set against releasing any of its technical information to anyone even the USA. No matter, the Air Service kept trying.

Brigadier General Billy Mitchell also complained about a lack of aeronautical information coming in from overseas in the early 1920s. In order to get Mitchell involved with the Washington Naval Disarmament negotiations that were going on at the time, General Patrick sent Mitchell with his aide Lt. Clayton Bissell, and one aeronautical engineer, Alfred V. Verville, for an inspection tour of France, Italy, Germany, Holland and England during the 1921-22 winter months. General Mitchell was received well on the trip but after the visits to Paris and London, both governments started to put forth demands for U.S. information, in exchange for what they had given Mitchell. Some questions however, went way beyond the technical issues. The French wanted to know the U.S. military opinions regarding what they termed "giant or powerful" military aircraft along with the need for multi-engines."

By 1928, one engineering officer Lt. Victor E. Bertrandis traveled to England and France and filed a report about the aviation factories that he had visited. Bertrandis concluded: "The U.S. surpasses England and France in production methods as and a whole our workmanship in aircraft practices are far superior to anything in England or France." With the New Air Corp created in 1926, all this had little impact on the air intelligence in a functional sense, although it did see some result with the restructure of Washington D.C. With that the Air Service was once again separated in to four sections:

a. Air intelligence
b. Photography
c. Publications
d. Press relations

The Information Division was charged with collecting all the essential aeronautical information from all possible sources. This would include "uses of aircraft in war including the various air forces around the world, tactical doctrines, tips on aircraft usage and the organization of personnel operation and maintaining aircraft" with the exception of the responsibility of the intelligence section routinely receiving foreign intelligence through the MID[12] and maintained a liaison with the Air Branch. In an effort to do that, a magazine and library was formed. The Intelligence section tried to compile the many digests from foreign sources on the European Air Forces and their aviation information. The workload was enormous since only two to five civilians handled the section at this time.

The K-20 camera used by the Army Air Corp.
(National Museum of the USAF)

---

[12] MID-Military Intelligence Division United States

Chapter Three

Air Intelligence in the 1930s and the Lead up to WWII

Since the assistant military attaches in the major European cities remained the principal sources of information on foreign aviation developments, the Air Corp sent an officer every year to visit far away Japan to write reports on what was going on there. The Air Corp by no means considered itself totally informed about aircraft development overseas even though the foreign nations were not imposing restrictions on information of military value leaving its offices. Italy, France and England, had far more stringent secrecy on information than the United States did. The Japanese actually imposed a particularly severe restraint on the acquisitions of military and naval information and had limited access to what they wanted foreign representatives (aka the United States) to see. One reason for this plan may have been the knowledge that in the 1920s, the U.S. was intercepting and translating Japanese messages to their negotiators in Washington D.C. Naval Disarmament Conference.

In 1929, the new Secretary of State, Henry L. Simpson learned of this Japanese secrecy and reacted harshly. Such interceptions of foreign government communications were "highly unethical". The reaction to the Secretary's order was that it had to stop immediately. Herbert O. Yardley, a former head of the War Cipher Bureau, wrote a book in 1931 that revealed the extent of the U.S. code breaking. The Japanese quietly went ahead, changed their cipher system, and were freezing cold to any U.S. request for air information. While the State department no longer participated in crypto analysis, the War and Navy Department continued to do so each on its own. The War Department code interception was handled as a communication function within the Signal Intelligence Service (SIGINT) of the chief signal officer who was outside the scope of the

MID and other military intelligence channels, which quietly solved the problem of the embarrassment of being found out on intercepting foreign signals.

Ideas Were changing

It wasn't just the United States that was concerned about what was happening overseas with their former allies. The Allies had a few concerns of their own. The Allies were directly concerned that they weren't giving out any of their strategic plans or what they had in their arsenal. It seemed like all the former Allies in arms were now thinking about strategic war planning. As far as the United States was concerned, they started revamping their own plans. Back in 1904, they had color-coded their war plans: Red for England, Black for Germany, and Orange for Japan. As the Japanese army started to develop in the 1920s, this forced the United States to go back and look at the ORANGE book with the Japanese war plans. The U.S. had already felt that at some point in time, Japan was going to be an adversary.

The Air Service evolved and moved ahead with its plans and revamping of the service following WWI. By 1938, their main objective had to be the consideration of reworking its air defense system by destroying the enemy in their home bases. This was going to cost something and would prove that the need for intelligence and the requirements for that had to be more than just supporting the ground forces in a war. One of the main problems however, was that there were not enough qualified officers to meet that demand for intelligence planners. There was also the issue that the Air Service had divided itself into two platforms: one being air tactical and the other air intelligence. The larger issue had the basic questions of what constituted air intelligence and which groups were best able to obtain, evaluate and disseminate the materiel coming in. These problems did not get resolved before the U. S. found itself in the throes of

WWII but the center for much of the Air Corp pre-war thinking fell to ACTS[13] which was at Maxwell Field, Alabama. There were many different fields of thought about how the Air Corp. should conduct all these new areas and plans. The officers of ACTS were saying that strategic air power "could be decisive by bringing about the collapse of both the means and will of an adversary to conduct war". ACTS officers felt that the destruction of the "meat and potatoes" targets that held within it a nation's industrial abilities would make the decisive turn to winning the war. However, as late as 1939, the need to gather the information regarding those industrial means had to be done via intelligence gathering prior to war condition, in short. Intelligence needed to be a full-time proposition, not just a course of action during a war. The ACTS officers recognized that the U.S.'s posture regarding war was always on the defensive; they also knew that being on the offensive would win the war. At the time however, the Military Intelligence Division (MID) and the War Department in general wasn't thinking along those lines. It was doubtful that ACTS officers could get the projected information that they felt they needed based on their idea of a strategic attack plan.

When looking back at the information that was available by July of 1935, the annual aviation report for Japan, which was filed by the attaché in charge of the mission there, found that Japan's army air force had a large number of obsolete aircraft. The statement "The unwise policy of some years ago of storing up an amount of spare airplanes in depots and the apparent failure to note the rapid changes which occurred in aeronautical development had been impressed upon the Japanese but it is doubtful if they will deliberately scrap planes which had some use even if obsolete." In an informed letter written by the military attaché' Major James F. Phillips of Tokyo, written to Wright Field Air Material Divi-

---

[13] ACTS- Air Corp Tactical School – Maxwell Field Alabama

sion, Dayton, Ohio, stated that "Superficial treatment was very courteous—including much blowing, kissing and gallons of tea drunk but verbal information was exaggerated or misleading". It was obvious the Japanese were not going to be forthcoming in any information gathering process. The Japanese showed this officer only what they wanted him to see.

The next step in the attempt to gather intelligence on the ground at least was not successful for the United States. There were not enough Air Corp Intelligence officers available to perform the duties of these intelligence units. The thought that these officers were really only useful during wartime was a fallacy. These officers were termed S-2 (S-2 lower level) in each of the three General Headquarters, Air Force combat wings that were feeling the cuts of a peacetime atmosphere in Congress, at least for the United States.

Japanese troops storming into Peking 1937
(NARA)

China vs. Japan

There were things to be learned even if the United States was not at war. It was definite that somewhere in the world, someone was fighting. That happened in November of 1936 when after signing an Anticom intern Pact with Germany and Italy. Japan was already planning to invade China. They made good on that plan in July of 1937. The Japanese forces marched into Northern China. Since the United States had passed the "Military Secrets Act", the job of the U.S. Military and that of the Naval attaches' in Japan was useless. Because of the problem of obtaining any military information from Japan, Lt. Cmdr. Ralph A. Ofstie who was the naval attaché for Air in Tokyo thought the attack of China by Japan was a "golden opportunity to see how and what materiel Japan used to carry on a war". Ofstie said:" *The Japanese have been bold and courageous, but they have exhibited a mediocrity in operations and in material which mark them as distinctly inferior to other major powers in the vitally important element of war.*" Ofstie felt that Japan would not use her Navy; she still had her Army aviation tucked up in Manchuria in an ever present fear of the USSR.

Ofstie basically downplayed the Japanese at every turn. He said, "I believe that there is no doubt that we are markedly superior to the Japanese in the air—in piloting skills, in materiel and in ability to employ our aircraft effectively on the offense and defense."

Claire Chennault wearing the famous
Flying Tigers patch on his A-2 jacket.
(U.S. Air Force)

However, by 1938, the reports getting back to Washington D.C. were not so brightly in the U.S. favor. What we see here is already the "split" in information getting to where it was needed and understood. While the Materiel Dept at Wright Field, Ohio got the specs of Claire Chennault's report, on the Chinese situation. The Intelligence Branch of the Information Division really didn't think much of it. In 1936 Chennault was in the Air Service of the U.S. and was in charge of Pursuit Unit that flew out of Barksdale AB in Shreveport, Louisiana. However, in his years of service, he was known for his many disagreements with his military bosses. He was asked to take a "Military" health retirement, which he accepted. Officially retired as a Captain, it was then that he was asked to take over the Chinese situation which he did to amazing results. Chennault was the leader of the famous "Flying Tigers" which was all volunteer unit flying to aid China He arrived in China in 1937 and worked as a civilian advisor.

It wasn't going to be the first of these types of incidents. Chennault felt that it was still his duty even though he was retired from the Air Corp to send information back to the United States. In January of 1938, he sent a confidential report to the U.S. Army that the Japanese had a pursuit plane, the I-96. Chennault called it the "most maneuverable monoplane, which has appeared in China." He also noted that it did support bombers in flights as far away as 250 miles. Chennault initially thought that the I-96 was a knock off a French fighter, but in May of 1938, he changed that conclusion to it being of original Japanese design. He called this new Mitsubishi fighter "Claude." Chennault said, "Japan is self-supporting and independent of foreign supplies in building airplanes." That statement in itself was a frightening precursor to what was coming down the road . . . WWII. As the war went on between China and Japan, in 1939 the Chinese managed to bring down intact a Nakajima Type 97 (known as a *Nate*) and brought the plane to Chengtu where Chennault flew many tests on it. He later brought the result to Washington in 1939. Chennault wasn't too surprised with what he found in Washington. He brought the report only to leave with the feeling that they were "flying swivel chairs and puttering with war plans." Chennault felt that no one in Washington had a clue as to what was going on. Chennault's report made the rounds, but no one took it seriously. Even the "aeronautical experts" made the claim that it was impossible to build an aircraft like the one Chennault described. That was lame considering Chennault flew the aircraft in huge amounts of tests.

On the left: The men of the A.V.G. Flying Tigers and their P-40. On the right: A Chinese guard watching the aircraft. (U.S. Air Force)

Chennault and the Flying Tigers

Working as a civilian advisor to China, Claire Chennault, of the "Flying Tigers" fame did much to aid China in their darkest moment. Chennault was a legend among the Chinese. He arrived in China in 1937, at the start of the Chinese-Japanese war. Chennault was making a survey of the Chinese Air Force and met with the infamous "Madame Chiang" also known as Soong Mayling. She was in charge of the *Aeronautical Commission* and was Chennault's supervisor. When war broke out in August of 1937, Chennault became Chiang Kai-Shek's Chief Air Advisor and trained the Chinese pilots as well as flying scout missions in an old Curtiss H-75 fighter. He also was in charge of finding and organizing the "International Squadron" which consisted of mercenaries who could and would fly anything with wings.

As China took a beating from the Japanese, the Soviets also aided in helping the Chinese. In the summer of 1938, Chennault went to Kunming, the capital of the Yunnan province in Western China, where he helped to train and organize a stronger Chinese Air Force. On October 21, 1939, Chennault and a contingent of Chinese advisors climbed on to a Pan Am B-314 "California Clipper" in Hong Kong and flew out to San Francisco, on a very special mission from Chiang Kai Shek. The Chinese

Air Force had totally collapsed due to no equipment or pilots. Chiang Kai Shek's plan in sending Chennault and his officials to the United States was to try to get some money to support the cause. They needed as many fighters, bomber and transport planes as they could get, along with crews to maintain and fly them.

Chennault 's mission for Chiang Kai Shek led him to the thought of creating an *American Volunteer Group* of pilots and mechanics to serve in China. Monetary plans were being made to support the program of buying materiel for China. On April 24, 1941, the United States and China formally signed a $50 million stabilization agreement to support the Chinese monetary system. The U.S. supplied China with one hundred of the American made P-40C aircraft. The aircraft were crated and shipped to Burma on freighters during the early part of 1941. When the aircraft reached Rangoon, they were unloaded, assembled and test flown by the crews from the Central Aircraft Manufacturing Company (CAMCO) before they were delivered to China. Chennault was able to recruit some three hundred U.S. pilots and crews who, posing as tourists were paid mercenaries who were in it for the money not for the Chinese. However, Chennault whipped them into a top-flight group and they became known as the "Flying Tigers." A year before the U.S. entered WWII, Chennault had developed a plan to make a sneak attack on Japan bases. The Flying Tigers would use U.S. bombers and pilots, all with Chinese markings. The U.S. military was not happy with the plan and kept throwing things in the way of the plan until President Roosevelt himself who wanted to keep China breathing finally adopted it. Because of Chennault and his Flying Tigers "flying the Hump[14]" in all conditions, China survived to fight another day.

---

[14] Flying the HUMP" was the term used for and by the American Volunteers Group A.V.G., the American pilots who flew over the Himalayas to deliver troops and supplies in support of China.

Europe Starts to Worry

While Chennault was helping to shore up the Chinese, the Military attaches' over in Europe were reporting on a constant basis regarding the affairs of their allies.

The British were not terribly open with their status to the United States on what their military was doing. By 1938-39, as Germany started her war dance, the British changed their mind and became more open to the U.S. In 1939, the G-2 of the Army Air Service asked the British for their air defense system layout. It didn't take long for Washington D.C. to get the complete story of what the British Royal Air Force was up to. The report the U.S. received stated that if Germany went to war, London and other cities would be defended by day fighters, ground observers would be on the watch along with the British Navy and the general reconnaissance aircraft running patrols. With the experiences that the British had in Spain and China the British gave some considerable thought to having fighters escort their bombers, which would allow the bomber crews to more easily get their job done and not have to worry about protecting themselves while doing it. The British also planned to send other teams abroad to France in order to get themselves a little better and more effective place to defend themselves. It also would allow these teams to check out the primary objectives for targets which would be the enemy munitions dumps, factories, aircraft factories, radio stations, bridges, foundries, supply and gasoline dumps along with the lines of communication. It was well known by the British that they were very vulnerable to German air attacks. While the British were worried about all the various problems discussed, they were not thinking about the "new" German air force that was just coming to be. Since the 1920s, German pilots were training secretly in the Soviet Union. The Germans were worried about the air disarmament, which was forced on them by the Versailles treaty and the fact they were surrounded by other countries air forces.

The twin-engine Messerschmitt ME-110 much like the Junker JU-88 was used by the Luftwaffe to combat the AAF bombers.
(National Museum of the USAF ™)

The Luftwaffe Rebuilds

When Hitler came to power in Berlin, the Luftwaffe went through an enormous rebuilding and restructuring phase. Germany had at least fifteen major factories in production and it was reported that they were putting all their time and effort in to building aircraft, while at least eight of them were devoted to building engines. May 2, 1935 during a dinner that was given by the General in charge of aviation, Herman Goring. Goring gave the story to the foreign press of Germany's forward push in aviation. Goering said that Germany had no aerial weapons now. However, when Hitler took over the government there would be a new modern air force, literally built overnight, by using the German ability and strength to the nth degree. Goering said, "I am not telling you anything surprising. When I emphasized that the German aerial forces are so strong that whoever attacks Germany will have a difficult stand in the air. What is possessed today in the aerial fighting forces in the war of airplanes and motors is the most modern in existence." Goering was just talking through his *Sauerbraten*[15].

It didn't take long for the United States to hear of the blowhard antics of Goering. By May 6, 1935, the U.S. attaché for Berlin, Major Truman Smith, sent a copy of Goering's statement to Washington. Smith added his conclusion that the German Minister' statements were true. Smith added: "It is not believed however, that the air fighting which he referred to is unorganized and equipped for immediate action but it is believed that the organization and equipment is well underway and that upon the completion of the construction of airframes, and necessary quarters and hangers, the picture of the German Air Force appointed by General Goering will be a reality…It is further believed that this force will be equal to that of France." In fact, the German Air Force surpassed it.

Lindbergh received the German Eagle award on behalf of Hitler in October of 1938 (Library of Congress)

---

[15] German Pot Roast dish

Lindbergh Visits Hitler's Germany

We all know that Charles Lindbergh was the darling of the United States. He was a hero of aviation when he flew the "Spirit of St. Louis" starting from Roosevelt Field, Long Island, N.Y. on May 20, 1927 across the Atlantic, non-stop, to land at La Bourget Airport in France on May 21, 1927. It was a brilliant triumph. Lindbergh later known as "Lucky Lindy," went on to serve in the Army Air Corp. as a reserve.

It was a shock to many Americans when they found out that Lindbergh had some other ideas when it came to America and her world status. As things started to heat up in Europe and many Americans felt that they didn't want to be involved in a war again. Lindbergh and his "America First" society, which dealt with keeping the United States out of war, and generally out of everyone's business, started to pick up a little speed.

In 1937, Charles Lindbergh decided to make a little side trip to Berlin while visiting Europe. On his ten-day visit to Germany at the behest of the U. S. Military and Army Air Force General Henry "Hap" Arnold, Lindbergh and his wife were very warmly received by the German high command that being General Herman Goering and other high ranking Luftwaffe officers. The Luftwaffe and their boss Goering gave Lindbergh a three star tour of the Luftwaffe stations and the aircraft factories and facilities. Lindbergh missed seeing the new Messerschmitt fighters that were at the prototype stage, however he didn't leave empty handed, the Germans gave him the specs for it. At the Heinkel factory, Lindbergh saw the Heinkel HE-111 bomber at Dessare. He also saw the Junkers JU-87 Stuka dive bomber. He also saw and examined the Junkers JU-88. With all of this, Lindbergh said he was not impressed with the quality of the aircraft but he was very impressed with the German vitality. Between September and October of 1937, Lindbergh went back to Germany several times and saw most the aircraft the Germans used in WWII.

Lindbergh then went on later to work with military attaches to prepare a "general estimator on November 1937" which was given to Washington D.C. Lindbergh signed off on the report which was written more dramatically which brought a lot of attention to the report. The report stated that "Astounding growth of the German air power from a zero level in the first four years. It is difficult to express in a few words this literally amazing size of the German air industry. Behind this industry stands a formidable group of air scientists, with large and well-equipped laboratories and test fields constantly pushing forward the German scientific advance. The actual November 1st strength of the German Force is probably from 175 to 225 squadrons." By March 1938, the Germans were optimistic on their end. In another report which described the action between Germany and Austria another statement on the German Air Force came from another Air Corp officer Major Vanaman; "Each cog and wheel functioned efficiently. Heavy bombers and swift fighters accomplished their mission by demonstration, troops were landed by airplane to initiate the attack, and the motorized troops arrived to complete the tasks and annihilate any resistance . . .Thus the Air Force has made history as an instrument adapted to quick decisive moments so necessary in modern warfare."

Lindbergh made a trip to Russia and Czechoslovakia in September of 1938. When he returned, Colonel H.H. Fuller who was the U.S, Military attaché in Paris interviewed him. Lindbergh was concerned. He told Fuller plenty about his concerns. Fuller remembered:" Col. Lindbergh believed that Germany had the outstanding air force of the world today (at that time) and that it exceeded in power those of Russia, France, and England combined. German equipment, machinery and factories he considered the best in the world." This didn't bode well for what was soon to come . . . the destruction of Europe under Germany's well-honed fist. Lindbergh went on to note later on that the Luftwaffe was not a long-range air force built to destroy cities and industry; it was designed to operate in close support of the German infantry. However, with all that said, more intelligence came back from the Germans that notes the Luftwaffe was having some personnel problems and issues with inexperience and inefficiency of many of the generals in the Luftwaffe proper. This was a huge problem for the Germans. Lindbergh missed one point about the Luftwaffe; it was not made for effectively carrying out independent strategic air warfare by heavy bombardment. By missing this crucial point when Lindbergh went on the political trail using exaggerated predictions of destruction and doom, he was one brick short of a load.

More Intelligence… More Confusion

The Germans didn't miss a trick when it came to trying out its fledging Air Force. As Spain entered into a civil war and General Franco requested Hitler's help to overthrow Spain's republican government, Goering was right there to try out the Luftwaffe. The German "Condor" Legion tried out all its new war toys and perfected its flying and air to ground communications later to be used in the European war that was coming.

The United States was watching closely what was happening in Spain and communications were coming back and forth. The Air Corp started to use some of this incoming information to set up training courses at the Army War College in 1937 to dissect what was happening in Spain. However, General Hap Arnold who was then Chief of the Army Air Corp in 1938, recalled that the reports coming out of Spain really weren't that precise. Now the arguments went on about whether aircraft were the answer, or should the U.S. be investing in more tanks.

As the intelligence started to roll in, it was obvious that there would be many hands stirring the pot. The Air Corp had its wishes for long-range bombers, fighters and more and of course, the Army had its wants for more artillery, tanks and trucks. Each wanted its own importance. It was the start of the something that turned out to be a lifetime virus in the U.S. military, the fight for "territory" and funding. What was more important, aircraft that snooped around or boots on the ground? Eventually both would have to work together, but not without a fight.

Two Types of Aerial Reconnaissance Defined

There were two types of aerial reconnaissance that was developing; the first was strategic reconnaissance, the second was tactical reconnaissance. Strategic reconnaissance was important as the wars being fought were now on a global scale. It was no longer over the border skirmishes. These were full blown intercontinental wars. Long range aircraft could now bring back, with newly developed high-altitude cameras, the order of battle for an enemy, along with vital internal targets like shipyards and aircraft factories that could become potential targets. Long range reconnaissance in peacetime also helped a nation forestall an enemy from developing a secret weapon. Aerial strategic reconnaissance is the most important source of overt intelligence that the United States could possess.

Tactical aerial reconnaissance supports the front lines of the armies during combat. This was needed for fast information assistance to commanders in the battlefield to find answers to command and critical problems as they were happening. In June of 1942, the USAAF (United States Army Air Force) was busy training its strategic reconnaissance pilots and teams for the work they were needed for. These training programs were running twenty-four hours a day, seven days a week, at the main aerial photography school at Lowry Field, Colorado. The Army Air Force used B-18s, F-2s, F-4s and B-25s as the basis for their reconnaissance aircraft. It took only months before the first reconnaissance units were operating in combat areas to stop the AXIS advances during WWII.

The USS Arizona sinking with hands aboard trapped below after being bombed by Japanese at Pearl Harbor on December 7, 1941.
(National Museum of the US Air Force ™)

Chapter Four

Air Intelligence at Pearl Harbor—the Night Before...

There were many deep holes in the United States version of military intelligence prior to WWII. The U.S. was in better shape to handle what was going on in Europe in 1941, than it could have even hoped to have been in the Pacific. This is regardless of the fact that there were major assets in the Pacific that the U.S. could have relied on. The Philippines, Hawaii, along with many of the outlying islands in the area were all valuable when it came to gathering intelligence on what the Japanese were up to. However, the Army SIGINT (signal intelligence) was picking up some very low-grade Japanese code and ciphers in early 1939 but nothing that gave a hint as to what was going to hit Hawaii in 1941. The Navy also managed to break the secret. Japanese diplomatic code. The project carried the code name MAGIC.

China was having its problems after being attacked by Japan in 1938. At this point the U.S. Joint Navy-Army Board started a revised ORANGE plan book which was based on the new and ongoing changes happening throughout the world at that time. It was urgent for the U.S. to hold onto its strategic triad which was made up of Alaska, Hawaii and Panama. It was obvious that in later 1939, the United States would most likely decide on a position of working with its many allies as opposed to taking on Japan alone. Because of that position, the U.S. came up with, yet a new plan book called RAINBOW 4, which both the Secretary of War and the Navy approved and would take the place of the single color code books for each nation. RAINBOW 4 was approved by President Roosevelt in June of 1941. This was based on the concept that the U.S.

would ally itself with Britain and France against the ever growing and ever spreading Evil Axis, Germany, Italy and Japan.

It wasn't much later that because of this issue, RAINBOW 5 was instituted for the Pacific region, which would contain its strategic defense posture in the Pacific until the war with European Axis was won. That would allow for resources to be sent to prop up defenses against the Japanese war machine. In the summer of 1941, before RAINBOW 4 came into being, the Army Air Corp had started to build up its resources in the Pacific. By mid-February of 1941, the AAF began to send some more of the modern fighters to the Pacific region. As time wore on and it got to early April, General Henry "Hap" Arnold committed twenty-one B-17s to Honolulu, with delivery of the last flight completed in May of 1941. Other things were going on; part of the Pacific fleet had been transferred to the Atlantic by the summer of 1941. War department planners suggested that four additional groups of B-17s should go to the Pacific region, two to Hawaii and two to the Philippines where their presence could act as a threat and keep the Japanese at bay. The Army Air Force had a total of 109 B-17s and with the bombers that were promised to Great Britain, General "Hap" Arnold agreed to this in hopes that enough of the new heavy bombers would scare the Japanese back to Japan. The decision, as well as all other decisions regarding the Pacific, had to be made on the basis of very limited knowledge about the enemy. All this was being done with a veil of secrecy. This action had halted just about every chance for the Army and Navy attaches to get any military intelligence on Japan. It was already known that in the Central Pacific region, the Japanese already had a marked advantage in maintaining their secrecy. Establishing an absolute control over the Pacific islands mandated that the League of Nations allow Japan to build an important naval bases in the Marianas Islands, Caroline and the Marshall Islands so that they could conduct naval maneuvers in this area without the West knowing anything about it. This area was given the name "VACANT SEAS" because few commercial ships and no U.S. Naval vessels moved through the area. Three seas lay between the great Southern trade routes that went from Hawaii to the coasts of Japan and China and the great northern circle routes that skirted the Aleutian Islands.

General Billy Mitchell, many feel was the father of the U.S. Air Force, made a tour of the perimeter of the islands in the fall of 1923 to get as much information as possible on it. In 1924, Mitchell predicted that the Japanese would probably use the islands eventually as a method for an attack on Pearl Harbor, the Hawaiian Islands and the U.S. While off the point for a moment but in the same time frame, Amelia Earhart was also involved with the Japanese efforts to cover up. In her July 1937 trans-world aircraft flight, Earhart and her navigator Fred Noonan disappeared at sea after a flight from Lae, New Guiana and went on to a 2556-mile flight to Howland Islands. They were never found and it was alleged that they were on a spy mission for the U.S. There was never any substance to the claim. In 1992, the International Group for Historic Aircraft Recovery said that they had found evidence the Earhart landed on Nikumaroro Island (also called Gardiner Island) around two hours flying time between Howland Island. Nikumaroro is one of the Phoenix Islands, which was controlled then by the U.S. and the U.K. According to the supposition, both Earhart and Noonan were picked up by the Japanese somewhere off the Marshall Islands and taken to Saipan where they died. U.S. researchers and writers who looked at the Earhart story were of a split opinion. Yet, those who suggested the Japanese involvement have offered little to support it. Earhart's story is still not closed and as much a mystery as ever.

Back to the summer of 1941, General Henry "Hap" Arnold found that Admiral Harold R. Stark, Chief of Naval Operations, was worried about what would happen with the Japanese and what they were doing at Truk

Island and Rabaul. Arnold approved for some of the B-17s going to the Philippines to fly of course and take photos of both islands. In the confusion of the Japanese attack on the Philippines in December, those photos were lost and no help to war preparations for the U.S.

In late November, the Army Air Corp ordered the B-24 Liberators equipped with photo ability and fully armed, to be sent over Truk island and Rabaul to take pictures from high altitude. The first B-24 arrived in theater without guns and it was not possible to switch armament from the B-17s that were already there. Before the correct weapons could be sent, the Japanese attacked Pearl Harbor's, Clark Field which became a desperate nightmare for the U.S. forces stationed there. The Japanese attack destroyed the B-24 Liberators on the field. General Hap Arnold said:

"Looking back on it, I am convinced now that we all assumed the Japanese would attack the Philippines. We were fairly sure that they would cut our air time because they had to cut our line to stop our heavy bombers from getting to the Philippines . . . . We were pretty sure that they would attack Wake and Midway when they did attack. So, I think that there was a general acceptance of the possibilities of Japanese aggression, certainly against the Philippines and against Wake, Midway and possibly Hawaii".

The evaluation of the intelligence failure at Pearl Harbor would reveal deficiencies not only in organization but also in interpretation. There are many who argue that the U.S. government somehow had some type of advance warning when it came to the attack on Pearl Harbor, which it chose to ignore. The most exacting examination of Pearl Harbor does conclude with the U.S. being genuinely surprised by the attack. That surprise resulted in no small way from the failure of intelligence analysis and looked at the probable enemy intentions, instead of accepting a broader range of assessments. If Pearl Harbor was an isolated failure in the pre-war intelligence of the U.S., it would have been a hard thing to explain to the thousands that lost their lives that day. As the United States found herself in a war after being attacked so viciously by the Japanese, General "Hap" Arnold saw it this way:" . . . *"one of the most wasteful weaknesses in our whole setup . . . our lack of a proper air intelligence organization."* Yet he knew as many others in the military did, that the problems with air intelligence in the years prior to 1942, had broader issues in the role of air power and its place in the national defense. In truth, air intelligence was treated almost as a second cousin until the hit on Pearl Harbor. It had been kicked about, bureaucratically bullied and had no true organizational place. The excuse of tight budgets, not enough manpower or aircraft and equipment, now paled in the light of what had happened on December 7, 1941. The confusion and uncertain responsibilities of the general staff and the Air Corp/Air Forces intelligence reflected in a search for some type of an organizational identity within the Army Air Corp.

As with any developing process, it happens in starts and fits, false leads and wrong adaptations of information. However, what exacerbated the process were the broader and more critical concepts about what actually defined and constituted the air intelligence and the determination of how it was acquired, interpreted and disseminated. The Airmen who built up the theory of strategic bombing in the "ACTS of the 1930s[16]", saw that it demanded more than just the traditional information like enemy order of battle or combat abilities. Their grasp did not include the depth of the information needed, nor any upshot of gathering and evaluating the information. It was obvious once strategic bombing operations started in 1942.

---

[16] Neutrality Acts passed 1935-36-37 & 39 to limit the U.S. involvement in future wars

Pearl Harbor . . . the Morning of Disaster

It was a typical Sunday on the Hawaiian island of Oahu, pure blue sky, cloudless, sparkling blue waters, as the waves broke on white sand beaches at 7 AM on December 7, 1941. The military personnel were already at their mess, some attending Sunday services, as some of the Hawaiian population were also doing. Both the Army Air Corp, the Navy and Marines were not prepared for what was coming. No one expected it, no one suspected it, no one would have believed it possible. The Japanese were already well on their way to their ground zero Oahu via air and mini submarines that were actually human torpedoes called *Kaiten*. The senior members of the Army staff did know and fear that there might be sabotage attempts by some of the Japanese sympathizers. They did not fear any type of military attack at all. Hence, the air bases at Hickam and Wheeler were not prepared for anything other than guarding their aircraft by setting them up pointing wingtip to wingtip on the flight line, instead of getting them in the revetments that were built for an attack just like that which was looming over them . Even the anti-aircraft ammunition was in ground storage, a long distance from the flight line, where it could not be loaded onto aircraft swiftly.

The bright blue morning of December 7, 1941 found both the Navy and the Army Air Corp ignoring signs that something was on the move out there in that beautiful blue ocean. The Naval destroyer *WARD* managed to sink a kaiten just at the mouth of the harbor sometime around 6:45 AM that morning. However, Admiral Kimmel, who was in charge of the Pacific fleet, wasn't told about it until 7:25 AM. Over at an Army radar station, a scout aircraft was detected. That scout aircraft had been sent ahead of the Japanese fleet at 6:45AM. Yet, the officer that was on duty figured this was a flight of B-17s that they had been waiting for, coming in from California and decided not to relay the information about the scout aircraft. At 7:53AM the party was on for the Japanese as the first of their pilots radioed in *"TORA, TORA, TORA!"* which was their signal for a successful surprise attack to the Japanese fleet. At 7:55AM, it was all history, a devastating painful part of United States history.

The first to go were the Army Airfields on Oahu. This was a basic part of the Japanese battle plan. The one thing the Japanese did not want was to start entering into dog fights with the Navy and Army Air Corp pilots, so they took out the airfields to make sure that was not an option. Hickam, Wheeler and Bellows airfields were the first to be targeted and destroyed by the Japanese. The first to go was Wheeler and Hickam fields. The Japanese destroyed the aircraft, maintenance hangars, and other buildings that supported the aircraft. The chapel, mess hall and the barracks at Hickam were badly damaged. There was a second wave of Japanese aircraft that hit Wheeler and Hickam just about an hour after the first attacks began. With the second attack, the Japanese wasted no time in strafing the buildings on the field, tents and anything else the moved. Bellows field suffered the same beating. By the end of the attack, the Japanese killed over 700 Army Air Force personnel, injured more and destroyed almost two thirds of the airpower that was based on Oahu. But it wasn't over . . . Not just yet.

While the Army Air Corp was being blown up on the fields on the air bases, Navy personnel were trying to organize some kind of retaliation, it was disorganized to say the least. One of the few pilots that managed to find a flyable aircraft, still in his pajamas, 2nd Lt. Philip M. Rasmussen of the 46th Pursuit Squadron Army Air Corp, managed to find a Curtiss P-36 Hawk and headed for the revetment at the end of the airfield. Joined by three other pilots in P-36s, they took off, with the Japanese still firing at them and were told by radio to head to Kaneohe Bay where they took on eleven Japanese fighters. Rasmussen got one hit against the Japanese and was attacked by two other Japanese in Mitsubishi A6M2 Zeros. Between the 20mm canon shell and regular gunfire, Rasmussen's canopy was crushed, his radio destroyed and the P-36's hydraulics lines and rudder cables were cut. Rasmussen headed for cloud cover and started back for Wheeler Field. He brought the P-36 in with no brakes, rudder, or tail wheel. The count on the bullet holes were a staggering 500! Rasmussen received the Silver Star for his efforts. He also shot down a second Japanese aircraft in 1943 and lived to retire from the service in 1965. The number of aircraft lost totaled 188. This is just one little example of what was happening that day on Oahu. The Navy was taking a horrendous beating with ships being sunk right in the harbor. The naval base was hit by 353 Japanese fighter aircraft. The battleship USS Arizona was not refloated. She remains today where she was sunk with her many crew aboard and turned into a memorial. Even now, she weeps drops of oil into the ocean where she lays, to remind all who visit her of those lost with her. Three cruisers, three destroyers and one anti-aircraft training ship and a mine layer were lost. The important base installations like power stations, the shipyard, the ammunition dump along with the submarine piers and headquarters were also destroyed. 2,043 Americans were killed. 1,178 were wounded. To say the least, the attack hit the U.S. citizens like a bolt of lightning. They were in shock that this could happen. It didn't take long for President Roosevelt to declare war. We ask the question: Were there signals? Were there any signs? Is it true that the Japanese diplomats knew all along what was going on and that the U.S. government allowed this to happen to make sure that the U.S. would enter the into the European/Pacific War? That smacks of conspiracy fodder that we will not address here. What we will address is the fact that yes, signs were missed that the Japanese were planning something huge and they did pull it off. Would the fact that the officer on duty that morning who sighted the Japanese scout plane and mistook it for a B-17 due to arrive, could have been more urgent in pushing his message through? It's possible. It's possible that if Admiral Kimmel had gotten the message about the sinking of the kaiten just at the mouth of the harbor earlier, he could have prepared or at least sent word down the line to be on alert for something. But it's all a sorrowful part of U.S. History now, as Roosevelt said, *"A date which will live in infamy"*. Had Signal intelligence been better, if the lines of communication not been so lax, there might have been a chance to save lives. However, what we should take away from Pearl Harbor's horror is that aerial intelligence, signal intelligence, human intelligence, is the meat and potatoes that will keep the U.S. from falling to its enemies. Intelligence was and is urgent and very important. With the United States now entering the War, it was more important than ever before.

Yankee Doodle - the B-17 commanded by Brig. General Ira C. Eaker on the first bombing mission over Europe-August 17, 1942
(National Museum of the USAF ™)

Chapter Five

World War II and the New Art of Aerial Reconnaissance—Lessons Learned

The worst had happened. With the dawn of December 7, 1941, the status of the Army Air Corp changed as it did for all the services of the United States. They were now engaged in a full-blown war against the "Evil Axis" Germany, Italy and Japan. Things needed to come up to speed and it had to happen right away. There had to be new methods of getting information which the Allies could use to defend and defeat against the Third Reich and the Japanese Empire. Pre-war United States military intelligence operations were just not adequate. The intelligence structure had no way of attaining the type of information needed for the building of a strategic air operations which the Army Air Corp could use for advanced planning. Getting that information became much more difficult than when the war actually started. As the war started to move on, the question of who was the best qualified to evaluate that information and be in a position to affect both planning and operations were not nearly as simple as the Air Corp would have believed in the 1930s. The U.S. air leaders and staff began to pull together their full range of the intelligence resources, methods of collection and analysis to get the most complete use of the image of the enemy that they could procure, hoping that they could find its weaknesses, abilities, objectives and strengths. These methods would include photo intelligence, economic breakdowns, wartime production levels, networking of their information officers, resistance groups, analysis of the enemy aircraft capabilities. That would include designs, technical breakdowns. And all of this had to be done thousands of miles from where the actual combat was taking place. The first on the list of tools would be SIGINT (signals intelligence) that would come out of Europe and the Far East. SIGINT would become the heart of the intelligence tool pack. However, it got there only gradually. It did succeed because SIGINT could reach into the most sensitive of the enemy's activities. For a good portion of the war, more of the intelligence that went into the planning and execution of strategic and tactical air operations came from other sources.

Tools of the Trade

The first on the list of tools was something by the name of ULTRA which was within the SIGINT list of goodies. We also had the diplomatic tool, called MAGIC. Both of these programs included the interception of intelligence, deciphering, translation and analysis of low-grade ciphers, the interception of un-encoded enemy radio and wireless traffic patterns, efforts to locate and catalog enemy electronic transmissions, direction finding equipment (DF). The process of determining the location of the enemy transmitters was completed with a process called triangulation. This process was based on the angle at which transmissions signals were received by two or more receivers and was of tactical value. It offered much to ground and naval operations. This was due to enemy Army headquarters, which was more like the enemy Air Corp headquarters, that would relocate its positions frequently. It was harder to hit a moving target.

Direction finding for the airmen was used to determine location and signal characters of their radar. This allowed the Air Commanders to judge the anti-aircraft defenses and fighter control abilities and then adapt their plans to root them out. Traffic analysis was used to secure some information about the enemy's presence and organization, when deciphering of messages wasn't available. Most closely guarded of all the secret war tools was ULTRA. It remained secret until almost three decades after the war ended. ULTRA also helped the United States with their MAGIC program and the penetration of the Japanese naval and diplomatic ciphers. The Germans succeeded in breaking the U.S. military attaché code in late 1941. Their decrypts of messages, starting with the U.S. liaison officer in Cairo, Egypt gave the Third Reich General Erwin Rommel important information about the 8th Army in the desert. It could be said the some of the SIGNIT just was not totally reliable and there were many chances that information could come through tainted or unclear. ULTRA did not influence the air war despite the insecurity of the Luftwaffe and ground fighting. It also did not garner much advantage.

Aircraft and Transformation

In 1941, based on a lesson from the British in WWI regarding aerial reconnaissance, the United States started to finally understand how much they needed to explore and expand this process. The first aircraft to go to the **F** series was the A-20 Havoc which was then called the F-3A. This occurred largely because of the director of Photographic Intelligence, Colonel Minton Kaye. Colonel Kaye also worked with one hundred of the Lockheed P-38s and changed those over to F-4s, using a trigonometric mount that he had been working on right before the war. While the F-4 looked like it might be a good deal, there were so many technical issues with the first models that it was rejected by the crews that had to use them on the front lines. The first U.S. operational use of aerial reconnaissance was in Australia. Colonel Karl Polifka, who was a pilot himself and noted to be rather on the belligerent side, developed many of the tactics that would soon become orthodox within the reconnaissance trade.

Colonel Karl Polifka responsible for many
of the tactics used in aerial reconnaissance
(National Museum of the USAF™)

Polifka worked out of Port Moresby and into Rabaul. His 8th Photo Reconnaissance Squadron had some very serious issues with their F-4s. If it wasn't one of them, it was all of them. However, Polifka used every bit of what he learned from those problems when he got back to the U.S. in 1943. The United States and Britain invaded French North Africa in November of 1942 and their quickly devised reconnaissance resources were faced with a myriad of issues. President Franklin D. Roosevelt's son, Colonel Elliott Roosevelt took over command of the U.S. assets. The F-13s out of the 3rd Photo Group, under Colonel Roosevelt, arrived at Steeple Mort in Cambridgeshire, England in September of 1942 and left for North Africa two months later. This group used the B-17 Stratofortress, which were now known as the reconnaissance version F-9. The Lockheed P-38 Lightning was soon converted to F-4s and the P-38G/Hs were converted to F-5s. By February Roosevelt joined together with the

British RAF squadrons in a multinational Northwest African Photographic Reconnaissance Wing (NAPRW). By this time, the F-4 was found to be inadequate. The F-9 was also not able to make it safely over enemy territory. The British had their new De Havilland Mosquito, which looked like it might be the ticket. The British Squadrons in the Mediterranean picked up the sagging end that the U.S. Air Corp had left. There were so many technical and tactical issues that the U.S. side of the Squadron was virtually at a standstill. However, the U.S. ricocheted back and by the time it came to invade Sicily in July with *Operation Husky,* the British and U.S. forces had knit together to become a viable unit. The NAPRW grew to include South Africa, Free French and New Zealand along with the RAF and the U.S. Army Air Corp. The new F-5 aircraft, which actually was another version of the P-38 Lightening were now accessible and they were beyond a doubt much more sustainable. By this time, the U.S. Army Air Corp, that was led by Colonel Roosevelt, got hold of the De Havilland Mosquito and developed a brand new version of a reconnaissance aircraft, it would unfortunately lead to the Howard Hughes aircraft, the XF-11.

The XF-11 actually came in too late for much help in WWII. At the end of WWII there were three types of dedicated photo reconnaissance aircraft that were under development for the United States. The first was the Northrop F-15 Reporter which had been developed from the P-61 Black Widow. The P-61 was a night fighter that carried a twin engine, twin boom design. The first "Reporter" was flown in June 1945, already too late for action, yet thirty-six of them were built. The original contract was for one hundred seventy-five, which were canceled and the F-15A never really went into service. That brings us to the second aircraft that was built for reconnaissance service again, too little, too late. The Republic X-12 (XR-12) Rainbow was designed in 1943, to a very precise requirement that was drawn up by the Army Air Corp photographic section of the Air Technical Service Command. This very large aircraft was close to ninety-four feet long and had a wingspan of over one hundred twenty-nine feet. It was powered by four 3500 HP Pratt and Whitney R-4360 WASP MAJOR radial engines which gave the Rainbow a top speed of over 425 mph and had ceiling of 40,000 ft. The first of the two prototypes flew February 4, 1946 but since the war was already over, the project was not considered urgent. The second prototype did not fly until 1947. The XF-12 was also being tested as a transatlantic airliner. We now get to the third aircraft, much like the F-15 Reporter, which was a twin engine, twin boom monoplane. The XR-11 was a large aircraft with a wingspan of one hundred one feet and a length of more than sixty-five feet. The airframe was streamlined, with every joint smoothed and sanded to make sure there was no additional drag on the aircraft. The aircraft was then sprayed with a shiny nylon based, clear coat finish. Dried and polished, the carefully prepared finish did add slightly to the 400+ mph speed of the aircraft. The first XR-11 prototype flew on July 7, 1946, with Howard Hughes, the aircraft's creator, at the controls. The aircraft had propeller problems and crashed into the Beverly Hills area of California. Hughes was severely injured but mended well enough to fly the second prototype on April 5, 1947. A victim of the post war economy altered requirements and progress into the jet age, the XR-11 even with the 40,000 ft. ceiling, was no longer immune to interception in the air. The XF-11 along with the F-15A Reporter and the XF-12 Rainbow were no longer candidates for reconnaissance work.

Original Aircraft	Reconnaissance Version
A-20 Havoc	F-3A
B-17 Flying Fortress	F-9
B-29 Superfortress	F-13
P-38 Lighting	F-4
P-38F	F4A
P-38G/H	F-5
P-38H	F5C
P-38 J	F5E/F
P38 L	F5 E/G
P-38G	F5A/B
P-51A/B Mustang	F-6C
P-51	F-6D
P51K	F6-K
P-61 Black Widow	F-15

Douglas A-20 Havoc
(courtesy Ebaumsworld.com)

Eagle Eyes

Boeing B-29 Superfortress aka F-13 Recce version
(www.ebaumsworld.com)

Lockheed F-4 Reconnaissance version of the P-38 Lighting
(www.ebaumsworld.com)

North American F-6 Recce version for the P-51 Mustang
(www.ebaumsworld.com)

Meanwhile Back in Europe . . . in the Midst of the War . . .

There were bigger problems facing the Third Reich war machine in the Fall of 1941. The Nazis were determined to go after the Russians. The Luftwaffe assigned some fifty-six tactical and armored division air/reconnaissance squadrons to the armies. By the end of 1941, only nineteen of those squadrons were in action due to Soviet fighters and their inability to work in Russia's extremely inhospitable weather. In short, they were freezing and ill prepared for the Russian winter, the units were sent back to the Luftwaffe control and there the commanders tried to re-equip them with the Junkers-88 and the Dornier Do-17 bombers. The first German aircraft developed for reconnaissance were the twin engine FockeWulf-FW-189, which had all weather capability. Due to the activities in Britain, the Luftwaffe began to modify their fighter planes for a two-mission role, and that was to perform photo-reconnaissance as well. The Messerschmitt ME-109G and the FockWulfe-FW190A were equipped with cameras and performed well under the pressure of war. The ten long range reconnaissance squads equipped with the JU-88 and the DO-17s were for daylight operations only. At the beginning of the Russian campaign, the Third Reich had three reconnaissance squadrons and were organized and equipped with the Dornier Do-17s. In the late days of the war, the Arad-234 which was a four engine jet reconnaissance aircraft used on a few missions, but the Luftwaffe much like the Allies had to "make do" with what they had. The Luftwaffe's main problems were much different after the Battle of Britain, which took place July 10, 1940. Looking to the east and to Russia, the Luftwaffe bombers no longer filled the skies over Britain and were now needed for long range reconnaissance work. Things were never the same. The lack of foresight and the stubbornness not to change also took its toll on the U.S. Army Air Corp. when it came to concepts. In late 1940, the general staff was still working on training aerial observers whose main function was to direct artillery fire like they did in WWI. The Army still had kite balloon squads that were stationed at Ft. Sill in Oklahoma.

Lessons learned in Europe were applied finally to the U.S. organization just before Pearl Harbor, when a reconnaissance squadron was assigned to each heavy bomber group and a photographic group was finally established. Slowly but surely, the U.S. was catching up. The U.S. Reconnaissance Squadron was equipped with the same type aircraft as the bomb squadrons. Their primary mission was taking photos but when not doing that, they were bombers. It seems that the Luftwaffe and U.S. Army Air Corp. were in the same boat. In early 1942, Boeing Aircraft Company started to modify their four engine B-17 for reconnaissance work. For a short time the B-17 was to become the Army Air Corp standard reconnaissance aircraft and on that premise, two of the aircraft were sent to England in the summer of 1942.

It was quite apparent that the B-17 flying alone would be easy targets for the Luftwaffe ME-109 and the newer Focke-Wulf 190 fighter. Since the fighter escort for long range missions was non-existent at the time, the reconnaissance version of the B-17 was shelved. Long range plans for the Army Air Crop were firm. There would be separate groups for photographic work with special aircraft assigned to them. By April of 1942, all of the reconnaissance units in the bomb groups were re-designated bomber squads. The 1st Photographic Group, was formed in June 1941, and was set up to expand the photo-mapping capabilities of the AAC and conducted long range photo-reconnaissance along the line of the Royal Air Force.

This new photo-reconnaissance group consisted of four squadrons equipped with the B-18 bombers, an offshoot of the Douglas DC-3 transport. The squad was assigned to each of the four allied air forces. At the war's outbreak these units found themselves involved in anti-submarine patrol work and mapping projects for the western hemisphere defense. The Army Air Corp found itself without a suitable high speed reconnaissance aircraft, a situation that was apparent in September of 1941 to the Wright Field officers at Dayton Ohio. These officers recommended modifying the twin-engine Lockheed P-38 Lightning fighter.

Right after the Pearl Harbor attack, the Mediterranean theater was very slow in getting used to using the B-24 Liberator for reconnaissance. The 16th Reconnaissance Squadron flew in support of the Allied landings on Sicily and in Southern Italy which pinpointed no fewer than four hundred fifty enemy radar sites. The 16th reconnaissance wing also pioneered the use of the RC-156 jammer, designed at the Harvard Radio Research Labs. The project that supported the jammer was known as *"Carpet"*. This program was known to close any gaps that might appear when project *"WINDOW"* (which constituted thousands of aluminum strips that were dropped from Allied aircraft to obscure a bomber's radar echoes) that were being used.

The AAF had neglected the reconnaissance function from the beginning of the war and attempted to patch it up throughout the war. It was a poor error and a costly one given the point that in the line of importance of intelligence to the precision daylight bombing campaign, it was literally life and death. It was almost an afterthought when the AAF decided to convert the Boeing B-29 Superfortress into the F-13 Reconnaissance aircraft. The B-29 was the perfect platform for reconnaissance because it had high range, altitude and speed with capacity for cameras and equipment. The B-29 was stripped down and called the F-13. The *F* designation was specifically for photographic work while the *B* for Bombardment and the *A* for Attack, *C* for Cargo and *L* for Liaison. The next step was to load her with camera equipment. The XXI Bomber Command had to wait for such an aircraft as the B-29, nothing could have been more perfect.

Eagle Eyes

On November 1, 1944, the first aircraft since the Doolittle Raid on Tokyo flew over the city in a very long, tough mission. A B-29 called the *"Tokyo Rose"* took off and flew over the city of Tokyo, Japan for about an hour at 32,000 ft. She took about 7,000 photographs that were vital to the mission. The Japanese tried hard to take down the F-13 (former B-29) but failed. They could not do anything but watch as the bird continued her mission out of range of their guns and flak, in broad daylight.

"Tokyo Rose" was having beginner's luck as the follow up missions were not as successful. When the reconnaissance arrived, the XXI Bomber Command flew a total of forty-nine missions in November and December. There were sixteen missions blocked by poor visibility. Fourteen more had partial visibility and in the others, the windows of the cameras iced up. The XXI Bomber Command flew a number of electronic reconnaissance missions to feel out the Japanese radar. This was basically called "lighting up" the enemy's radar. With all this, two of the F-13s were lost.

The Army Air Force entered WWII poorly equipped and under prepared to support ground commanders. With photo and visual reconnaissance, it really could not employ aerial reconnaissance effectively from the beginning. In the Mediterranean theater, reconnaissance use was done in support of ground forces. The Operations in North Africa frequently failed because of de-centralized control and inadequate aircraft.

Photo reconnaissance improved for the Sicily invasion, but it lost its pertinence after the invasion when the Allied ground forces were ahead of the photo coverage. Visual reconnaissance supplemented this coverage during mobile operations, but it didn't have the sufficient detail for wide enough area coverage. The same situation in Italy occurred when aerial reconnaissance supported the 5th Army. Because the 5th Army had achieved a greater degree of success by securing a tactical control over photos that were coming in, it made things work more efficiently. The 5th Army had to have it right the first time.

Tactics and Aircraft—Tactical Reconnaissance and the 10th Air Reconnaissance Group

This section is a closer view at how a tactical reconnaissance unit would operate during WWII.

The tactical reconnaissance pilots of the 10th Photo Reconnaissance Group, for example, worked with the P-51 Mustang that was converted to a photo reconnaissance aircraft, which was then called the (F-6). The designations for the P-51 were as follows: F-6b (P-51A); F-6C (P-51A/B); F-6D(P-51D); F-6K (P-51K). Obvious was the conversion from fighter to photo reconnaissance, which was the camera installation in the fuselage. The F-6 version held on to the four to six-gun armament that it had as a fighter, which was something the that P-38 Lightning did not do. A tactical reconnaissance pilot was told to stay out of combat at all costs. When doing vertical reconnaissance photography, the F-6 would carry the K-22 camera with a 12" aerial lens cone. It really turned out some fine detailed photography for an altitude of 6,000 ft. The K-17 camera carried a 6" aerial lens cone for altitudes of 3,500 ft. The K-17 was replaced by the 6" version of the K-22 that allowed for a two second rewind cycle for any overlap photography at very low altitudes.

The missions that carried the oblique photography equipment in the F-6, used the K-24 camera, which used a 7" or a 14" aerial lens cone, or a K-22 with a 12" cone. The K-24 was used for low altitude oblique images of the railway tunnels, bridges etc. These images were basically used in all the fighter-bomber briefings that were given to those pilots who were assigned to attack those targets. These images were usually taken at altitudes from 2,500 ft to 4,000 ft and at angles of 12-17 degrees. The images were gridded (boxed out in squares) so artillery and field commanders could plan assaults.

For a normal tactical reconnaissance mission, the plan would work with a two plane flight called the *SECTION*. The plan would be commanded by a seasoned pilot that would be held responsible for navigation, observation and shooting the images of the target area. The second pilot would provide the protection for the first aircraft against any attack or give a warning against flak. He was always about 200 yards behind the lead aircraft and covered the lead pilot's tail from the sun which was usually where the Luftwaffe showed up. The visual reconnaissance missions SECTION would fly were between 3,500 and 6,000 ft altitude, even though the tactical reconnaissance mission sometimes did go higher. However, a visual reconnaissance mission was usually held to 6,000ft. Anything above the 6,000 ft. would not provide sufficiently good images. Sometimes, it was necessary to go in way below 3,500 ft. to make observations of the possible cargo of a train or fleet of trucks.

Tactical reconnaissance was broken down into these types of missions:

Area Search: This would give a General in charge the immediate information of a troop movement within its boundaries. This flight was given a complete briefing on the situation by the Army ground liaison officer who would tell them what and where to look for specific targets.

Route Reconnaissance: This mission was flown for a view of any railroad lines and highways to a depth of 200 miles behind the enemy lines. This would allow the reconnaissance team to figure out the enemy's supply route and watch the troop movement.

Artillery Adjustment: Tactical reconnaissance pilots would fly these missions to adjust the fire of long-range artillery like Howitzer guns, in areas where the light aircraft like the L-5 could not fly safely. These missions would produce photos of the targets. It could also run by a ground station, asking for information from another tactical reconnaissance section about the targets in the area.

Merton Oblique Photo Cover: These missions were special request flights from the artillery commanders of a certain area. It produced gridded photos that were used in planning fire ranges for guns.

Photographic Missions: These flights went up to 4,000 ft. or made a penetration flight of 50 miles, since it was impractical to send unarmed F-5s in to get high altitude images. The tactical reconnaissance sections were used for these missions.

Photo Reconnaissance

The 10th Photographic Reconnaissance Group used the F-5 which was the reconnaissance version of the P-38 Lightning. The F-5s were not armed as the F-6s were. Any pilot flying an F-5 flew alone and had to rely on altitude, speed and evasive maneuvers to stay alive. The F-5 (see below for chart of various aircraft and codes) had a range of 100-150 miles from their base, but sometimes went as deep as 250-275 miles.

For the F5, the cameras used were either the K-17 or K-22 with a 7-degree side lap. In most of the variations, the cameras used had longer focal lengths for very high altitude photos or 12" or a shorter focal length camera when the ceiling was too low caused by clouds, bad weather or when flying a special mission called "dicing".

Dicing missions had the F-5s carrying the 12" focal length nose camera, tilted in a down position at an angle of 10 degrees and two 6" focal length oblique cameras, one on either side, aimed forward from the right angle of the aircraft line of sight. This allowed for 180 degrees of coverage. To allow for the 1:10,000 scale images with a camera carrying a 24" lens, the F-5 pilot usually found themselves at 24,000 ft. Sometimes they worked as high as 35,000 ft using the 40" lens. On many of the high priority flights when the weather was not cooperating and high altitude could not be flown, straight line courses were flown at 6,000 ft. and used the 6" camera that gave the 1:12,000 scale photo. When the 12" camera was produced, they could work as low as 5,000 ft. These missions were few and far between due to the flak and that was serious and prolific. If photos were to be low level urgent close-ups, the F-5 pilots would use the "dicing" plan, which would constitute a high speed pass over the target at approximately 50 ft. and leave before the flak gunners could warm up their guns.

Photo Reconnaissance Missions:

Strips and Mosaics: This allowed for missions that involved photos of an entire battle area and other sections of proposed operations, communication lines or just plain nothing on the ground to make a difference.

Pinpoints: The F-5 pilots would fly specific target missions for airfields, bridges, roads, gun positions command posts.

Front Line Coverage: These missions allowed for detailed images of the front line to figure out the enemy defenses, their gun positions, and top targets. These were flown daily.

Bomb Damage Assessment: This mission allowed for targets to be examined literally minutes after they had been struck by bombs to see the extent of the damages.

Night Photo Reconnaissance: The 155th Night Reconnaissance Squadron used the F-3 (A-20J Havoc) aircraft. The crew carried three; pilot. gunner and navigator. These missions were flown singularly, with almost 400 miles of area to cover. Initially, the F-3s were flown with a twin 50-caliber machine gun in the top turrets, but later on this was replaced with a tail warning device that would ring a bell in the cockpit telling the pilot that an aircraft was on his tail. Usually the "bogey", if it got close to the F-3, was met with a rather fierce evasive action. One of the biggest headaches for the night flying F-3 was navigation. Of everything that was tried on board, only the **GEE**[17] system worked. Flak attack was the biggest issue and problems in navigation didn't help the issue. Flak that went after night photo missions left behind a painful loss of men and equipment that were either destroyed or damaged. Later in the war, the *Microwave Early Warning* system, could check the enemy for aircraft before a mission and some cases had the F-3s escorted by the devilish P-61 Black Widow night fighters. However, even with all of this and the coordination of all Allied anti-aircraft batteries being on alert, the AA (flak) fire still wreaked painful loss among the F-3s.

The F-3 had two different types of cameras and had two types of missions. The camera used was the K-19 or the K-29 camera with a 12-inch lens. This camera made 180 exposures when timed to a Edgerton Lamp, also called the D-2 Flash Unit, that produced a 200,000,000 candlepower light which came on every three seconds during the photo mission and produced excellent images. The F-3 also carried the M-46 flash bomb unit which operated between 6,000 and 10,000ft. and carried two 12-inch

---

[17] Radio navigation system that used a time delay between two different radio signals to produce a "fix" on a target up to 350 miles. Also used by the RAF during WWII

cameras. This camera gave the F-3 two M-46 flash bombs which lit off from a fuse preset after release. The 800,000,000-candle power light which was generated by the flash bombs turned on the cameras through a photoelectric cell.

The F-3 flew both the **Pinpoint** and **Strip** photo runs as described in the tactical reconnaissance section above.

How Photo Interpretation Analysis Evolved

As earlier discussed in opening chapters, in May of 1862, General George B. McClellan used balloons to take photographs in several of the Civil War battles around Richmond, Virginia. He made huge maps and then superimposed grids over them to better slice out the areas he needed. He also has a telegraph connection between division headquarters and the balloon borne observers, who could watch and anticipate what was going on near or around a battle area. He could also gather information about ensuing troop movements of the enemy. It was a huge gain for reconnaissance in the Civil War.

As the technology changed throughout the years and various wars, the means for aerial reconnaissance grew in giant steps. In 1906, at a meeting in Stuttgart, Germany, Mr. A. Bujard presented a paper entitled, *"Rockets in the Service of Photography"* which noted concerns with the work of Alfred Maul, an engineer who wanted to use camera carrying rockets for military reconnaissance. Maul started in 1906, with his first test model rocket that carried a camera, which had a 40mm square image, and is the same size as the picture taken by a Rolleiflex miniature camera.   Maul had problems and lots of bad luck. His problems included things like the shutter freezing up, the parachute delivery system not working and it went on. He finally worked up to an 8"x10" camera that could shoot at about 2600 feet. However, as Maul was trying to gear up, the airplane came into play and rocketry photography for reconnaissance sort of fell off the map when it came to its uses as reconnaissance platform. As the methods and madness went on to find the ultimate in aerial reconnaissance, by World War I other discoveries were coming to light. Research prior to World War I which came from the use of a dirigible, the existence of aerial haze at high altitudes was discovered and came into play. The need for more sensitive film emulsions that allowed for contrast and of course, the use of color sensitive plates and color filters were also being explored. The development of aerial photography had advanced slowly from a balloon to the dirigible, which was just superior for photographic purposes, but was not going to be enough as World War I and World War II came into view. The oncoming Cold War had its roots in the Bolshevik revolution of 1917. The United States found Bolshevism repulsive. By the mid-1930s, the Nazi threat was worldwide, along with the Japanese threat that was taking over the Pacific islands and nations. The need for more precise aerial photography was needed, but along with that was the need for specialists that could read those photographs and tell the military just what secrets those photos held.

The British took the lead in World War II in developing aerial photographic analysis, thanks to the work of Constance Babington Smith and a number of other British military and civilians that were essential to the development of the art of photographic analysis and interpretation.

All of the photographs in the world taken of enemy installations or troop movement, meant nothing if there wasn't someone who could take that photograph and actually read it. That person is an image analyst or photo interpreter. This art form, and it is an art form, actually came into its heyday during WWII. The British were the lead in acquiring and developing this process. Thanks to people like Sidney Cotton who came up with the aerial reconnaissance camera concept and Constance Babington Smith, the forerunner of image analysts, the birth of true aerial reconnaissance was born. It was due to Babington–Smith's excellent work with the Allied Photographic Intelligence Group, that made the art of image analysis a real item that could be used to defeat the Nazis and Japanese. As the reconnaissance pilots flew and returned with their "take", it would mean nothing unless the eyes that viewed those images could pick out the varied details of tank movements, troop movements, changes in the landscape that could show an encampment or possibly a storage depot of the enemy. The secrets that the photographs gave to the Allies allowed for the decision making processes of the Generals who would be able, within twenty four hours of receiving this treasure trove of information to make plans for troop movement or bombing runs. As discussed earlier, the Allies without the aid of the British in this new means of finding out photographically what the enemy was doing, would have lost much and gained very little. Thanks to the British and their work, the art of aerial reconnaissance/photo interpretation and analysis came into its own.

As an example of just what the British had devised, Britain had faced the threat of German invasion before and now in WWII, it was a common thought. However, as of 1940, the Brits stood a chance of getting ahead of the threat. The summer of 1940 was the first in the line of proving the worth of photo intelligence. Just as the Germans were thinking about crossing the channel to invade the United Kingdom, most of the various methods used to get intelligence were worthless to both the War cabinet and the Chiefs of Staff for the British. On June 10, just before the Battle of Dunkirk, the Photographic Development Unit working with the British Admiralty, wanted all of the enemy ports watched. However, the British Bomber Command didn't feel the same way. The Admiralty felt their priority should come first, and the Bomber Command felt that theirs should be first because of the need for damage assessment. The argument was on between the Admiralty and the Bomber Command as to who should control the photographic unit. It didn't take long for the Air Staff to finally come up with a solution and that was for the Coastal Command, which was already managing the RAF's visual reconnaissance of all enemy ships. They would take command of the photographic units. This move let Sidney Cotton, the man who created the concept of aerial reconnaissance for the British, to step back out of the limelight. He was awarded the Office of the Order of the British Empire as a thank you for his creative and magnificent service. Now it was up to the military to build on what Cotton had left them.

An RB-29 from Ramey Air Force Base, Aguadilla, Puerto Rico.
(Ramey Air Force Base Historical Society)

Chapter Six

The Start of the Cold War

The End of WWII and the Beginning of the New War

As the European theater of World War II ended in the spring of 1945, there was a treasure trove of information that followed many of the repatriated POWs, most especially those of the Soviet Union. The Soviet Union was a "fair weather" ally in World War II but to be sure, that was something that wasn't going to last when it came to sparring with the United States in post war positioning. While the material received from these Soviet POWs was somewhat outdated due to their incarceration, it was nonetheless valuable. The war may have been over but the need for intelligence was not and the United States had to find a way to do it. The Cold War was closing in and fast.

Now that the war was ending, there were new challenges emerging. It wasn't until 1945 with the atomic bomb drop on Hiroshima, Japan, that would finally close the Pacific theater for the United States. It was then that the United States would finally be faced by its newest foe. The Soviet Union was not the friend that the United States thought it was, and it didn't take long to find that out.

A PB4Y-2 Privateer of the U.S. Navy.
(U.S. Navy)

The U. S. knew that it had to finalize its policy of reconnaissance issues, if it was going to protect itself. The USAAF and the Navy needed to revamp the plans and methods for reconnaissance. However, in facing the plain reality that the United States was tired of war, its hardware was worn out and the only way the U.S. could accomplish this task would be to take its used hardware and reuse it, at least for now. The United States had to face the fact that its people were exhausted, its hardware was at its productive end and most of all, its pockets were low on cash.

During the war, the services did try to reuse aircraft for different purposes. There just was no other way to do it. The services also were not shy about loaning equipment out to each other. In the examples below, you will get the idea of how these aircraft were used. It's necessary to see this in play to understand how these same aircraft was used after war duty. The Navy decided to use its PBY Catalina rescue aircraft and refitted them for reconnaissance work. The PGB-1W held an AN/APS 20B search radar in a large radome. It had a limited capability and detection range of sixty-five miles against low flying aircraft. The military was growing anxious regarding how to fine-tune its aerial reconnaissance structure. Even during the war, the Army Air Force loaned aircraft out to the Navy to aid them with supplying the reconnaissance that they needed. The B-24 Liberator bomber became the F-7 or F-7A because they could carry cameras. The Naval conversion totaled some one hundred eighty aircraft each of which held eleven cameras mounted in the bomb bay and rear fuselage. This was done to help stop the Kamikaze attacks that decimated shipping lanes during the war.

This was known as Project "Cadillac" and it was successful enough and really became the first of the AEWs or airborne early warning systems for Navy aircraft. The F-7A was used in the Pacific theater for photo mapping of Japanese held islands before the allied attacks. Both infrared and color photography were rarely used, however on occasion the Liberators used the photography to pick out targets.

Feb 4, 1944 found two B-24s from VMD-54 of the Marine Corp Photo reconnaissance squadron made a twelve-hour night flight from the Solomon Islands of Truk to prepare for a carrier strike much later that month. April 18, 1944 with aircraft loaned from the USAAF to the Navy, the Liberators that were loaned to VD-3 Naval reconnaissance squadron made a thirteen-hour round trip to photograph Saipan, Tinian and Agrihan islands in preparation for the invasion of the Marianas Islands. The VD-3 squadron was accompanied by the USAAF B-24 Liberators that bombed the island as a diversionary tactic. The Consolidated Aircraft Company B-24Js were also converted to carry six bomb bay cameras and used for reconnaissance of Japanese homeland in the closing months of the war.

B-17G Shoo Shoo Shoo Baby
(National Museum of the U.S. Air Force ™)

Another upgrade program to aerial reconnaissance for the military was started by the U.S. government, and taken over by the Massachusetts Institute of Technology. "Cadillac II" used thirty-two Boeing B-17G flying fortresses fitted out as airborne combat reconnaissance information centers to fly countermeasures against the Kamikaze suicide attacks. This was the precursor of our now well-known "JOINT STARS" idea of forward air control. With these examples of how the United States military started to transform itself into a reconnaissance ready service, we see the ingenuity used and the methods employed which led to a successful end to World War II for the United States. However, the war was now over and not only did the plans for gathering intelligence change, there were now two new services that would deal with it.

The National Security Act being signed by President Truman 1947
(CIA Archives)

USAF and the CIA Created

With the end of WWII, the United Stated gained two new services in the shuffle of the post-war government. The United States Army Air Force had shown its mettle during the war and wanted more than anything to be separated into its own autonomous service. It was a long, hard political fight but in 1947, the Air Force got its wish.

The second major organization that came into being was an intelligence unit, which was created under the National Security Act of 1947 (Public Law 253), which established both the U.S. Air Force and the Central Intelligence Agency. The USAF was established on July 26, 1947 after a brutal political battle and became official on September 18, 1947.

Stuart Symington, first Secretary of the Air Force and Gen. Carl Spaatz, first Air Force Chief of Staff at a press conference announcing the new organizational set-up for the Department of the Air Force, 1947.
(U.S. Air Force)

Along with the new Air Force, the National Security Act also brought with it more funding for the Navy, Army and Air Force and also allowed for a newly created Secretary of Defense to control all of the military services under one roof.

The National Security Act gave each service its own Secretary, which would control each branch of the military. Each service would now be answerable to the new Secretary of Defense. Public Law 253 also created one other organization, the Central Intelligence Agency. The CIA would replace the Office of Strategic Services, which was disbanded shortly after the War's end. As far back, before the start of World War I, the United States didn't have an intelligence service. It was just about the only country in the world that didn't have some form of an intelligence agency to rely on. At its inception, the OSS was a military office. The history of this office began with this statement:

Eagle Eyes

"The Office of the Coordinator of Information established by Order July 11, 1941, exclusive of the foreign information activities transferred to the Office of War Information by Executive Order of June 13, 1942 shall hereafter be known as the Office of Strategic Services. In addition, is hereby transferred to the jurisdiction of the Joint Chiefs of Staff. The head of the Strategic Services will be appointed by the President of the United States and shall perform his duties under the direction of the U. S. Joint Chiefs of Staff. William J. Donovan is hereby appointed as Director of Strategic Services."

This made it official and put the newly formed OSS in the espionage/intelligence business with no civilian government authority to answer to and only the military controlling it. After the German defeat and the complete end of the war in 1945, with President Roosevelt gone, President Harry Truman felt it wasn't a necessity for the OSS to exist. President Truman was not enamored of William (Wild Bill) Donovan who was the head of the OSS and the father of the CIA as we know it today. Truman and Congress were worried that someday, some organization like the OSS could be used against the country. Truman felt that the U.S. wartime intelligence process was built on ENIGMA and the busting of codes, which the OSS really had nothing to do with. SIGINT (signal intelligence) which was the heart of the Army and Navy, who of course were in their own interservice rivalry, was given the win when it came to signal intelligence.

Truman could have tried to turn the OSS into what the CIA became doing clandestine operations out of country and analysis overseas. Many felt Truman foolishly dissolved the OSS out of ignorance and spite. Even the Presidential aide, Clark Clifford, complained that Truman prematurely, abruptly and unwisely disbanded the OSS.

Truman wanted to think of rebuilding the country after the war and wanted desperately that all "secret organizations" like the OSS to just disappear. He did acknowledge his mistake later, when he approved the reassembly of many of the OSS services in the newly planned Central Intelligence Agency. Congress saw Truman's earlier rash decision to disband the OSS as agreeable to them. Most of the legislators felt that the OSS was marked for disbanding because so many of the different sections were needed in a peacetime economy. The OSS was technically a wartime agency, used for national emergencies, in this case a country on a wartime footing. Congress was ready to release it and forget about the OSS in entirety. When Truman got the final report from Congress on the OSS situation, he was stunned. The document said that the OSS was "bumbling, and had "lax security" and complained that Donovan had proposed intelligence reforms that had "all the earmarks of a Gestapo system." The report recommended abolishing the OSS save for the Research and Analysis branch, which would be salvaged and turned over to the State Department for supervision. Congress passed the legislation requiring the White House to look for specific Congressional funding for any new agency operating longer than twelve months and allowed any presidential wish to preserve the OSS or to create a permanent intelligence agency, just a wish.

That legislation, when signed into law wouldn't allow for Donovan to create an "American Gestapo". Donovan was insisting that this intelligence branch should report directly to the President first. The Truman White House decided the solution was to create a new peacetime intelligence office without Donovan's involvement. Many of the White House advisors also felt the nation needed some sort of an intelligence organization, but not the type that Donovan was famous for. After all this, what was left of the OSS now belonged to the War department. Donovan found out that the original date of October 1st, for closing down operations was no longer valid. This gave him less than two weeks to dismantle everything that he had worked for all those years. Donovan had officially gotten his walking papers.

Major General William (Wild Bill Donovan) head of the OSS (NARA/USAF).
As all these changes progressed, the OSS transformed into the
CIG Central Intelligence Group

The new CIG had two purposes:
a. Strategic warning
b. Covert actions

The CIG didn't exist for long. Twenty months later, it was disbanded in favor of the newly minted CIA (Central Intelligence Agency) completed the "1947 National Security Act "which instituted the need for an agency like the new CIA. Now that both services, the USAF and the CIA were in place, the intelligence capability of the United Stated started to look like a reality.

The New Air Force and Reconnaissance

The New U.S. Air Force stepped into its role and the 72nd Reconnaissance Squadron carried out photo reconnaissance and ELINT (Electronic Intelligence) over both the Soviet Arctic and the Far East. The United States was using the venerable B-29 from the wartime version as a bomber and transforming it to a reconnaissance platform. Just like the USSR, the WWII aircraft were doing double duty as reconnaissance aircraft. The RB-29 was equipped with oblique cameras that allowed them to photograph Soviet territory while staying in international air space. Long-range photography revealed very little of what was truly going on. By the end of 1948, some RB-29s were stripped of these weapons and other necessary equipment, allowing them to get to higher altitudes and make penetration flights over the Soviet Union on behalf of the CIA with the approval of President Truman.

The first of the over flights was made on August 5, 1948. The 72nd Reconnaissance Squadron of RB-29s took off from Ladd AFB and made surveillance flights over Siberia, landing in Yokota AB, Japan, after a total of 19 hours and 40 minutes.

There were some longer flights of up to 30 hours, which soon became routine with the aircraft operations at 35,000 ft or more on missions covering at least 5000 miles. However, the RB-29s were seriously in jeopardy when the Soviet MiG 15 showed up in 1948.

A B-29 waiting to be released, her crew waiting to board
(Department of Defense)

The United States was using the B-29 from the war as a reconnaissance platform. Just like the USSR, the WWII aircraft were doing double duty as aerial reconnaissance aircraft. At least the Soviets and the United States were on the same playing field when it came to using WWII aircraft as their temporary if not new reconnaissance tools.

Development of Aerial Photographic Analysis after WWII

Thanks to all the work done by the British and American photographic services during WWII, the art of aerial reconnaissance had grown. Something else that had grown was the adversarial relationship between the Soviet Union and the United States. After the end of WWII, that relationship between the erstwhile allies had deteriorated into a Cold War. The Cold War began when fear of the Soviets power started to take affect. The intrusion into Berlin and splitting Germany into East and West was the Soviet's prime move. The East part of Germany, claimed by the Soviets and run like a concentration camp, had no regard for the German populace that was caught there. Families were literally torn apart from each other once the Soviets decided to claim the East for themselves, causing great tension and angst with the United States. President Truman, who succeeded Roosevelt, was completely unprepared for the nightmare facing him and this was due in no small part to Roosevelt's keeping him so isolated from any involvement in foreign affairs while he was vice president. Hence, the CIA and the need to find out what was going on with the Soviets became more urgent. Spies on the ground were not going to be enough. The U-2 Dragon Lady created by Lockheed's Kelly Johnson, helped to aid that situation up until the time of the *May Day Disaster*. However, the other immense item that became the heart of the Cold War was the development of the Photo Interpreter or Image Analyst.

Properties that Aerial Photography Produced

There are some very important gifts from the process of aerial photography. It can capture and freeze a second in the life of an enemy. This meant that this image could be held and studied and restudied at length, allowing for a more precise record of the area involved. The imaging also could be studied by many people in the imagery analyst's department which allowed for more depth in figuring out exactly what was being shown. It also would become a record of the area for later study, should the landscape change. The image could be duplicated, enlarged and reproduced for many departments to see.

Along with the properties discussed there were also five very important breakthroughs for the imagery analysts. The development of the tough, thin, *ESTAR* plastic base, created by Eastman Kodak Company, now allowed for large quantities of film to be spooled onto a single roll or magazine. This allowed for reconnaissance to be done over a larger territory and for extended time periods. The film referred to as TBF or thin based film, was a specialty that was ordered directly through Kodak.

The Eastman Kodak scientists, Joe Boone, Ford Tuttle, Raife Tarkington, Al Soren and Ed Green worked on development of the film base, and also designed the cine' film processing machines to develop this new thin based film.

Arthur Lundahl—The CIA's Magic Weapon

As the Cold War started to really take form, the need to develop the means to understand what was in those photos taken from the U-2 and the Discoverer satellites became crucial. Arthur "Art" Lundahl was a former naval intelligence officer who came to the CIA in 1952, to develop and head the CIA's first photo-interpretation group, called the "Photo Intelligence Division" (PID) which was the forerunner of the *Office of Imagery Analysis*. The new division was actually housed on the corner of 5th and K street in downtown Washington, D.C. in the Stuart building. This part of town was not what you would call the more fashionable section. In fact, it was in a part of Washington D.C. often called the ghetto. As the new division started to form, the name changed yet again to NPIC or the National Photographic Interpretation Center. It was comprised of more than two hundred interpreters taken from the CIA, Air Force, Navy and Army. The official name change happened in 1991. The term *"Photo Interpreters"* from aerial photo interpreters, lasted until the 1970s when it was dropped and changed to *"Imagery Analyst"*. This change reflected in part the fact that the new reconnaissance satellites like NASA's LANDSAT or the CIA's KH-11, no longer employed the camera system with film. The satellites used "electro-optical" scanners. The analysts were working with images created from electronic data instead of the photographic image produced from film. The new term was meant to enhance the status of the government photo interpreters, who increasingly worked not only from just images but many other intelligence sources. The new non-photographic or electro optical systems like the LANDSAT or KH11 satellites had many types of resolution. Spatial resolution, which it is called, stands for "the dimension of the ground projected, instantaneous field of view (IFOV) from the sensor system which collected the information"[18] There is also radiometric and spectral resolutions used to collect information. There are two forms listed below:

Radiometric resolution: referred to the sensitivity of the detectors acquiring reflected or emitted resolution from the earth's surface.

Spectral resolution: defined the number and width of the spectral bands for which the sensor system gathers data. The remarks made about the electro optical system was used to produce "useful information from the data.

In working with photo interpretation, most analysts continued to depend on the many techniques that were created out of WWII such as the use of stereoscopes to magnify objects, although today, these devices are much more sophisticated and can magnify objects up to 500x. They also use "soft copy" analysis, which uses computers to analyze the digital data from hard copy. While the quality of images (in terms of spatial resolution and frequency of acquisition) and analytical enlargement (computers, stereo microscopes) improved dramatically since the start of the program. The task of imaging analyst has not become any easier but better imaging has led policy makers to ask tougher questions.

---

[18] Jensen (1986)

Imaging Analysts and Their "Responsibilities"

In an essay written in 1952 by Amron Katz, who was a U.S. physicist specializing in aerial reconnaissance methods, was this statement: "...take a million dollar airplane, a hundred thousand dollars worth of cameras, fly a hazardous, expensive mission, get back... run the film through comparably expensive processing machinery...and when the photo interpreter gets around to extracting {intelligence} information on the photographs, he uses a ten cent magnifying glass". It was a major point about the reconnaissance world of the 1950s, early 1960s. In the 1950s there was a slew of different format films that were being used: 35mm, 70mm, 6"x6", 9"x9" and 9"x18". Photo interpreters had to deal with each of those formats.

The CIA had a three folder system for material:
1. *Installation data*—text information
2. *Plant data*—aerial and ground photos and maps of installations including blueprints of targets
3. *Town Data*—ground and aerial photos of a city including maps the installation target was held in.

The USAF used the CIA files to build their *Encyclopedia of Bombing.* SAC (Strategic Air Command) used these folders to prepare target bombing charts with different types of metals embedded for radar return. In fact, they kept a sample of metals in a Plexi-glass display so that bombardiers could set up target shots, knowing what type of bomb they would be using.

After WWII, the reconnaissance photos called GX Aerial Photography, created by the Nazis and that were collected by the U.S. Military from Luftwaffe headquarters and installations, were plotted by the U.S. Military. There was now a full picture of the AXIS captured images along with Allied images and material from China as well. There were even photos from the Soviet Union, gotten by Allied bombers for the perfect targeting of Europe and Russia.

When the Korean Conflict broke out in June of 1950, the CIA had images for tactical use in the field. However, they all had to be reinterpreted to look for caves, bunkers, artillery used by the North Koreans and the Communist Chinese.

The Cold War in Europe and most especially Berlin, was a major factor in CIA aerial reconnaissance. The Berlin Air Corridor which was called RED OWL or CREEK MISTY in the photo intelligence community was flown and intelligence gathered almost every day. This allowed the U.S. Military to see just how fast the Soviets were doing things. At this time, SAC reconnaissance aircraft were flying along the Soviet coastline and in the Arctic area. Since there were no detailed maps of the area, these images gave the first ideas of what this real estate actually looked like. Even deep penetration photos of Siberia were able to show the infamous Gulag Archipelago.

Strategic Air Command, using the rest of the USAF aircraft, applied oblique aerial cameras in those areas. Long range photography or (LOROP) consisted of the K-30 100 inch focal length camera, mounted in the RB-50s, RB45s and the 240" focal length cameras were mounted in the RB-36Ds, RC97 andRB-57Cs. The code name for this operation was **PIEFACE** and **SHARP CUT**. These new cameras were designed by Dr. James Baker[19]. The huge **PIEFACE** camera was flown in the RC-97 Globemaster, later used as an aerial tanker. The 36"x18" photos were called *"Texas Postcards"* for obvious reasons and were super difficult to analyze. Properly interpreted, this was invaluable for city targets and mapping.

---

[19] Dr. James Gilbert Baker was a renowned astronomer and optical physicist that designed started with the US Army in WWII to establish an aerial reconnaissance branch. He also designed lenses for the U-2, A-12 and SR-71 blackbird cameras.

Eagle Eyes

The advances made in the 1950s in both film and cameras made it obvious that newer forms of equipment were needed to support the photo interpreters. Duplicate positives were used now instead of paper prints in the 1952-53 period. When the U-2 came into being, new light tables were created by the Richards Company to allow for better lighting. Medical microcopies were being used, but photo interpreters felt them ungainly to work with. Bausch and Lomb created the micro stereoscopes for use in the U-2 work.

The aerial photo interpreter was the first to see the enemy territory, after the pilot who shot the film. He had specific targets to shoot, but the photo interpreter had to had to find, examine and interpret the ground and naval facilities, airfields and missile sites. If they didn't find anything, the film was stored for re-examination later on. However, the photo interpreter could have missed a vital piece of military information, which could adversely affect military intelligence. While it could sometimes be tiring, you knew that you could find that one little thing that could make it all worthwhile.

Two instruments used in the 1950s for interpretation work was the 2x/4x stereoscope and the slide rule. You would lean over the light box with the photo, one eye in the stereoscope and your finger on a counter. When you found something, you punched down on the counter and punched out a little chad on the edge of the film. When done, you counted the chads and the number of items that you found. Yes, it was extremely low tech, but it was precise enough to get the job done.

October 1958, the "Pickle Factory" or the "Brewery" as it was called, was the photo interpreter building located in the Pentagon's south parking lot. The U-2 Dragon Lady's reconnaissance film was brought there. Teams worked day and night going through the load which even though it was days old, was still within the realm of real-time.

The film lab, stationed in Yokota, Japan, was another Reconnaissance Technical Squadron that was used for the film loads of the A-12 Blackbird before the processing rules changed and the film was sent to Kodak in Rochester, New York for processing. With cine' processors that ran at 9 ft. a minute, a 1000 ft. film load could take some time to process, that barring any breakdown in equipment, like a splice breaking or something getting caught in one of the racks in these very deep chemical processing tanks. The 15th Tactical Reconnaissance Squadron processed the film for the RF-86 missions that used the horizontally mounted cameras. All film that was shot was actually reversed. It took a lot of work to straighten out the film for the photo interpreters to be able to view and comment on. At Photo Interpreter's School, in the 1950s, there really wasn't much taught about the various types of film, cameras, techniques that were used in the processing and shooting of reconnaissance targets. Much of it was learned as you went through the process day by day.

This brings us back to the start of the CIA program of Photo Interpreters/imagery analysts that were building up the USAF's **Strategic Library Bombing Encyclopedia** (BE) for use in generating target maps for the SAC bombers and later on the target coordinates for intercontinental ICBMS. Within, was included the index of Soviet missile sites, command craters, air defense systems, airfields, naval bases and the largest commercial petroleum storage facilities, factories, power stations, all rail yards and bridges. When the image quality started to get much better, the analysts started to develop more methodologies for estimation of the production of enemy aircraft, factories and missile plants right down to the agriculture. Without high resolution images and near real time reconnaissance systems, information could not have been produced for Iron Curtain countries during the Cold War. The technology of getting a high resolution image had grown exponentially, but there was also the political side to the intelligence process which had caused innumerable disputes between those in the various intelligence community about weapon capabilities.

Politics and the Photo Interpreter

Many of the arguments that developed because of political wrangling caused the DIA (Defense Intelligence Agency) to be at the throat of the CIA (Central Intelligence Agency). The DIA, along with the military services and intelligence groups were reproached for resorting to "worst case scenario" assessments to justify the high defense spending that went on in the 1960s, due to the missile gap and the bomber gap. Both of which were "pumped up" by the USAF to make sure they got what they needed budget wise. On the other side of the fence, the CIA critics accused the CIA of being just as guilty of putting its own ideas in about what the Soviets were up to. By CIA standards, there was a less hostile interpretation of Soviet "dealings" which made arms control with the Soviets more of a reality, in which the United States was a huge factor.

Yet, arms control was also steeped in politics and the imaging analysts who usually found themselves caught between a rock and a hard place when it came to dealing with any of these political issues. The biggest hang up for the analysts was the fact that part of their job was to monitor certain activities to find out whether there were violations happening. Along with that, was the responsibility to "monitor" and not "verify" a situation that might be occurring. Verification was a political decision and not in the course of an analyst's job. That decision was made by the National Security Council, better known by the acronym, NSC. Should there be a possible violation of an arms controls agreement that was found by any of the CIA analysts, that information would be sent to the NSC where their decision to do something or nothing was made. It could also be determined as part of a pattern to cover up or possibly deceive what a situation was actually showing. The other part would be to bring this violation to the public, discuss it privately with the "party in question" or just let it drop without any response. However, if the violation did go public, the imaging analysts could be blamed for letting it slip in the first place, so the analyst was in the middle, damned if they did or didn't. There is also the matter of time for the analyst. Monitoring a situation could take months to develop with no "real interest" outside the intelligence community, when all of a sudden that site being watched, could become a major political issue in the hands of a journalist or some political figure hoping to make hay from it, blowing it out of proportion and beyond the handling of the NSC.

Much of what an imaging analyst saw could affect some political campaigner who would use it in order to add something hot to his re-election campaign, like the concept of a Soviet battalion in Cuba, which played a significant part in preventing the ratification of the SALT II Treaty.

At the time of the Cold War and after the Cuban Missile Crisis, the CIA knew some Soviet troops were allowed to stay in Cuba, after the October 1962 debacle. However, this fact had been forgotten in the ensuing years. Yet, when the item was brought up in 1979, the CIA was caught out in total surprise. That forced President Jimmy Carter to hold up on signing the SALT II treaty. It was a real issue and caused a ton problems, most of them very expensive. The Soviets had already made their push into Afghanistan[20] and the SALT II Treaty was never formally ratified, even though both sides of the treaty agreed on all points.

---

[20] The Soviets and Afghanistan in 1978 thru 1992 were involved in a civil war in which Afghanistan and its allies were fighting the coalition of anti-communist groups called the Mujahedeen that was getting support from the U.S. Pakistan and Saudi Arabia.

Eagle Eyes

There is yet another incident that came up involving the Soviets. The fact noted was the Soviets had built a long line of civil defense shelters, which indicated that there could be a threat of a first strike on the United States via Cuba to Florida in the 1970s. A retired USAF general wanted to know why nothing was done about this. It caused a total meltdown of angst and aggravation inside the intelligence community as to why this had not been picked up by analysts. The incident showed that the construction was being monitored by no one and in Washington D.C., no one gave it much credence until this USAF general got hold of the information and questioned it. It took literally thousands of analyst hours to document the Soviet construction. The Soviet were still doing it, even with the Cold War totally over!

Even with the huge advancement in imaging technology, there is still some limitations as to what kind of overhead reconnaissance an intelligence system could actually give. That is a point in question which we will examine later on in this book.

While it is possible to figure out a nation's military ability with satellite imagery, it is still impossible to figure out the intentions of the country's military/political leaders. It is still difficult to do real time reconnaissance. Yes, there are UCAVs that can do some kind of real time reconnaissance. However, what is missing? Could it be eyes in the cockpit? Aircraft like the SR-71 and the A-12, which we will discuss later, were synonymous with real time reconnaissance. The USS PUEBLO was taken prisoner by the North Koreans in January 1968. The PUEBLO was found by the CIA's A-12 OXCART high altitude, high speed reconnaissance aircraft, when a satellite could not find the ship. The SR-71 with its enormous range of not only reconnaissance cameras, ELINT packages and sensor packages allowed for even more intelligence to be collected in one flight and processed just as quickly.

Imagery analysts are not gods. While a photo, digital or paper, might sometimes give an indication of a certain issue, it can only narrow the window of when the event took place. The fact that if the intelligence is good, it does not guarantee that there will be a perfect outcome. There is a certain fact regarding intelligence. Poor intelligence inevitably leads to poor policy. The biggest issues that image analysts face is just getting the facts through to the policy makers. The intelligence produced by imaging analysts is spun into an "all source" report which is sent to the policy makers in Congress and other intelligence agencies. It is received in many ways, but mostly via written reports. This includes intelligence memos, photographic intelligence reports, (PIRS) and the usual monthly, weekly or daily reports which include the President's daily briefing (PDB) and National Intelligence Daily (NID). Yet, most of the problem of interpreting the material is in the review process. The written documents are edited, re-edited, rewritten as they go through various department heads which by the time it reaches Congressional level, the strength of the document has been homogenized, totally twisted or lost. Only the most senior of the imaging analysts know how to break through the maze and get the real message out.[21]

More Consolidation

The National Intelligence Estimates (NIE) are the most important of the analysis and prepared by the CIA's Office of National Estimates. The NIE became the responsibility of the National Intelligence officer's system after 1973. During the time of the annual estimate on Soviet Strategic force capabilities, it became the intelligence community's most influential document. While the projections of the Soviet weapons

---

[21] Ranleagh John CIA 1986 (p685) The Agency—Rise and Decline of the CIA–Simon-Schuster NY

systems were frequently criticized for underestimating the wealth of the Soviet arms buildup in the 1960s, there was no place in the strategic arms control and reduction process that would have been possible without these estimates.[22]

With the Cold War over in 1991, the overhead reconnaissance program lost its basic mission. Congress approved a consolidation of most of the imagery resources into a single new organization called the ***National Imagery and Mapping Agency (NIMA).***

With all the Congressional hoopla around the reorganization, it became truly obvious just what the imagery community accomplished during the Cold War had been lost, due to the secrecy surrounding the programs at that time. In the case of the CIA's Black programs like the OXCART program and the A-12 Blackbird, it took 40 years before even the most rudimentary information could be FOIA'd[23] out of the CIA.

In February of 1995, President Clinton ordered the declassification of intelligence imagery from the earliest satellite systems, which would be the CIA's CORONA project. CORONA ran from 1960 to 1972 and gave the most complete coverage of the USSR, China and other denied territories. The CORONA satellite program was one of the most successful the CIA ever ran.

Nuclear Nightmares

Atomic energy was on the forefront after the use of the atomic bomb on Hiroshima, Japan in 1945. The USAEC (United States Atomic Energy Commission) was concerned that the United States had little or no intelligence on the Soviet Union's nuclear program. The Soviet Union

---

[22] Steury 1996(p 502) The Intelligence War, Metro books, NY
[23] FOIA Freedom of Information Act—where a civilian may put in a request to declassify a black program or piece of information from a Govt. Agency. This process can take years to complete, usually dependent on the program.

had accomplished some research on atomic weapons as early as the 1930s. In February of 1939, the Russian scientists learned that the United States and other foreign countries were working on the same problem. By the 1940s, the Soviets had managed their first chain reaction by using U235 on natural uranium with a moderator of heavy water (deuterium oxide). The Soviet Union was now in the atomic weapons race. By June of 1940, a Uranium Commission was established by the Soviet Academy of Science. The premise was to start research for the "Uranium Problem". Soviet Dictator, Joseph Stalin began a small scale project to study uranium, under the auspices of the great Russian scientist, Igor Kurchatov.

By 1943 Kurchatov made up a research plan with three main objectives:
- Achieve a chain reaction using natural uranium
- Develop ISOTOPE separation
- Study design of U235 and create a plutonium bomb

In the meantime, the United States held its first nuclear test on July 16, 1945. President Truman told Stalin that the United States now possessed a new weapon of unusual destructive power. Stalin's rather harsh reply was to "try it out on the Japanese". Truman did just that, but not because Stalin made the suggestion. Stalin pushed his man Kurchatov to step up their research. August 6, 1945, the first atomic bomb exploded over Hiroshima, Japan with a huge death toll. After receiving no response to surrender from the Japanese, Truman authorized the Army Air Force to carry out the second atomic strike of Nagasaki, Japan on August 9, 1945. Shortly after that, the Japanese Emperor agreed to his nation's surrender on august 14, 1945. The formal surrender was signed on September 2, 1945. The B-29 Enola Gay, with Colonel Paul Tibbets at the yoke, dropped the first bomb and Bock's Car, flown by Major Charles Sweeny, dropped the second bomb.

Major Paul Tibbets and the Enola Gay
(Dept. of Defense)

In 1947, the United States developed a new long-range nuclear detection program. With the new and separate USAF in control, using an airborne monitoring system that could detect and pinpoint a nuclear detonation on the Soviet Mainland or the Arctic, there wasn't much the Soviets could hide. The USAF was using the WB-29 (former B-29), a weather reconnaissance aircraft, that flew at some 18,000 feet altitude between Japan and Alaska. It was able to detect any unusual radioactive debris; the aircraft was also fitted with a filter system that could pick up radioactive particles, which was carried east from Central Asia. Analysis of the debris by the United States staff of atomic physicists, which included Robert J. Oppenheimer from the famous and secret "Manhattan Project," confirmed the detection of any atomic particles.

It wasn't too long before the Soviets had created their own version of a nuclear device. The Soviet test called JOE I, named after leader Joseph

Stalin, was announced to the United States by President Truman on September 23, 1949. Somehow, the U.S. completely missed the test and detected it too late. It wasn't until the middle of 1953, that the U.S. found out that the test actually took place on August 29, 1949. There were obvious issues in the U.S. reconnaissance program that needed to be revised and revamped.

The news of the nuclear test was compounded by the fact that the Russians blockaded Berlin from June 23, 1948 to May 12, 1949. It made the need for United States reconnaissance to step up its game against the Soviet Union. The American commitment to the security of Europe and to stop the spread of communism increased. With nothing else to fly but left over WWII aircraft, the U.S. continued to extract the secrets of the USSR using any aerial reconnaissance tools they could get their hands on. As the 1950s crept in, the United States and the Cold War made it reality that both the world and the Soviet Union had changed. However, the United States military analysts were still stunned by the fact of the Soviet Union's weakness in so many areas. The Soviets really had nothing long range in their air force, their atomic bomb was still in the works and way behind the United States and their own air defenses were weak at best. Even the Soviet Navy was considered weak and slow next to the United States. The only claim to fame the Soviets did have was their submarine power. The U.S. Joint Logistics Plans Committee and the Military Intelligence division of the war department felt that the Soviet Union would need at least some fifteen years to pull themselves up by their bootstraps, and at least another ten years to develop the manpower to do it. However, the United States was still worried about an attack in Europe and Asia. There was also worry that the Soviet Union's communist party would try to exploit the countries that were in the grips of famine and disease, offering a "better way through communism". All these things added up to the need for aerial reconnaissance and intelligence gathering. There was no trusting the Soviets and the United States knew that well. The basis of the Cold War was to stop the spread of communism to Europe and Asia and to stop the Soviets from taking over European neighbors and allies, along with Asian countries, as we will see with the Vietnam War later on. Reconnaissance could never be more needed.

A Deadly Trade

In April of 1950, a PB4Y-2 took off from the U.S. base in Wiesbaden, Germany as part of the VP Naval Patrol Squad and headed out on a reconnaissance mission over the Baltic Sea. The mission was to gather intelligence on the Soviet naval installations off the Port of Libau. A Soviet Lavochkin LA-9 and LA-11 plus MiG 15 fighters intercepted the flight. The Soviets shot the PB4Y-2 out of the air claiming that it was an RB-29 penetrating Soviet air space. Anyone looking at a RB-29 and a PBY would know right away there is a huge difference in those aircraft that can't be mistaken unless the Soviet pilots were that badly trained, which was highly unlikely. The Soviets claimed that they told the flight to land and they didn't. Of course, this was a total Soviet fabrication and it wasn't the first time that it happened. No Americans were recovered from this flight. Oct 22, 1949 found another LA-9 intercepting an RB-29 over the Sea of Japan and fired a warning shot over the RB-29 to chase it out of the area. However, the PB4Y-2 incident was viciously different. It was clear the Soviets would not tolerate any intrusion and any intelligence gathering by the aircraft of non-Soviet denomination. All comers to the Soviet airspace were shown no mercy, no quarter.

A beautiful example of the B-26C "Dream Girl" from (National Museum of the US Air Force)

Chapter Seven

The Korean Conflict—Aerial Reconnaissance Comes of Age

The Korean "Police Action".

When the Korean Conflict broke out on June 25, 1950, communist forces tried to break through from North Korea into a very shocked and surprised South Korean army. It was a hot and humid Sunday in the early morning hours, right before dawn when the North Koreans crossed the 38th parallel to attempt to grab all of South Korea. The United States did have a very small contingent of troops in South Korea and quickly brought them up to speed to fend off the North Koreans. In the meantime, the political machine called the United Nations was listening to the United States as it put out a resolution for military assistance for South Korea. U.S. President Harry Truman sent U.S. Army and Navy and Air Force to the South Koreans aid. Here the term "Police Action" became a real time war, although the United States never really said so. Korea was never anything but an all out war, it was never a police action. Men were bloodied, many died, many were shot down and many fought with a vengeance. That does NOT happen in any police action. However, Truman had just ended WWII with the atomic bomb and wasn't prepared for the term "WAR". With the U.S. in the fight, the North Koreans were beaten back. However, it didn't take long until they revamped and reloaded with a massive number of communist forces including Red Chinese. It didn't take long for this "police action", which was the first of the "HOT" wars of the Cold War era, to stall like a concrete block. The United States did want to limit its size and scope because the thought was, here was the start of WWIII, and no one was looking for that.

This "Police Action" was a dirty, cold, hot, steamy and filthy mess. That was the best of it. As the American troops showed up and realized what they were up against, they also found out that there was one big issue... reconnaissance. Because of the terrain, it was virtually impossible to find many of the enemy hold outs. The only thing that would help would be aerial reconnaissance. That was something that would change the tide. As discussed, there are two types of reconnaissance; strategic which became more important with global warfare, it provided what was necessary for finding out just what the enemy had, aka the order of battle. In peacetime, it helped to find out what the enemy was producing for secret weapons. The other type of reconnaissance was tactical: it helped to support the front lines troops during actual combat. It was needed as a fast aid to military commanders who needed to make on the spot decisions and find answers for command and control of their forces. It also took a special kind of pilot. Reconnaissance pilots were usually of the "lone wolf" variety. Some reconnaissance pilots were on their own most of the time. He had to make decisions for procedures, airspeed, and tons of other minutiae' that would make their mission successful. Once the larger aircraft were used, there were crews that needed to work together to accomplish what was needed, finding and controlling the enemy.

Here, serious deficiencies in the U.S. reconnaissance, both strategic and tactical became clear and apparent. They need to be quickly corrected. With 180,000 Communist Chinese troops already in North Korea, more had come in from Manchuria, U.S. Intelligence claims of only 60,000 Chinese troops was nothing more than a myth. The error was apparent when the Communist Chinese started to beat back the U.S. and Allied forces. However, by then, it was already too late.

There were obvious reasons for the failure of reconnaissance and intelligence in the North Korean war. The first had to do with Communist Chinese forces, which moved across the country in small groups at night and reached their assembly area. There were no allied spies on the ground in North Korea, so this movement went undetected. Second, the shortage of aerial reconnaissance assets and the fact that there were no detailed maps of North Korea, which became a massive problem when it came to interpreting what aerial photos there were. Even the USAF's headquarters in the Philippines couldn't deploy effective reconnaissance flights. The USAF relied on the RB-17s of the 204th Photo-mapping flight at Clark AFB, Philippines for gathering information and to carry the workload.

The U.S. Strategic Command Unit at Kadena, AB, Okinawa did bring some relief. The Lockheed RF-80 Shooting Star aircraft that was serving in the 8th Tactical Reconnaissance Squadron was sent in to help. August 1950 brought the Douglas RB-57 Canberra, based at Yokota AB, Japan, which brought in night reconnaissance ability. The next to arrive was the 45th Tactical Reconnaissance Squadron, with the P-51 Mustangs but they were not used because of operational shortage. The role of the 45th Tactical Reconnaissance Squadron was visual battlefield reconnaissance. Thus, the nightmare of beefing up aerial reconnaissance grew for the United States. On the other side of the U.S. Military, the Army and the North American Aviation T-6, a trainer used in WWII, carried out reconnaissance on behalf of the 8th army, at great risk to both men and machine. At one point, an RB-29 crew out on a reconnaissance run said that there were seventy-five Chinese aircraft parked on North Korea's Antung airfield. By the next morning on the return flight, all were gone. It was a clear indication that the Chinese were getting involved in Korean Air War.

RB-57D Canberra covering a nuclear test
(USAF)

In November 1950, six Soviet MiGs crossed the Yalu river and ran straight into a P-51 Mustang flight. The next incursion occurred November 9, 1950 when the MiGs attacked an already damaged RB-29. From this date, the RB-29s were forbidden to fly into the territory alone or otherwise. The job was passed onto the Lockheed PF-80A Shooting Star. On and on it raged as the "Korean Police Action" tore up the skies over North Korea. Another reconnaissance disaster occurred November 9, 1951. An unescorted RB-45C Tornado was attacked by nine MiG 15s near Haja-dong, North Korea and barely got out with its tail feathers, thanks to the poor gunnery skills of the enemy. The RB-45C Tornados were no longer permitted to make any penetration flights into Northwestern Korea, known as "MiG Alley". One by one they were pulled from reconnaissance duty, because they were too slow, could not fly high enough and could not outrun a MiG.

More Reconnaissance and New Tricks

Korea did allow for new tactical reconnaissance methods to be applied. When the Soviet MiG 15 showed up over Korea, the already outdated RF-80 from the USAF, was lining up to be a MiG dinner. The next up was the RF-84 Thunderjet fighter, which was a swept wing version that should have replaced the RF-80, but it was just too late to the war. The RF-86A was brought in. With a camera mounted parallel to the longitudinal axis of the Sabre jet, and a mirror arrangement for vertical coverall of an enemy target area, things started to get better. While photo quality wasn't the best, she was fast enough to stay alive in MiG alley and come home with some images.

The RB-26s (Douglas A-24 Invader) were being used for night reconnaissance. They had problems because of the methods that had been used since the end of WWII. Night missions were usually route surveillance sorties that included photos of already chosen objectives along a particular route. In order to accomplish missions successfully, it was necessary to have precise navigation and artificial illumination that was carried on the RB-26. There was a cartridge ejection illumination system which used the A-14 magazine and the M-113 flash cartridge which was used initially, but proved to be insufficient. Another basic defect in the night reconnaissance procedure was the aircraft were using whatever flash equipment was available and they had to fly at 3,000 ft. altitude, which was not high enough to be safe from mountains or enemy antiaircraft fire at night. Before the night crews could shoot, they had to find the target and the navigational equipment was just not accurate enough to do it. The receivers could not pick up the beams at the altitude. Without proper navigation ability, the effectiveness of the missions were limited. Even with all the problems, the reconnaissance record for the Korean War far outweighed the reconnaissance performance during WWII.

The highest number of sorties flown in one month of WWII was 1300, while Korea stood at 2400. The average sortie rate per month was 604 but in Korea, it was 1,792, which was three times as many photographic negatives produced in Korea.

When the U.S. realized that the Red Chinese were now involved in the Korean fighting, aircraft were ordered to photograph the Yalu River area not only for bomb damage assessment but for communist forces that were infiltrating South Korea. However, by this time, the enemy was already encamped. Some photos showed heavy traffic south of Kangqye, all the way to the Chosin reservoir. Traffic not seen in the daylight hours was showing up at night. The 162nd Tactical Reconnaissance Squadron went out on daylight reconnaissance because the night was not bringing back anything worth the trip. The RB-29s of the 31st Strategic Reconnaissance Squadron tried to operate on the Yalu River but the size and speed of the RB-29 was so slow the MiGs just made it impossible. At Taegu, the 543rd Tactical Support Group interpreters studied some 27,000 photos that were sent to them. The 98th Engineer Aerial Photo Reproduction Group joined the 8th Army and handled 5000 negatives and 25,000 prints a day at the Seoul Headquarters. The 8th Army demanded some 3600 photo negatives a day from the 5th Air Force which was three times what they asked for prior to this. The 5th Air Force reduced the number of negatives to be delivered to the forces to average at least 2,000 a day. Imagine the amount of intelligence to be gleaned from each and every one of those negatives and prints. It was mind blowing to think all this was done without the aid of computers.

There were problems with photographic quality. For the first time ever, jet aircraft were now taking aerial reconnaissance photos. The RF-80's cameras and the magazines designed for speed of conventional aircraft were having a hard time keeping up with the fast moving jets. The pilots had to actually throttle back to be able to keep the cameras in sync and get a good photograph.

The 8th Army was the client of the 15th Tactical Reconnaissance Squadron and they flew frontline coverage at least once a week. The 12th Tactical Reconnaissance Squadron known as the "Blackbirds" flew during the night in early 1952. They flew RB-26s which kept the pilots up for three-hour long night missions during which they show pre-picked targets. However, the crews had problems with illumination systems which were as bad as the navigation systems that were supposed to help find targets in the blacked-out areas of North Korea.

Air reconnaissance counted for 44% of all the reconnaissance used by U.S. ground troops. The Navy was not sitting idly by, they too were working aerial reconnaissance. The Navy relied on the 67th Tactical Reconnaissance Wing for a large amount of its photo coverage. The Navy also had their own reconnaissance units working. The Marine Squad VMJ-1 which was stationed at Pohang Airfield, Korea, use the F-2 Banshees which did some excellent work for them. The PBM Mariner Seaplane was used for reconnaissance sorties during the Korean War especially for mine spotting at sea. The Marines also used helicopters for reconnaissance.

No story of Korea and aerial reconnaissance would be complete without the **MOSQUITO** missions. These missions were of vital importance which taught the military experts a lesson. Daylight bombing during WWII using the B-17s and B-24s that used the Norden bombsight proved they didn't need a "seeing eye" aircraft to help them.

However, when jets came into the picture, it was clear during the Korean war that it wasn't going to work like before. There was not enough time or fuel to let pilots hunt for targets and bomb them if needed without help.

The F-80s, F-84s, and the F-86s were way too fast and burned up fuel just as fast to be able to get any photos that were worth it. Tactical air control tried to operate from jeeps with officers controlling air strikes from there. However, with Korea's non –roads and enemy fire from every side, this made it virtually an impossible task. Jeeps were replaced by the L-5Gs and the L-17 Liaison planes which is how Tactical Air Coordinators became literally standard operating procedure. They were good aircraft and later were replaced by the heavier T-6 Trainer, both fast and reliable.

When Operations sent the order from the 5th Air Force and gave the airborne controllers the radio call sign "MOSQUITO BAKER; MOSQUITO HOW; MOSQUITO ABLE," from early missions, the names stuck and from then on, airborne controllers and their aircraft were known as "MOSQUITOS." As of August 1950, MOSQUITOS were grouped together as the 6147th Tactical Control Squadron and worked out of Taegu Airfield in Korea. Pilots controlled the airstrikes and also provided aerial reconnaissance for the Joint Operations Center. The 6147th Tactical Control Squadron kept one aircraft called "MOSQUITO MELLOW" circling to relay messages for other aircraft that were too far out to do it themselves. The Joint Operations Center could get valuable reconnaissance intelligence which could be worked on right away. After the fighter/bombers did their job, the MOSQUITOS went back in to do some bomb damage assessment photos. There were many losses for the MOSQUITOS due to enemy ground fire, bad weather and of course, the never ending Soviet MiGs and Yaks that gave no one any rest.

A Truce

The age of jets had arrived and were tested out in the skies of North and South Korea during this three-year war. For the first time, jets were used in a combat area. Not really built for reconnaissance work, the RF-

80 and the RF-86 did the job and solved many of the problems which allowed for better air reconnaissance. The 67th Tactical Reconnaissance Group Citation that was awarded for heroism covered well their efforts and gave credit to all the members. After the Korean War was over, the 12th Tactical Reconnaissance Squadron remained at Kimpo Airfield until November 8, 1954 when they moved to Itami Air Base, Japan. After two years of flying over the Korean DMZ [24], putting together a photographic file of the many areas needed and looking for changes or communist violations of the truce, the unit moved to Yokota, Japan where they started to fly the RB-66B Destroyer and remained as a night reconnaissance group until they were deactivated in March 8, 1960.

Those are just a couple of the many reconnaissance units that worked the Korean War. They worked hard and sometimes it just didn't go right. However, these units were successful in transitioning aerial reconnaissance into the jet age. It is only now, literally 2018, that we are now getting some of those killed in Korea, repatriated to the United States. It took sixty-five years to do this. President Donald Trump and his administration worked hard and well to start the process of returning our lost soldiers. We have only fifty-five remains being returned to Hawaii, and are hoping for the rest of the 7,800 lost in Korea that were never returned and are still listed missing in action, to finally come home from the longest of wars that has never really been closed.

It Never Ends . . .

From 1951 through 1952, RB-29 reconnaissance forces suffered very heavy losses due to the MiG 15s during daylight operations.

Emphasis was switched to night runs, which showed up more problems in the U.S. bombing techniques and equipment. The 91st Strategic

---

[24] Demilitarized zone

Reconnaissance Squadron, using the RB-45C Tornado, which was equipped for radar mapping, could not use this aircraft for night duty, which was just another illustration of the weakness of U.S. reconnaissance efforts in night photography.

North American RB-45C Tornado
(USAF)

From 1950 to 1954, the USAF ELINT (electronic intelligence) Operations began in earnest using the Convair B-36 Peacemaker for reconnaissance duty. The aircraft, which is a huge aircraft, with dimensions of length of 162 feet, and a height of 46 feet 8 inches, weighing 357,500 lbs. stripped, carried some fourteen cameras which alone weighed 3400 lbs. The cameras were used in the forward bomb bay. The second bay contained eighty T-86 flash bulbs, and extra 3000-gallon fuel tank was installed in the third bay. Electronic Countermeasures (ECM) was used in the fourth bay. The RB-36D did carry a standard gun armament with an AN/APQ24 radio navigation unit for target location. It had a crew of eighteen that later increased to twenty-two crewmen. The RB-36D Peacemaker was most assuredly ready to catch some Russian bear.

The Boeing RB-50 appeared on the scene and the flight line on July 12, 1950. The RB-50 went into service with the 91st Strategic Reconnaissance Wing at Barksdale AFB, in California. On August 26,1950 the 91st SRW also took delivery of the RB-45C Tornado. The RB-36 Peacemaker flying out of the British base at Sculthorpe, England was making over flight of the Soviet Arctic bases. The island of Novaya Zemlya was a reconnaissance target because of the information that the Soviets were building what looked to be a large nuclear weapon test complex there. The Soviet nuclear weapon testing went on from 1955 through 1964.

Yakovlev Yak-25 Flashlight (NATO code name)
(Dept. of Defense)

The Soviets were also trying to find a fighter capable of protecting their bases. The Soviet Air Ministry sent out an urgent specification for an "all weather fighter" which could be fitted with long-range radar. The "Isumro Emerald" air radar that "Flashlight" (NATO Code name), a fighter with improved radar, came into service with the Soviet fighter squads.

An RB-50 Superfortress used for Aerial reconnaissance (USAF)

FERRET

Both the RB-50 Superfortress, which was the revised version of the RB-29, and the RB-45 were flying "FERRET" missions over the Soviet Union. The JOE II atomic bomb was tested by the Soviets in a Central Asia site during September of 1951. The only U.S. success in getting information on the Soviet work, was to look for the gaps and holes in the Soviet research radar. Listening in on the Soviet stations from U.S. covert stations in Europe, the Mid East and Far East did this. The United States continued to fly the FERRET missions and aircraft out of Rhein-Main AB in Germany, Mildenhall and Lakenheath in England, Misawa and Iwakuni in Japan along with Kadena in Okinawa and Sangley Point in the Philippines. That also included bases in Norway and Libya. Ferreting was always a nasty business at best and Ferret crews were aware that should they go down during a mission, there was no hope of rescue. Cloud cover was the Ferret mission's best friend; a severe clear sky was its worst enemy.

The aircraft used in U.S. reconnaissance was building up quickly. In 1953, there were four heavy strategic reconnaissance wings built up by the USAF, the 5th, 28th, 72nd and 99th Wings were all packing the RB-36 Peacemakers. The earlier B-36 had now developed into the B-36F and the RB-36H, which now counted as twenty-four RB-36Fs and seventy-three RB-36Hs. In May 1953, a new contract was awarded to Convair and Republic Aircraft companies for new modifications to ten of the RB-36Ds that were turned into a mother/carrier aircraft and twenty-five RF-84s to be turned into parasite aircraft. The designation was changed to RB-36D and RF-86K.

December of 1954 had the 91st Strategic Reconnaissance Squadron, which was attached to the 407th Strategic Wing at Grand Falls AFB, added into the picture. More squadrons were activated in January of 1955. The 71st Strategic Reconnaissance Wing began operations at Larson AFB, Washington with two squadrons. The 25th and 82nd Reconnaissance Squadron was finalized with RF-84s from the 91st Strategic Reconnaissance Squadron. More of the RB-36D aircraft were delivered to the 99th SRW at Fairchild AFB. With all of the repositioning and influx of additional aircraft, the reorganization lasted just about a year.

Bad Day at Black Rock.

The 91st SRW changed out its aircraft and got a new designation in 1956. It remained part of the 71st SRW until July of 1957. The USAF added another reconnaissance unit to the list. the 55th SRW was actually a SAC (Strategic Air Command) unit that was primed for the ELINT (electronic intelligence) missions using the RB-50. The 55th SRW was sent to Yokota, Japan, and became known as Detachment 2. The 55th SRW used the RB-50G which was specially configured for ELINT operations while the older RB-50Bs and Ds were used for photo mapping and photo reconnaissance. The RB-50Gs from the 343rd SRW out of Japan took off on a mission to Vladivostok, Soviet territory, on an ELINT mission. The aircraft carried a total crew of eleven. Six crewmembers called "Ravens" were dedicated to listening for Russian intelligence.

The date was July 29, 1953 and it turned out to be one of the most gruesome reconnaissance missions of the Cold War. At 6:15 a.m., June 29, 1953 a reconnaissance mission from hell was about to take off. An RB-50G from the 343rd SRW took off for a mission to cover the Soviet city of Vladivostok. The aircraft had just approached 20,000 feet and was south east of Vladivostok, when MiG 15s attacked the aircraft. The MiGs took out two of the RB-50 engines with the starboard wing catching fire. The RB-50G started to break up. The pilot, Captain John E. Roche, called to his crew to bail out. Some twenty hours later, an American destroyer combed the waters and picked up two of the survivors from the American crew. The Soviets had already picked up the rest of the crew, the worst scenario possible. The USAF claimed that their RB-50 flight was a routine navigation-training mission when it was shot down in international-al waters. The Soviets just laughed off the protest. When the USAF gave the Soviets a bill for 2.7 million to cover the loss of the aircraft, the Soviets countered with $1.8 million bill for an Ilyushin IL-12 that was shot down by an F-86 Sabre on the last day of the Korean war. All twenty-one crewmembers on the Ilyushin were killed.

The Soviets were not tolerating anyone in their airspace. The Soviets even made sure to cover the waters with ships just in case there was a shoot down of a U.S. aircraft, so they could be there first to pick up to downed crew. It was a gruesome tactic on behalf of the Soviets. After the shoot down on June 29, 1953, U.S. fighters escorted the RB- 50s recon-naissance flights.

This tactic saved a U.S. aircraft when an RB-50D, in 1954, was chased by MiGs over the Yellow Sea. The F-86s chased off the MiGs, actually knocking one down. Three days later, two AD Sky raiders from the aircraft carrier Philippine Sea, was attacked by a pair of Lavochkin LA-7 or LA-9 fighters, which were capable of 413mph and over 35,000-foot ceiling.

Not all reconnaissance flights were successful. On July 23, 1954, Communist Chinese fighters off the Hainan Islands shot down a Cathay Pacific airliner. The U. S. Naval aircraft destroyed both. By April 1955, Soviet fighters got their first victory against and RB-47E, which was shot down, over Kamchatka by MiG17s. The MiG 17 Fresco was a new aircraft from the Soviets and replaced the MiG15 Fishbed since early 1954.

National Security

National Security was the game to play in 1954. Many in Washington D.C. were on constant alert against the Soviet Union. Defense against unprovoked attacks by the Soviet Union was always on the minds of U.S. Government officials. The President, Congress and the Defense Department were constantly working against a surprise attack by the USSR. It was time to create a committee to review the problem. The membership of this new committee consisted of the best and brightest the U.S. had to offer. The one thing missing however, was critical intelligence on the Soviet Union. There were two famous intelligence gaps in the 1950s, the Bomber Gap and the Missile Gap. Good, solid intelligence was the one thing the United States didn't have enough of and needed to close that yawing fissure, lack of real time reconnaissance.

Edwin Land, father of the Polaroid Camera system (Polaroid Corp)

On November 5, 1954, Edwin Land (father of the Polaroid Land Camera) became Chairman of the *"Project 3 Technical Capabilities Panel"* (Subgroup under the office of Defense Mobilization Surprise Attack Committee). Land wrote to the CIA director Allan Dulles and asked for photographic over flights of the Soviet Union. He also recommended that the CIA, with USAF assistance, should create a program for high altitude reconnaissance. The Land Panel proposed in a paper which was titled, *"A Unique Opportunity for Comprehensive Intelligence"* outline over flights might bring. With the danger involved, should the military engage in this activity, especially in light of the very tense political situation with the Soviet Union? The paper went on to say, *"Because it is vital that certain knowledge about industry growth, strategic targets and guided missiles set should be obtained at once, we recommend that the CIA as a civilian organization undertake(with USAF aid) a cover program of selected flights".*

The flight for control of airspace raged throughout the 1950s. Both the USAF and the Navy were constantly taking the lead for missions over the Soviet Union or China from wherever the call came from.

Silent Warriors

Silent warriors were the new soldiers in the Cold War. These airmen both the USAF and the Navy and civilian from CIA, were fighting on the leading edge of the Cold War. Their roles were not like regular soldiers. These men and women were not allowed to discuss the nature of their missions with wives, husbands and family members. The people back home never knew what the missions were about until some brave soul was lost and his family received that heartbreaking knock on the front door that told them their loved one was lost in the line of duty. It wasn't until many years later and only after many hours and much research through declassified documents, that a loved one's family even got an inkling about what they had been doing out there. The shoot down score card was adding up rapidly in the mid to late 1950s.

P2V Navy Neptune aircraft US Navy.
(Courtesy US. Navy)

July of 1955 found a Navy P2V-5 Neptune aircraft from the VP-9 Squadron, which was on a mission off the Aleutian Islands. The flight was viciously attacked by two MiGs and brought down. August of 1956 had a P4M-Mercator aircraft out of Navy Squadron VQ-1, on a night patrol, some thirty-two miles off the Chinese mainland, attacked by enemy fighters over international waters and never heard from again. In another incident, September 1956, the Soviet Union shot down an RB-50 on a photo-mapping job over the Sea of Japan. June 1956, brought another P4M-Mercator from the VQ-1 Squadron, flying near the edge of the Korean Peninsula was downed by Soviet MiGs. The list grew on, silently as the crews of these missions died in the line of duty . . . silently.

RF-101 Voodoo
(U.S. Air Force)

B-57 Canberra

In the middle of 1959 both the aircraft and equipment used by the U.S. was starting to change. Modifications were made to better the systems and make it safer for the reconnaissance crews. The RB-57D

Canberra and the RF-101 Voodoo were now taking over the job of ELINT catching and photo surveillance over China.

The USAF had also upgraded to the B-57 Canberra, but it happened by accident. The Canberra was selected for Tactical Air Command Squadrons. There were design changes and after the first Canberra rolled out in July of 1953, the Glenn L. Martin Aircraft Company, maker of the B-57 got instructions to proceed with the design revisions under the designation B-57B. Only eight were built to bomber configuration while sixty-seven were made for the reconnaissance role as the B-57A.

By 1954, the RB-57 was sent to the 363rd Tactical Reconnaissance Wing at Shaw AFB in South Carolina. They were used by the 10th and 66th Tactical Reconnaissance Wing of the USAFE (USAF in Europe) based in Germany and France. Most of the aircraft were left in the natural metal state but some were painted black matte, formerly used on the P-61 Black Widow, which rendered them virtually invisible to searchlight beams.

The 10th and 66th Reconnaissance wing were using the RB-57 to replace the RB-26Cs they had been flying. The 10th and 66th Reconnaissance wings were attached to the 4th Allied Tactical Air Force on NATO's central front. Their many jobs were night photo-reconnaissance along with target markings. However, a high accident rate had the Canberra grounded in March of 1955. The closing out of the RB-57 was completed by November 1958. The 66th Tactical Reconnaissance Wing had changed over to the McDonald RF-101A Voodoo. Many of the remaining RB-57s were sent to the Air National Guard units and kept on flying until the early 1980s.

Bigger and Better

The Department of Defense constantly tried to refine the requirements for the consummate reconnaissance aircraft. A GOR#53-WC-

16507 (General Operational Requirement) had been posted by the Defense Department. The program known as **"Black Knight"** asked for a single seat, subsonic, high altitude reconnaissance aircraft capable of carrying a 700 lb. payload over 3000 miles at 70,000 feet altitude. Three companies answered the GOR.

The Martin Aircraft Company proposed a stepped-up version of the RB-57 Canberra, Bell Aircraft Company and Fairchild Aircraft Company, submitted new designs for consideration.

What Martin proposed to the Department of Defense was accepted. It was considered a stop gap measure, not so much as advancement, until a new design was started, Martin's design was called Model 294, which translated to RB-57D designation. This aircraft carried the standard B-57B fuselage melded into a new wing with a span that increased from sixty-four to one hundred eight feet. The J-57P-9 turbojet engine built by Pratt and Whitney powered the Model 294. It was a single seat version equipped with a K-38 and two KC-1 split vertical cameras. Six Model 294s were ordered along with seven Model 744 RB-57Ds that were almost the same. The next RB-57D had a flight crew of two, an ability of in-flight refueling and carried a specialist in SIGINT/ELINT role. The last design for the RB-57D was a single seat used for day and night radar mapping and was equipped with AN/APQ 56SCR side looking radar. Only one aircraft was delivered of this type. Even with initial wing problems, the first RB-57D was accepted by the USAF and delivered to the 4025 Strategic Reconnaissance Squad of the 4080th Strategic Reconnaissance Wing. On March 19, 1956, a detachment of this unit was sent to Yokota, Japan and Eielson AFB in Alaska.

ELINT operations continued around the Kamchatka peninsula for a short time, before retiring to Ramsey AFB in Puerto Rico. The Japan detachment remained in Yokota, Japan from October 1956 through September 1957 and was involved in *"Operation SEA LION."* This program monitored radiation samples from Soviet Union nuclear tests and pulled whatever ELINT it could record. The 4025th SRS sent more RB-57Ds in a detachment of four aircraft to Rhein Main AFB in Germany *(Operation Bordertown)* for ELINT and SIGINT missions along German border over the Baltic Sea. These flights were usually intercepted by the British Hawker Hunter aircraft squadron, which was scrambled to make an identification of the mission of the RB-57D, which was flown in secrecy. By 1959, progress had moved the RB-50Ds out of the 4025th SRS and the unit was deactivated.

Some of the aircraft were purchased by NASA to be used as high altitude test flights and terrain mapping. They were assigned to the 7677th Radar Calibrations Squadron for NASA; six more leftovers went to monitor the last of the U.S. atmosphere nuclear tests in 1962. Three more RB-50Ds were assigned to the 1211th Test Squadron for the U.S. Weather Service at Kirkland, AFB New Mexico and re-designated WB-57s. The RB-57Ds wing structural problems forced the aircraft into retirement.

Martin Aircraft Company got a new contract from the USAF to rebuild wings of eight-stored RB-57 aircraft with 3000 airframe hours on them. They were refitted with ECM (Electronic Counter Measures) equipment and used by the U.S. until the 1970s and placed in storage as the RB-57D. The versatile RB-57 answered many of the United States tasks that were given to the aircraft at a time when it was very much needed.

Chapter Eight

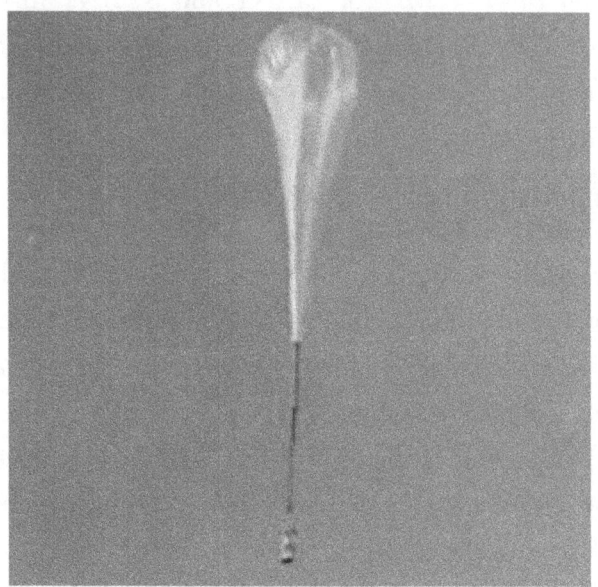

SKYHOOK Balloon
(Office of Naval Research)

The Cold War and Balloons

GENETRIX and the Balloon Generation

In the backrooms of the CIA the idea for the U-2 Dragon lady was coming together. The USAF was busy with reconnaissance plans of their own. Their idea wasn't a brand new one, but it was a new concept in how to do it right. The idea for balloon reconnaissance went way back into the Montgolfier brothers and straight into the Civil War. The USAF brought the concept into the 20th century. While the USAF did do that, there was also the load of international complaints that went with the idea. There was so much angst about it, that the U-2 project was nearly canned before it ever got started due to the complaints about international over flights, which was what the U-2 was all about.

The GENETRIX concept used camera carrying balloons to get high altitude images of the Soviet Union, People's Republic of China and much of Eastern Europe. The idea wasn't all the USAF's, but actually came from their think tank, RAND Corporation from a study back in 1951. It took until the end of 1955 for the USAF to iron out the myriad of problems in camera design and recovery technique. They also had to manufacture a large number of balloons to use in the project. On December 27, 1955, President Dwight Eisenhower approved the project. Two weeks later, the launches started to take place from Air Force bases in Western Europe. By the end of February 1956, the USAF had launched five hundred and sixteen balloons. However, even with the large number of launches, the GENETRIX program wasn't the total success that the USAF was hoping for. Most of the problems began with something that only Mother Nature controlled, and that was the weather. Because of the variance of winds, balloons tended to drift toward the Southern part of Europe, all the way across the Black Sea, missing the targets which were all at different parts of the map and flight plan. The USAF's large number of balloons didn't get across to the Soviet Union and China. Most were either shot down, some others ended up on the ground because the ballast exhausted, causing them to just crash. Forty-six payloads were recovered from the five hundred sixteen missions that were flown. Only four of the payload cameras were non-functioning. Eight others proved that the imaging quality was really poor and had no valuable intelligence on them. Only thirty-four of the balloons actually managed to get something worth viewing. The poor rate of return wasn't the only problem GENETRIX was having. The international community was protesting in force. The publicity wasn't good either. The USAF came up with a cover story that the balloons were being used for weather research that was connected with the International Geophysical Year. The CIA was also using this as some of their cover story for the U-2. Most of the Eastern European countries were opposed to the balloons, claiming the balloons were jeopardizing their civilian aviation. The Soviet Union sent the usual harsh letters to the U.S. government condemning the balloon launches. As usual for the Soviets, anytime one of these balloons "were found" on their territory, they were the first to do a "show and tell" to the Moscow press about all the cameras, payloads and anything else they found on the balloons.

President Eisenhower was getting the message that the balloons just weren't worth all the aggravation that they were causing. He said, *"the balloons gave more legitimate grounds for irritation than could be matched by the goods obtained from them."*

On February 7, 1956, Secretary of State Dulles told the Soviet Union they no longer had to worry, and no more "weather research balloons would be flown", but he didn't apologize for any of the earlier over flights. GENETRIX was causing upheaval just about everywhere you looked. However, USAF Chief of Staff General Nathan Twining was thinking about another balloon project that would fly higher than the GENETRIX and could be ready in as little as eighteen months. Twining's plans were shot down by Eisenhower who told him he was *"Not interested in any more balloons."* The GENETRIX photos didn't add up to the number of missions flown. The small quantity that could be used, however, were some of the best of the Soviet Union that they had gotten since World War II. Those images were actually given the title *"Pioneer Photography"* because they were the foundation of all further Soviet Union images in aerial reconnaissance. These images did prove valuable many years later when both the U-2 aircraft and the satellites showed images of further construction.

One of the better things that GENETRIX did give in its program, was a boon to the U-2 program that was up and coming. GENETRIX did get information on the Soviet Union radar systems at an altitude of 45,000 ft. which helped to plan the U-2's flight path. GENETRIX balloons did manage to light up the Soviet radar system that was known as **TOKEN**, and which helped both U.S. and NATO to find many unknown Soviet radar sites. All this information went right into the U-2 operation plans.

All of the good things that came out of the GENETRIX program weren't a match for the political headaches the program caused. There were many in the CIA who were very concerned that the bad feelings over GENETRIX would put a hex on the U-2 program and would cause Eisenhower to backtrack on any and all over flights. The CIA told the USAF to back off of the balloon flights because of the "additional political pressures" being generated against all balloon operations and over flights which would increase the problems of policy decisions which would hamper any operations in the future. A memo was sent to General Nathan Twining, USAF Chief of Staff, in February of 1956, by the Deputy Director of Central Intelligence, Charles Caball, that warned against further balloon flights because of the "additional political pressure being generated against all balloon operation and over flights, this increasing the difficulties of policy decisions which would permit such operations in future."[25]

The CIA had feared that Eisenhower had some anger over the whole balloon fiasco and could curtail not only the balloon program, but the Free Europe Committee, which was a covert agency based in West Germany used to release propaganda over Eastern Europe, could also be

---

[25] Philip G. Strong: Attachment to Memo DCI Dulles," Project GENETRIX Summary" February 1956, OSI records.

affected. GENETRIX was not only cancelled, it was officially over and hopefully would not curtail the U-2 in the process.

SKYHOOK and Strange Goings On

The Air Force's re-use of WWII aircraft as reconnaissance wasn't the only trick in the bag for trying to get the goods on the enemy. There were other things that were happening. However, it was happening in the commercial world NOT the military. Balloons were again looked at as a possible solution to some other everyday issues. However, there hadn't been much in the line of technological development for balloons. The 1950s brought us the plastics revolution; cellophane, polyethylene, and Nylon. The new plastics were being developed by the Union Carbide Company, and the DuPont Chemical Company. Plastics were not expensive to make and lent themselves to many different shapes, moldings and other uses. Plastics could be stretched to $.1000^{th}$ of an inch in thickness and all were extremely light in weight. It would lend itself to the development of balloon technology. On September 25, 1947, one of the very first test balloons was ready for a run. The balloon was large, holding 30,000 cubic feet of gas and had a 63lb payload. However, there were many tiny pinholes in the film sealing the seams with adhesive tapes. The balloon reached 100,000 ft and after taking off from St. Cloud, Minnesota. It landed in Eau Claire, Wisconsin. The next two trips failed miserably. There were some meetings held and the whole process was in question until NYU (New York University) stepped in with their experiments in plastics for balloons. The meteorologists of New York City were working with NYU in the hopes of developing some new meteorological tools that could sustain going up into the higher atmosphere. While these devices were made for weather forecasting, it would be more plausible that those meteorological devices were looking for particles of Soviet testing of nuclear explosions. The NYU balloon needed to fly at a specific altitude for a long time. These balloons were made out of "carrot grade plastic bags" meaning those bags that supermarkets used to bag carrots in, basically polyethylene. Later in 1947, with the success of the NYU project, the General Mills Corporation and a man who worked for General Mills by the name Otto Winzen stepped in to work on a new balloon/plastics project.

Flying Saucers! Or Was it SKYHOOK?

On June 24, 1947, a pilot by the name of Kenneth Arnold was flying alone in his aircraft, along the Cascade Mountain range of Washington State. He was actually trying to find a downed C-46 transport aircraft belonging to the US Marine Corp. that had crashed somewhere in the mountain range. There was a hefty $5000 reward for the person who found the aircraft. Arnold was on his search when he saw nine disc shaped objects flying in a loose formation toward Mt. Rainier. Arnold said that they "flew like a saucer would if you skipped across the water.' Hence the nomenclature of "flying saucer" was born. Of course, Arnold was laughed at by his friends when he finally landed at his destination, an air show in Yakima, Washington. Chiefly, Arnold was laughed at by everyone, even though another resident of Yakima, a lady by the name of Mrs. Ethel Wheelhouse, also said that she had seen something like Arnold described. Some suggested that Arnold had seen a reflection from aircraft possibly a mirage, which distorted the mountain peaks or disc shaped clouds. The USAF actually put the sightings in their "Blue Book" as extraterrestrial, which was the byword of the of the late 1940s' 50s due to quickly changing technology like jet fighters, rockets and of course the atomic bomb. It didn't take long for many of the science fiction magazines to pick up on the story and run with it. In three months, the "SKYHOOK" balloon launched again. The size made it look like a UFO. This flight caused a total disaster. An F-51 Mustang pilot was scrambled from a local base to find the UFO claim. The pilot passed out due to lack of oxygen, during a spiraling steep dive and crashed into the ground while trying to follow the SKYHOOK.

The USAF investigation unit **PROJECT SIGN** was trying to find out what they were chasing and tried to intercept the "disc". The first public announcement that there was some kind of something going on came on March 3, 1948, with the unveiling of **"SKYHOOK."**

SKYHOOK did get a lot of publicity. *Aviation Week Magazine* published a scientific paper which said there were fifty-two flights made with SKYHOOK, and the top altitude reached was 98,400 ft. What does this have to do with aerial reconnaissance? Hang on, its coming. On September 7, 1950 the Chicago Tribune published photographs of the SKYHOOK that was launched from Stagg Field at the University of Chicago, with the caption *"That "Saucer" you saw was a SKYHOOK!"* However, the public chose to not believe it and decided to run amuck with the theory of it being a UFO.

On February17, 1955, General Mills Company had advised the Chief of Nuclear Physics for the Office of Naval Research that they could locate some of the SKYHOOK balloons that had been lost in flight and were fueling the fire of UFO and flying saucers. Of course, the country was now in a UFO frenzy. This is to say nothing of what occurred in Roswell, New Mexico in mid-1947, when a U.S. Army balloon crashed in a rancher's field. All kinds of craziness ensued there, purporting little grey men and secret autopsies at Wright Patterson AFB. So, truthfully, the "disc" shaped balloons were really causing issues everywhere. By November of 1950 a telescopic photo was taken of a SKYHOOK balloon. When seen from below, the balloons really did have a definitive saucer shape and even LOOK magazine jumped into the Saucer/UFO hysteria by doing an article on how one could interpret these balloons via the "lateral rays of the sun." The craziness went on and continues today, albeit more sophisticated sightings of lights and ships flying at enormous speeds. However, in the 1950s, the SKYHOOK balloons were playing hell with everyone's nerves!

The SKYHOOK balloons were constantly chased by aircraft to find out and make sure someone knew where they were. In one flight, a RB-17 was tracking a balloon launched from Holloman AFB in New Mexico. The crew watched the balloon as the sky went to dusk and later into the evening. The pilots saw the balloon drift off. At that point, the planet Jupiter rose in the evening sky. The pilots watched Jupiter for an hour before they realized this "balloon" hadn't moved very much! That just goes to show how anything could be misinterpreted.

SKYHOOK caused more havoc when one was "lost" over central East Texas and got caught in a wind current. The RB-17 crew that was monitoring the SKYHOOK looked for it and just could not find it. They called in to Barksdale AFB, Louisiana, requesting the base call the newspapers in Shreveport, Louisiana to see if there were any reports of a sighting of SKYHOOK in the 5000-mile radius it could have traveled. Meanwhile, newspapers were besieged by phone calls of "flying saucers" around Waco, Texas, also around the northern port of Louisiana and over the Mississippi River. It was here the balloon's radio beacon was finally picked up. But it was late evening and the gas in the balloon had cooled causing it to shrink about 5% which called the balloon to drop several thousand feet. When the balloon reached 70,000 ft, it stabilized and stayed at that altitude for the night. When the sun warmed up the balloon in the morning, it rose again.

SKYHOOK was really the start of space science. It surely got the imaginations of the United States populace in a tizzy. It was the first object to really explore the atmospheric border of air and no air. SKYHOOK experiments led to the creation of Satellites. However, the Cold War was here to stay, and balloons could carry reconnaissance cameras beyond the reach of a fighter jet and without harm over the United States prime adversary, Russia.

While it was difficult to control in many situations, SKYHOOK was a breakthrough to the next step in aerial reconnaissance. Yes, it did help to start the 1950-60s craze of flying saucers and did help the Movie industry in turning out many "B" movies telling of the horrors of space visitors. SKYHOOK was really the true start of looking past the usual attainable heights by aircraft and gave scientists a look at what happens beyond ... where the air gets thin and then melds into a darkened sky of no atmosphere. SKYHOOK does deserve a place in aerial reconnaissance history.

MOBY DICK PROJECT

Thanks to the escapades of SKYHOOK, technology in plastics and in balloon technology did change for the better. Life went on and the Korean War was a big part of it in the 1950s. What was just a rival between two parts of the same country turned into a hot war. The United States information on the Soviet military equipment and strength was in question. What information the United States had went back to WWII, at least the solid information did. The photo reconnaissance library that was captured from Germany at the end of the war did help, but these photos were limited to Eastern Europe reconnaissance.

All postwar photos were largely limited to the Siberian coast by United States aircraft flying outside Russian territorial waters in RB-29s. RB-29s carried 100-inch focal length, K-30 cameras with oblique angle ability. When cloud cover was bad for photos the aircraft's radar would be used to find targets on the ground. Echoes showed coastline and built up areas. The aircraft also flew with receivers which picked up Soviet radar and radar signals (ELINT or electronic intelligence).

The aircraft conducting the photo reconnaissance or the ELINT had to remain 12 miles off the Soviet Union's coast. In the fall of 1950, the Joint Chiefs of Staff had a plan for systemic probing flights over Russian territory. The Air Force Vice Chief of Staff, Nathan Twining, brought plans to the White House. President Truman asked if the Joint Chiefs all agreed. The answer was yes and that allowed Truman to also jump on board with his agreement. A new program was born, its name . . . GOPHER

GOPHER

The MX-1594 project called "GOPHER" was a covert mission to overfly Soviet Union with balloons. From September 11 to 15, 1950, the Air Force Scientific Advisory Board held meetings to extend the photographic coverage to the interior of Russia. There were major diplomatic and technical problems. The use of manned aircraft to overfly the Soviet Union in peacetime could be viewed as an act of aggression. The use of the Snark missile, with an inertial guidance system set up for photo reconnaissance, was a distinct possibility in 1953. A reconnaissance satellite was looked at, but that process would take years to develop. The only feasible means of doing this was to use reconnaissance balloons. A balloon for this purpose would be ready by 1951.

The concept of using balloons for aerial reconnaissance over the Soviet Union was going around for a while. The idea started in 1946, with the RAND Corporation and the help of General George A. Goddard, who was a pioneer in the development of reconnaissance cameras and systems since the 1920s.

In 1949, Goddard proposed that ELINT equipment should be put on a balloon. But, due to lack of funding and questions of feasibility, the idea sort of hung out there. By July 1950, the General Mills Company test flew a camera package to over 90,000 ft, which took excellent photographs of the ground. On October 9, 1950 the balloon reconnaissance go ahead was finally given.

The general characteristics of this new program were:

Camera System: Scale of 1:100,000 with time of day, altitude and directions recorded if possible. Cameras did shut down at night.

Flight Profile: Altitude was between 60,000 and 80,000 ft. Flight time was several days at a specific altitude.

Recovery: Balloons and equipment had to be recovered. Air, Land and Sea pick up were looked at. A timed beacon was used to locate the balloon then another timer would vent gas from the balloon to lower and raise the balloon. Development of a recovery system was not in the initial test program. They would use off the shelf items for that.

Camouflage: Minimized detection from ground to air. This would be under development of the equipment division by the Directorate of Research and Development. Major J.J. Pellegrini who was in charge of the GOPHER Project Office.

By October 1950, GOPHER was expanded which would include ELINT. Balloons would be released to drift over the Soviet Union radar sites. As of January 8, 1951, the briefing on GOPHER Project was in the office of General Donald N. Yates who was then director of the Research and Development office.

A Five Phase Schedule Was Produced for GOPHER
Jan 18,1951—Balloon vehicles delivered.
February 1951—Upper air trajectory test
March 1951—Gondola Design

April 1951—Test flight across the United States
July 1951—Balloon Recovery Test.

The reconnaissance balloon was ready for operational flights over Soviet Union during the winter of 1952, but all was not that simple. There were problems. In July 1950, the camera test was run by General Mills Company. It was a success and General Mills was given the first GOPHER contract for $97,000, to develop a balloon system with a gondola.

In November 23, 1951, a conference was held on GOPHER. The two main questions were:

a. Was there an interest in GOPHER and what further requirements were needed. The first answer was yes.
b. The second question totally depended on the status of other projects and world conditions. It was felt that GOPHER should proceed on a "crash" basis. Yet, GOPHER was still in difficulty. It was a year behind in progress. The problems of the defective polyethylene plastic were solved, and General Mills could now start its flight test of the various Gopher components. The balloons were launched from Minneapolis, Minnesota, Holloman AFB in New Mexico, Peyote, Texas and Tillamook, Oregon. One of the major problems was designing a balloon able to carry a very heavy payload for a very long duration flight which was raised by the USAF to 14 days in May of 1951. The balloon used for the long duration flight was 116 ft. in diameter and volume of 711,000 cubic feet. Its shape was a modified sphere in a core which reduced stress on the balloon. The plastic was .0025 inches thick, pay-

load was 500 lbs. and 1,000 lbs. of ballast. This was for 14 days aloft.

Of the balloons launched, the best the test got was 8.75 days with a gross load of 2,366 lbs., of which 955 lbs. was the actual payload. After the launch, the maximum altitude reached was 74,000 ft. with the altitude controlled by solar engine control system. This allowed the balloon to descend at a controlled rate during the night hours. Each day the balloon descended from a maximum altitude of 54,000 ft. to 40,000 ft. The maximum altitude dropped about 3,000 ft per day due to the air getting into the balloon. The flight ended when the ballast system power supply failed.

During 1951, the test flights were done at WADC (Wright Air Development Center) Wright Patterson AFB, Ohio, but this caused a lot of conflict with the General Mills Company. WADC felt that General Mills was showing poor management and inadequate technical supervision. This resulted in both money and effort that was spent in areas that did not advance items that the USAF wanted. The Gopher Project was now in jeopardy because General Mills Company ignored its obligation to the contract.

Oct 9, 1951, a nine month/$1 million contract was signed with General Mills and the USAF in order to test the gondola system independently of the other General Mills order for thirty of the 70ft. balloons designed by Winzen Research. The contract for development of the gondola was issued in November of 1951 with the winner of the project bid, Stanley Aviation Corporation. The work completed cost $387,498 was also completed by July 1, 1952.

A complete prototype system was designed, and nine production gondolas were delivered. The gondola arrived in two parts with an outer shell or hood. The outer shell was a load bearing structure, which used a hydrogen peroxide heater that worked on a thermostat and helped to keep the systems warm. The ballast container was on the underside of the gondola and like the MOBY DICK balloon would use steel shot as the ballast substance. The camera use on the test flight was a K-17 modified to a reduced weight and power. WADC was not happy with the outcome of the test flights for the gondola. By April 17, 1952, it was agreed that General Mills would continue with the remaining funds, after WADC pointed out the poor performance, with no more funding coming forth in future. By August of 1952, the General Mills contract was terminated, and the balloons were then made by the Winzen Research Company and launched from Holloman AFB in New Mexico. Things didn't improve.

The test flight and procedure produced the same image quality, but the program was fraught with problems. It was time for Gopher to end. Gopher was finally transformed into WS119/L project called *Grandson* which was an operational reconnaissance balloon project.

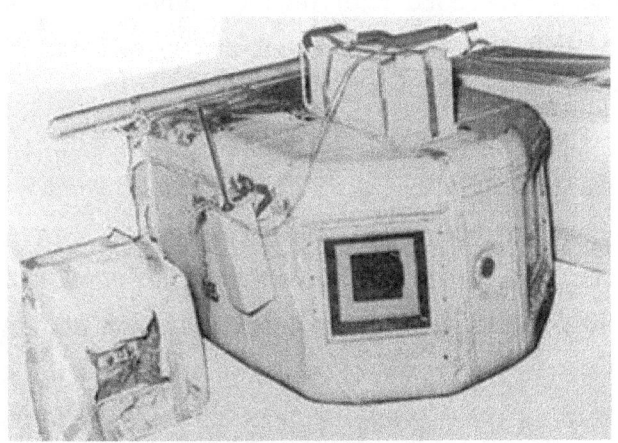

The AN/DMQ -1 gondola with camera
(R.W. Koch)

MOBY DICK Comes of Age

Another project under way, one that would play a major role in the manufacture of the U. S reconnaissance balloon venture. Before WWII,

10,000ft was considered high altitude. Development of the Boeing B-29 Superfortress raised this to 25,000 ft. A jet aircraft doubled this in the early post war years. 1950 showed that there was little data available for the conditions over 50,000 ft. in altitude. Some things were known, like at 50,000 ft., the ambient air temperature was equal to -70 degrees F. Yet, at 100,000 ft., the air became hot again. Winter jet streams flowed west to east and winds from west at 50 to 60 miles per hour at 70,000 ft during the summer months. The problem was there were no systematic studies of these air currents available. Soon aircraft and missiles would be flying at these altitudes. It was a good time to study the effects and SKYHOOK had provided the means. In May 1951, Colonel Paul Worthman, who would later head the CORONA project at U.S. Air Force headquarters at the Pentagon, wrote a directive to the USAF Cambridge Research Center asking to study high altitudes. Aided by the RAND Corporation meteorologist William Kellogg, this experiment took the name of MOBY DICK. The experiment proceeded with floating hundreds of polyethylene, helium filled balloons, with their gondolas loaded with all kinds of scientific experiments.

By June 1, 1951 a contract was issued to New York University to again design a suitable vehicle as a balloon. Tufts University, Massachusetts, was signed on to develop a gondola transmitter; power supply and ballast system. Dr. Alvin Howell designed the gondola and used a compass fluid as a ballast. This ballast fluid was made of a kerosene type liquid that was supposed to withstand low temperatures. It was found that at a temperature of -94 degrees F., the compass fluid did freeze. With that, work was stopped, and ground tests were made with dry ice. The fluid was totally unusable. The decision was made to use a very fine steel shot (which was fine as dust). This steel didn't freeze, had a low volume for the given weight and actually poured like a liquid. Ground tests were made, and a new "magnetic" valve was created to allow a controlled amount of ballast to be released. The use of an aneroid switch was used to detect a drop in altitude. It was turned out with an electromagnet which neutralized the permanent magnetic field allowing the steel shot to fall. The Gondola had an empty weight of 150 lbs. and could carry 250 lbs. of steel shot with two hoppers on its sides. The Gondola's main payload was a transmitter built by Ultrasonic Inc. There was considerable effort made to reduce the risk of midair collision with a MOBY DICK Balloon. Sixty percent of the payload weight was safety devices.

A timer allowed for the balloon to take 100 minutes to reach 28,000 ft. If it was still below altitude at the end of it times, the balloon would be automatically cut down. That would prevent a leaking balloon drifting into the air lanes of commercial traffic. The gondola also carried a flashing light for visibility at night. Great effort was made to reduce the risk of a midair collision with a MOBY DICK balloon. Various systems and test flights were made by mid-1952 allowing quantity production to start. Due to the number of launches planned which was a thousand plus in quantity, more people would be needed to service the program. The call went out the USAF for three squadrons to support air supply and communications and aid with the additional work. The new unit was called the 1300th Air Resupply and Communications Squadron, Mountain Home AFB, Idaho.

The balloons were manufactured by General Mills and traveled 50,000 to 100,000 ft to measure all the wind field at these very high altitudes. The balloons were 65 ft. in height when blown up and loaded with radio beacons that bleeped out every two minutes or so and were tracked by the USAF meteorologists. This method tracked the jet streams. By 1952-53 the United States meteorological scientists now had a method to understand those jet streams that so affect our weather even today. By November 13, 1953, the 1110th Air Support Group was formally established replacing the 1300th Air Resupply and Communications Squadron.

The 1110th Air Support would have responsibilities for all the USAF balloon launches (science and military). In 1953, four hundred and eighty-two MOBY DICK flights were made.

While MOBY DICK was revving up for action, there were other things going on. The Soviets were busy blowing up their test hydrogen bombs. The first three were in August 1955. During 1954, the Russians managed to do at least two more H Bomb tests. The Soviets were also increasing their large-scale facilities to produce more fissionable material in the volume needed for a stockpile of H bombs. The Soviets were also giving the U.S. a run for the money, or at least we thought so at that time, with the building of MYA-4 Bison bomber which made a flyover during a May Day parade in Moscow. The U. S. also had some new things to show, there were the two prototypes of the huge B-52 Bombers. The first production model was already flying, and Boeing was in full scale production by 1956. The estimate for the Soviet Bison bomber was upgraded during a May Day 1955 air show where there was a flyover of ten of the Bison jets. The Soviets also brought along the TU-95 Bear prototype bomber. At this time, the United States did have thirty B-52s ready to go. A report that came out on May 16, 1955 which put the Soviets with heavy bomber forces -twenty MYA4-Bisons, and twenty TU-95 Bears. That number would rise to eighty of each by 1956 on to two hundred Bison and one hundred fifty Bears in 1957 and thirty-five Bison and two hundred fifty Bears in mid-1958. This "growth" was also known in the U.S. as the "Bomber Gap." When compared to SAC's plans, the current B-52 production gave the lead to the Soviets. Of course, these estimates were unnerving in the White House when shown against U.S. current defenses. The F-80s, F-86s and F-94s would be alright against the Soviet TU-4 but lacked the speed and altitude to intercept the Bison. The Soviet numbers were also up with ICBMs. The

Eagle Eyes

Kapustin Yar test range near Stalingrad was pushing the Soviet test programs by mid-1953.

In the summer of 1955, the United States had their balloon launch crews working on balloon reconnaissance program. The 456th Troop Carrier Wing, Beale AFB, California, was starting to sort itself out and by June 1, 1955, personnel were organized into combat crews which had one aircraft commander, two pilots, a navigator/flight engineer, radio operator and a winch operator along with four pole handlers for a total of eleven in each crew. This along with fifty of the C-119F Boxcar transport aircraft back from the factory, production gear started to come in and the balloon crews could start training again. Training also brought up new dangers. August 23, 1953, brought a tragedy. A C-119F took off and crashed in a residential area destroying several houses. The damages ran up to $10,000 which was a lot of money in the 1950s. The accident review board said the left engine on the C-119F could have been the cause, after being written up for several excessive back firings. The engine failed due to a faulty carburetor.

With the crash of the C-119 and the death of half of her crew, this was a turning point for the balloon program. Again, there was public attention to UFOs and little gray men starting up all over again. The first "leak" started September 11, 1953, when the C-119 "Weather Plane", as the newspapers called her, caught up over Indiana with a MOBY DICK balloon that was launched from Lowry AFB five days prior. It was cut down successfully, but the mid-air recovery did fail. The gondola and boxes landed and some of the crew bailed out to protect the packages, when a group of bystanders came by, they were told that the balloon was brought down by "electric impulse guns" and the boxes had "small animals" inside to deter their interest. Two trucks from the nearby Chanute AFB, Illinois, showed up to pick everything and everyone up. Lowry AFB denied the small animal story and said they "couldn't talk about it". This all brought out so much speculation and tabloid frenzy of UFOs the, USAF "BLUE BOOK" Project was running into overtime!

This notice was tagged to all the packages that the MOBY DICK balloons carried. (US NAVY/Public Domain)

The MOBY DICK test recovery trials of the midair and water pickups were made in September and October of 1955. The first series dropped 175 packages of which fifty-four were picked up. The second series were tests at the "water stations" which successfully extended fifty-one packages that were dropped off, of which twenty-three were recovered. The third test was an ocean recovery with 38 training packages sent out and twenty-one were recovered.

As the program went on, shortages again started up. This time it was the tools that were the problem, there just weren't enough to go around. Many times the C-119 would have to come back from a chase and would be intercepted at some distant base in order for new aircraft to "borrow" a set of tools from them. There were also maintenance issues: wings had defective propellers, 30% of the blades were defective and 50% of the C-119s had defective props. As it was, the propeller shop was working 24hours a day to rebuild and restore props that were defective.

The deployment of the MOBY DICK balloons, and the C-119 recovery aircraft started with the first unit to go overseas, which was the 6926Th RS(M) which started in June 1955 and completed in August 1955 moved out with seven hundred twenty five personnel.

There were 10 tracking sites:
Guam
Wake Island
Clark AFB in the Philippines
Okinawa
K-6 Korea
Chitose Air Base Japan
Shiroi Air Base Japan
Midway Island
Shemya Island in the Aleutian Islands
Elmendorf AFB Alaska

The MOBY DICK Far East balloon flights were scheduled August 1, 1955 but were pushed back to September 1, 1955. The launches officially started on September 7, 1955. By October 15, 1955 the launch crews at Chitose AB, Japan moved to K-6 AB in Korea. By the end of October, 70% of the objectives for MOBY DICK had been completed.

The Deployment of the 456th TCW (Troop Carrier Wing) and the 1110th ASG (Area Support Group) started in early October 1955. By October 15th, the 746th TCS headed by train to meet with the US Navy Transport ship the "General A.E. Anderson", which set sail October 23, 1955. Conditions on the ship were austere to say the least. There were serious issues of ventilation in the crew bunks, no recreation, 2 movies were shown each night and 3 bingo games were held each week. Not much enjoyment there, so the crew tried for a variety show but the attempt failed. Finally, ten musicians aboard got together and formed jazz and western music bands. To keep the airmen busy, they were given tasks on the ship like chipping paint, rust removal, guard duty and washing the decks. The ship did stop in Okinawa and Yokohama, Japan to drop off the 744th Personnel. The others went on to Itszuke AB, Japan where they had no blankets in freezing cold. The crew used their overcoats as blankets to keep warm at night. This went on and on until all the crews finally were dispersed. The final move was to C-119F destinations

Call signs:

Detachment 1—744th TCS Okinawa—ASCOT
Detachment 1—744th TCS Itazuke AB—CENTER
                  745th TCS Adak AB—CLOVER
Detachment 1—745th TCS Misawa— Japan EASY
                746th TCS Kodiak— Alaska GIRLIE
Detachment 1—746th TCS Johnson AB—Japan MDHEN

The End of the Story

The outcome of the MOBY DICK program was up for grabs. There were three balloons that were lost and that meant no more operational flights. The rest of the WS-46L balloons were put into storage. Throughout 1958 and 1959, there were sporadic flights for the U-2 over the Soviet Union and that was to find out how many Soviet SS-6 ICBMs were really available. This was what was known as the "Missile Gap". The WS-46L flights of 1958 were the end for the 1110th Balloon Activities group. The phase out started 1959 and officially closed out on January 1, 1960. There was some more information that was released on two other MOBY DICK programs that were flown:

ASHCAN—April 1, 1957—1110th ASG took over the fallout (nuclear particles) collection.

GRAB BAG—got the whole air samples. This program provided a total worldwide sample of radioactive materials in the atmosphere.

Both programs were taken over by other units during the massive Soviet nuclear testing that went on 1961-62. NASA used some of the released 1110th personnel and continued launching balloons for NASA's National Scientific Facility in Palestine, Texas. What was left of the WS-46L project was now in storage at Norton AFB, California by 1968 and still considered a very top-secret project.

The history of balloon reconnaissance started with the French Revolution through the United States Civil War, two world wars and the Cold War. However, it had outgrown its usefulness. The program's technological limitations were really what downed the balloon usefulness.

The U-2 was on the way to taking over the skies and the CORONA Satellites were also in the works. It took Kelly Johnson's brilliance to bring both the U-2 and the up and coming Blackbirds to life and this would be the way aerial reconnaissance would work in the upcoming years. However, the really good thing about using the balloons was the fact that the United States could continue to call them "weather" balloons and if one got lost or downed, there was that little thing called "plausible denial." With the U-2, as we would find out, there was no such thing. If she went down, the Soviets and the rest of the world would know it. Balloons did have some advantages, however slow. Altitude was also an issue for balloons. They did have limitations. There was also the amount of balloons that could be launched in a day and how much it was going to cost, yet the United States had been flying the balloons for years. There were assessments at the end of the MOBY DICK program. The harshest came from the CIA who called it a disaster. A lot of that had to do with the competition that the balloons presented to their new item, the U-2. In a statement by Robert Burch who was one of the 1110thASG's launch crewmen:

"From what I heard later on, our efforts were really of little value . . . I really don't believe we did much good for the intelligence community." However, the USAF was more positive in their view. They felt the balloons were effective and a means of getting reconnaissance at a cheap cost. As for the photographic end, the product was a good source but still had a lot of limiting factors. What it all boils down to is; the balloons were a good source to start out with. It was a cheaper means to try to see what could be gotten out of this type of aerial reconnaissance. It wasn't a failure by any means, despite the limitations the system had. The MOBY DICK, SKYHOOK, GOPHER, programs all had given something back to aerial reconnaissance. It was a stepping stone to newer more precise methods of finding out what the adversary was doing.

Chapter Nine

Satellites Around the Earth

CORONA Satellites

The United States of the 1950s was a country in deep fear about what the Soviet Union had in the ways of military weapons and missiles. Critical information on what was happening in the Soviet Union was not only scarce, it was often erroneous, and the United States needed to find out the truth. The Soviet Union drove that fear home when they when they launched the little Sputnik satellite in 1957. The people of the United States lived in a fearful nation after that announcement of hearing the little Sputnik Satellite beep its Russian greeting to all the world. Many Americans felt that the Soviets might start dropping bombs any minute. This would not stand, and newly re—inaugurated President Dwight D. Eisenhower decided that the time had come for the United States to find a solution.

In 1953, the USAF Advisory Board in a statement made a note of a method to create a small, lightweight, thermonuclear warhead. It was then that the Atlas ICBM was given the highest development priority available. GOR 80 was another *General Operational Requirement* that called for *"providing continuous surveillance of pre-determined areas of the world to determine the potential status of an enemy's war making capabilities."* The USAF Air Research and Development Command (ARDC) had taken over the RAND program in 1953. It then assigned the program over to the Ballistic Missile Division. The WS-117L program called for the development of systems and subsystems for reconnaissance purposes; basically the collection of photos and infrared surveillance material. This program separated into three segments.

In 1956, the project awarded to Lockheed Corporation had already begun work on all three sections for WS117/L "VIDICON" film recovery and infrared observation for Ballistic Missiles Early Warning System.

Each of these satellites would go on to its own upper stage rocket and carry its own restartable rocket engine and steering thruster. All three of these satellites in this reconnaissance system would work under the name of *"PIED PIPER."*

This system set the precedent for every other satellite system to follow. The first in the series of tests was the THOR missile, which would begin in 1958, the second the ATLAS/AGENA missile series which would begin in 1959, the third and the operational series would begin in 1960.

It was obvious that this program was breaking new ground and quickly fell behind schedule. The program also fell into problems with security. It didn't take long for the press to create the popular stories of "Big Brother is Watching You" from the skies above, as they alluded to when describing the reconnaissance satellites. This gave an already nervous American public more tabloid nightmares to think about.

At this time, Eisenhower's presidential consultant board was already looking at the feasibility of two reconnaissance programs. The CIA manned reconnaissance aircraft program would call for better RCS (reduced radar cross section) and greater speed, the second being considered was WS-117L. Since neither program would be ready for 1959, the list of the three that were involved in WS117L would be sorted out of the rest and designated Project "CORONA." This would be the best of the photographic subsystems. CORONA would be comprised of six similar but distinct satellites and three different intelligence systems.

CORONA's name came from one of the people drafting the program. He had looked down at his desk at his Smith Corona typewriter, a very efficient and popular machine in the 1950s. The name CORONA was now the official name.

Richard Bissell, who was already the special assistant to the Director of Central Intelligence for planning and development, headed the developments project staffs. Along with Bissell, his co-director was General Osmond Ritland, who also served as Bissell's first deputy in the beginning of the development's project staff.

Ritland was made Vice Commander of USAF's Ballistic Missile Division. Bissell's early instructions in the new office were vague. He was told only that there would be new subsystems that would be branched off from WS-117L program and that it would be covert management. One of the distinct things he was told was that no monies from already established Air Force programs would be on issue in the means of supplying the THOR missile for the program. Since the USAF owned all of the missiles, the CIA was forced to return to the President's office and admit that the money situation was a problem, in fact it needed more money, pure and simple.

The WS-117L program was an advanced reconnaissance system that had been divided into the SAMOS (Sentry Optical Reconnaissance Program) and the MIDAS (Missile Defense Alarm System), which was the early warning satellite program. The optical phase of the program was projected to recover the film from orbit and via re-entry trajectory with its parachute recovered. Lockheed was the prime contractor for the program. Eastman Kodak developed the cameras for the SAMOS system. The unique camera gimbaled for point and was activated by radio command from a ground station.

Since the split off from WS-117L program, the Department of Defense now found it imperative that it was the time to restructure its space activities management. February 28, 1958 brought the granting of space management activities ceded to it. The Advanced Research Projects Agency (ARPA) was established. This allowed the WS-117L reconnaissance program responsibility to be turned over to the USAF and the WS117L provisional reconnaissance program, which used the THOR missile as a booster was dropped totally.

This allowed the USAF program to be dropped, while the covert program could not begin. The cancellation of a military program such as the WS-117L brought with it individual issues such as notifying the contractors and. There was a great deal of shock amongst the contractors when they got the word. However, some of these contractors were picked right back up again as soon as the subsystem program was working. A very limited group including the USAF were again told of the new project and cleared to work on CORONA.

Eisenhower approved CORONA in 1958. It was pretty much an all-out rush to get the new program up and running. The program was brought together with quick decision-making. Just as quickly a meeting to approve those decisions was called. It took the Director of Central Intelligence, Robert Gates, only three very short paragraphs to consign seven million dollars to the first phase of the new project. In retrospect, there is no possible way today with the current state of political bureaucracy, that a program like CORONA could ever be launched that fast and that quietly.

However, the perception to be noted here is that there was a need to be filled with great speed. It should be noted that with today's political machine decisions can be made quickly, when it is essential to get critical information that is imperative to national security. It took little more than two years to go from first plans of CORONA to actually recovering film from orbit.

August 18 and 19, 1960, saw the first film payload delivered from space and caught by means of a parachute catch. This was Mission 9009 and flown with the KBH-1 camera and this marked the start of the CORONA satellite system. The first target was a military airbase near Mys Schmidta on the Chuckchi Sea in northeastern Russia. While the images might have been not the best quality, it didn't take long for those imaging problems to be corrected.

It stuns the mind when we consider the achievements of the CIA/USAF/Project CORONA which had produced so much so quickly, and we look at the recent results of our current forays into intelligence gathering. Brig. General Ozzie Ritland was the head of USAF support of CORONA. Of course, there were the other technical geniuses like Lockheed Missiles and Space Co., ITEK Corporation, Fairchild Camera and Instruments Co, Eastman Kodak, General Electric and Douglas Aircraft. With a team like this, CORONA was destined for greatness.

It wasn't all an easy trip, however. The technical challenges were huge and there was no time to go to the usual route for studies and more testing. Mission failures did happen, but they were reversed. This was all done in the darkest halls that the CIA secrecy could manage. Program success came fast. The first payload recovered from CORONA brought back 3000 feet of film, which covered a total of 1,650,000 miles of Soviet territory. This total footage was more than the U-2 Dragon Lady aircraft had collected in twenty-four of its flights. This was just the start. Consider that during the beginnings of the Cold War, decisions were made bereft of good solid intelligence.

This broken down "collection gathering" led to the Missile Gap and the Bomber Gap. The onset of CORONA allowed the U.S. to find and maintain a higher form of intelligence that kept the Soviets and the U.S. nuclear dogs of war at bay.

What should be noted, is that as good as your intelligence photographs might be, they were only as good as the photo interpreters that read them. These men and women would analyze these images and got the information to the services that needed it. There is not enough that can be said about the people who analyzed the photographs. It was due to their talents that were the hard won images from space, could be used to settle many of the deepest issues of the Cold War.

The CORONA program was initially announced by the USAF as the "DISCOVERER" series of satellites to actually disguise it from the CIA project. The "buckets" of film were caught in their drop, via parachute by the specially adapted aircraft, the Fairchild C119 "Flying Boxcar." Should the air catch be missed, the "buckets" could float in the ocean until pick up could be arranged.

The film used was black and white, but sometimes infrared and color film would be carried for experimental testing. DISCOVERER did not only make CORONA surveillance flights. The program also made many flights in the name of developing a new type of technology to fix problems in support of the MIDAS early warning satellite system. After DISCOVERER made its 38th flight, the program was ended and the shroud of concealment would cover all the satellite work.

A C119 aircraft recovery "bucket" catches take from the Discoverer satellite.
(Courtesy US. Air Force)

The KEYHOLE designation was used to refer to all satellites during photo reconnaissance work. The KH description would include the type of camera system used. This system started in 1962 and started with the fourth camera system used. The first system to use the new designation was KH-1, KH-2, KH-3, and KH-6. These satellites carried a single panoramic camera or a single frame camera which were calledKH-5, KH-4, KH-4A, KH-4B and used two panoramic cameras set to work thirty degrees apart (one forward, one rear looking). KH-6 was programmed to tilt forward and back, so it could cover the same land mass twice during a pass and allow for stereo coverage.

The first satellite used the one-bucket system while later satellites were built with two buckets. KH-4A used multiple buckets with the front and back camera films were packaged separately, for missions that used twin panoramic cameras.

The CORONA payload used a vertical looking, seventy-degree panoramic camera, produced by ITEK Company, used Eastman Kodak film. The camera scanned at the right angles, to the line of flight. In early flights, resolution was only 35 to 40 feet. By 1972, CORONA was able to produce resolutions of 6 to 10 feet. By the 1960s, satellites could remain in orbit for 19 days with precise attitude position and mapping information, gaining coverage of 8,400,000 nautical miles squared per mission. However, on May 25, 1972 CORONA was closed out after this final mission despite the enormous success this program had. CORONA had an amazing legacy to leave behind:

- CORONA covered all Soviets submarine classes from deployment to operational bases.
- CORONA covered all Soviet medium range, intermediate range and ICBM complexes.
- Provided inventories of all Soviet bombers and fighters.
- Provided evidence that there were Soviet missiles in Egypt that were protecting the Suez Canal.
- Produced evidence that the People's Republic of China was receiving Soviet nuclear assistance.
- Monitored the SALT I treaty.
- Identified the People's Republic of China missile launching sites.
- Produced exact locations of Soviet defense missile batteries.
- Produced evidence of construction and deployment of Soviet ocean going vessels.
- Produced evidence of the Plesetsk missiles test range north of Moscow.

CORONA also has quite a space history to be proud:

- the first photo reconnaissance satellite.
- first recovery of an object from space.
- first midair recovery of an object from space.
- first mapping of earth from a satellite.
- first stereo-optical data from space.
- first program to fly more than 100 missions in space.

CORONA (KH-1, Kh-2, KH-3, KH-4, KH-4A, KH-4b) ARGON (KH-5) and LANYARD (KH-6) encompassed a series of satellites programs that change the outlook of the Cold War. Without them, the face of the Cold War would have looked much different for the United States.

Of course, the USAF wasn't too happy about the CIA crossing into their sacred territory of the skies and above, but the President was more than happy to give the CIA the job.

One hundred twenty of the one hundred forty-five missions were total or partial successes. CORONA exposed close to two million feet of film and produced some eight hundred thousand images. To add to the list of success, probably the biggest of all the goods CORONA came up with, she resolved the problem of the "Missile Gap." CORONA verified that the missile gap was there, except the problem was on the side of the Soviets, not the United States. That was a huge relief for the United States. CORONA had managed to locate all missile sites, ship bases and other unknown Soviet military /industrial complexes, the United States never knew about. Considering without all this information, the United States military would have been making war plans that would have been useless, without even knowing the basics of the Soviet layout and what they truly had and didn't have. CORONA took away much of the fear and doubt about the Soviets through her years and missions. For a satellite program named for a typewriter, that was not half bad work.

A very rare image of the U-2 at Groom Lake facility early in the program. You can see the NACA markings on the tail to disguise the aircraft as a weather observation plane instead of reconnaissance (USAF)

Chapter Ten

Project Bald Eagle
And the Start of the CIA's Reign in Reconnaissance

Project Bald Eagle

When General Dwight D. Eisenhower won the presidency, he knew that times had radically changed from his time as the Supreme Allied Commander in Europe during WWII. Eisenhower had to find a method and a means of getting the information and reconnaissance needed to protect the country. The Cold War had become an official item and no one understood that better than Eisenhower. The Department of Defense put out a request for a design study marked 53WC-16507 in March of 1957. It called for a subsonic, single seat aircraft that was able to carry at least a 700 lb. payload (mainly cameras and ELINT equipment) and fly at an altitude of 70,000 ft, with a range of 3,000 miles. That was a tall order and the order's name was given "Bald Eagle". The rest of this requirement called for daylight reconnaissance, which would leave the aircraft without armament and no ejection seat. That was a very scary prospect, indeed.

The USAF Speaks

The U-2 unfolded because of the U.S. Air Force. In March of 1954, Kelly Johnson had submitted the CL-282 design to Brigadier General Bernard Schriever's office of Development Planning. The design was studied further. It went back to General Schriever, who wanted Lockheed to present a specific proposal. By April of 1954, Johnson arrived with a new complete CL-282 plan. This included construction to support thirty of the aircraft. This plan was given to Lt. General Donald Putt, who was Schriever's boss. Putt was the deputy Chief of Staff for Development.

Trevor Gardener was a special assistant for research and development to the Secretary of the USAF. Johnson found out the civilians loved the plan for CL-282 while the generals were not so pleased. At that point, SAC's Chief, General Curtis LeMay stepped in. According to Bud Weinberg of Development and Planning, LeMay, with his characteristic cigar drooping out of his mouth, stood up and told all present that if he wanted high altitude photos, the B-36 loaded with cameras, could do the job. He had no use for an aircraft that carried no bombs or guns. He left the room, saying that it all was a waste of money. Not good news for Kelly Johnson.

The CL-282 made its way through the USAF development offices and reached Major John Seaberg. who initially gave the U-2 a good going over but was not in favor of the J-73 engine built by General Electric that Johnson planned to use. It seemed that the Wright/USAF engineers were more in favor of the Pratt and Whitney J-57 engine, which was much stronger and the rest of the competition, meaning Bell, Martin and Fairchild were all using that engine. of the unconventional landing gear, really spooked the USAF quite a bit. This, along with the fact that there was only one engine, really dropped the CL-282 out of position. The USAF always liked an aircraft that had at least two engines, just in case an engine would fail. Since the U-2 had only the one engine, the USAF backed off from the plan.

In 1953, Major John Seabury of Wright Patterson AFB, Ohio was the Chief of New Project Development. He was convinced that the USAF needed a reconnaissance aircraft, that could fly high enough to avoid detection by enemy interceptor or missile. Seabury went to his boss, William LeMarr, who brought in a few smaller companies like Bell, Fairchild and Martin to come up with an idea. They said they were confused and concerned about the altitude and the flight demands. The best engine out there at the time was the Pratt and Whitney J-57. The higher the altitude, the less density in the atmosphere. LeMarr and Seabury saw the engine was not going to be enough to keep any aircraft flying. Any engine required air and how could an engine survive in a no air atmosphere in a high altitude. With a new airframe, the engine might look good. Seaberg and staff went to the Killian Committee (James Killian was the Chair at Massachusetts Institute of Technology) which were charged with discovering if the Soviet Union was planning another Pearl Harbor type of attack, something that new president Eisenhower was totally in fear of. However, it seemed that no one, including Secretary of Defense, Charlie Wilson, Allan Dulles of the CIA and Eisenhower just didn't know the answer to that question. Eisenhower wanted a very simple military order. He hated spying and the way the CIA did business, he wanted direct results not unpredictable outcome. Eisenhower had heard about Kelly Johnson at Lockheed. He asked his Chief of Staff, "What's his real name? "The response was "Clarence, Mr. President." By the time that Kelly Johnson made his way to the White House, he was already in the top realm of the aeronautical world. He delivered the P-80 Shooting Star in record time for WWII, along with the P-38 Lightening and the F-104 Star fighter jet along with the beautiful commercial and military Lockheed Constellation. When Kelly Johnson finally reached the Oval office, he was also known for not being pushed around, or for being anyone's easy mark. Truly, he wasn't sure that he wanted to get involved with Eisenhower and his plans. Kelly Johnson had his own "spy network" to let him know what was going on. Eisenhower let it slip to Johnson that he was looking for an aircraft that would go high, so no one could touch it. Johnson admitted it was a big order but with the right amount of money, he could make it happen. Eisenhower gave Johnson a figure of $30 million. Johnson thought it was a nice amount, but he wanted to know who was going to hold the purse strings. Johnson told Eisenhower he was not up to working with committees or groups of any kind. Eisenhower assured Johnson that it would be only the USAF, CIA and of course, the president. That was three too many for Kelly and he opted out. His adage of too many cooks spoil the aircraft was right on the top of his list. Johnson told Eisenhower that the whole thing was unacceptable. Eisenhower tried to reason with Johnson and asked him not to be so obstinate and if it would close the deal, only the president would handle it. Kelly finally agreed.

Three contractors decided to put in for this requirement. Bell Aircraft, Fairchild and Martin were now working under the secret code MX-2147. At this time, Lockheed was not even involved with this project, a slight that really got under Kelly Johnson's skin. He went ahead, using Lockheed money to set up and start design of CL-282 which was based on the Lockheed F-104 Star-fighter. While Bell and Fairchild came in with new designs, Martin Aircraft stood by with the venerable RB-57D Canberra. Martin was already the pick for the provisional decision while work on the new aircraft went on. The new idea had a very long wingspan for that super high altitude the CIA was looking for and was subsonic speed with a long range.

Using the General Electric J-73 turbo jet engine for Johnson's concept, he soon found out that the USAF had already decided on using the Pratt and Whitney J-57 engine. Kelly Johnson went back and redefined the fuselage of the CL-282 to accept the P&W J-57 engine and brought his CL-282 into the competition as an unsolicited entry. Since Martin had already tied up the provisional deal for a high altitude aircraft, the RB-57D, the competition was now against Bell, Fairchild and Lockheed.

A U-2 landing on the deck of the USS Kitty Hawk aircraft carrier.
This was a truly rare event for the U-2 and the Navy.
Program's name was called WHALE TALE (USAF)

The USAF was in favor of the Bell Model 16 and ordered twenty-eight aircraft in September of 1954. The first of the aircraft flew some eighteen months later, but it was totally a research issue known as the X-16. While all this was work continued under the *"Bald Eagle Project"* it had now changed to the code name, "AQUATONE."

With Lockheed's CL-282 fuselage change to accept the Pratt and Whitney J-57, she no longer looked like the F-104 Starfighter and was more in the line of a glider than a fighter. The best part of the entire change was that the CL-282 was far from looking like any kind of a threat to the enemy. She was more like a weather observation aircraft that could not protect herself, and was basically cloud catching. It was all the much better for the secret AQUATONE bird.

Kelly Johnson continued with the CL-282 working with only twenty-five engineers on the project. It had to be kept quiet at all costs. One person, Ben Rich who was an aerodynamicist for Lockheed, would one day become Kelly's right hand for years to come, was on hand for the work. After doing all the figures, Johnson told the USAF that he could deliver twenty aircraft with spares included, for approximately $22 million. The first aircraft, he promised, would be flying in eight months. That was quite a promise. Lieutenant General Donald Putt, (USAF) went to bat for Lockheed and the truly outlandish offer Johnson had made. Putt said "He (Johnson) has proven it several times already-on the F-80, F-80A, and the F-104." It didn't hurt Lockheed's chances of getting the deal for AQUATONE.

The next piece of this secret puzzle would soon be added. Richard Bissell was an MIT graduate and economist, who was working in the CIA as a Special Projects Director. He did have some aviation experience but it wasn't extensive. He was known in the CIA and college circles but not all that well. However, as the Special Projects Director for CIA, he was chosen to carry the books for AQUATONE. Kelly Johnson found out what had originally been a USAF project, was part of the CIA, who eventually took over the entire thing, much to the ire of the USAF. Eisenhower was still having his concerns about the U-2 and the AQUATONE project from the very start. He just wasn't comfortable and was truly worried about a shoot down of this fragile aircraft. His worry was basically prophetic. It would happen. To calm Eisenhower's fears at the time, General Nathan Twining tried to explain to the president how reconnaissance flights were taking place over the Soviet Union for almost ten years with no incident. That wasn't helping the Commander in Chief to quell his nerves. Eisenhower was having second thoughts about the entire program and stalled on giving it approval for days. Even adding in the clause that the pilot must be civilian. He wanted NO "military uniforms" in the cockpit. Hence, "AQUATONE" pilots now were removed from their USAF blue suits and "sheep-dipped" into a civilian pilot's status, working for the CIA.

SECRETS

The development of the U-2, better known as Project AQUATONE was totally secret. Kelly Johnson and the rest of the small team that developed the U-2 were told the minimum about the project and asked to sign the non-disclosure form. In essence, once you signed on, that was going to be a lot of months missing from your desk calendar, not to mention your home life. Johnson told those lucky few that the new aircraft he was designing would fly over the Soviet Union, higher than anything a Soviet fighter could chase and be able to get the photographs that Eisenhower and the CIA so desperately wanted. There were some on the Lockheed team that naturally thought this aircraft was a new one for the USAF. The word was out that it wasn't the USAF's bird at all, they were all working for the CIA. That shook things up in the proverbial Lockheed lunchroom. As things were discussed between the blessed few, it was found out that Lockheed was going to supply the test pilots, mechanics, all the ground crew and it was all going to happen . . . somewhere. That was something no one really knew. There were other strange things going on. There were Lockheed employees that were no longer getting their checks from the home office. It was coming from some strange account. The CIA was signing their checks and these guys were sure that was actually happening. The story going around was that this new bird was going to be a high altitude weather aircraft. Lockheed was using secret funding. Kelly was getting personal checks for over a million dollars sent directly to Johnson's home! The money then went into a new account for a new company no one ever heard of before called, C & J (for Clarence Johnson). All kinds of strange boxes, letters etc. were showing up someplace out in the San Fernando Valley, so much so that the local postmaster was so nervous, he started looking up the name in the phone book and found nothing. This was very secret stuff, and it was strange. It was also going to protect the aircraft that would make the difference in the United States security against the Soviet Union.

At the time, the Soviet Union was developing an ICBM which was a liquid fueled monster. The fact that they had already tested the "H bomb as the U.S. had done proved the Soviet Union was rapidly catching up, if not already on the doorstep of U.S. technology.

According the John Foster Dulles, who was Eisenhower's Secretary of State, the Soviet Union had more in the back room as far as the number of aircraft, tanks and soldiers available to them than the U.S. had. However, Dulles said that should the Soviet Union want to go to war, it would mean instant retaliation on the part of the U.S. Instant retaliation translated to "*MAD*" *Mutually Assured Destruction*. That heinous acronym was forcing many Americans to build fallout shelters in their basements and backyards in the late 1950s and early 1960s.

The U-2 was going to be the aircraft that would put the Soviet Union back in the U.S.'s pocket. We needed to know just what they had in those frosty areas of Siberia where no human spy could traverse. The U-2 would allow us to see what was in those frozen wastes and it couldn't hide from our cameras.

Eisenhower was briefed constantly on the U-2 project and he made sure that Allan Dulles, John's brother and head of the CIA, knew he wanted this project moving quickly. Eisenhower was always afraid of having another surprise attack like Pearl Harbor hit the U.S. He knew that the Soviet Union would be just up to doing it. Many of us remember when Premier Khrushchev banged his shoe at the United Nations and screamed "We will bury you" etc. Of course, some of the intelligence that we did have claimed that the Soviet Union was literally loaded for Bear or Bison, as the case may be. The Tushino Air Show produced twenty-eight of the Myasishchev Bisons to wow their audience which included U.S. generals. The kick to the story was that the Soviets flew those aircraft around and around making it look like there were just dozens of these aircraft. The U.S. later found out about the trick.

The first of the U-2 flights would hopefully change the assessment of what was really going on in the Soviet Union. You need to consider if the U-2 had not turned out to be a viable aircraft that she was, the United States would have been pointing all their armament at a mound of snow in Siberia and not even hit that.

The Aerial Reconnaissance Issue of the 1950s

Aerial reconnaissance in the United States in the 1950s was not what you would want to call state of the art. While we were sending RB-50s, RB-57 Canberras, RB-29's near to or over the Soviet Union, they were turned to shredded wheat by the Russian MiGs that were patrolling and looking for anything that had the USAF or NAVY on it, While these aircraft were not only searching for photo opportunities, they were also looking for ELINT or electronic intelligence, basically signals and sniffing the air for the trace of any Soviet nuclear testing that might have been going on. The aircraft, that had been converted to reconnaissance aircraft, were not swift enough to deal with the MiGs. If not for the hope of the U-2, that was critical to the Cold War, even with fighter escorts these lumbering aircraft were still getting nailed by the MiGs at every turn. Silent Warriors were going down and many of the families of those Silent Warriors never knew what became of their loved ones until many, many years later after painstaking letter writing to the services to ask for a declassification of the mission, that many never got.

The promise of the high altitude U-2 would give the U.S. what they really needed clear, precise images of the areas of the Soviet Union and in good, real time, making the efforts even more viable to United States aerial reconnaissance and the CIA.

The U-2 in air superiority gray camouflage (USAF)

The Angel with the Eagle Eyes

After hearing the doom and gloom of the WADC (Wright Air Development Council) on the CL-282 prospects, Allan Donovan of the Intelligence Systems Panel met with General Putt on Oct 19, 1954, to fight for the CL-282. Via this meeting, Putt met with fifteen scientists from the Technological Capabilities Panel[26] on November 18, 1954 to look at four proposals for reconnaissance aircraft. Major John Seaberg who was at the meeting, recalled:

"What I did was present the results of my comparative analysis of all four designs. I showed the relative high altitude performance abilities in all four aircraft. I pointed out aerodynamically the Bell, Fairchild, Martin (B-57 Canberra), and Lockheed design were close. The Martin B-

---

[26] Scientists stayed active in advisement of the government on overhead reconnaissance. Feb 1955, Technological Capabilities Panel made a final report which pushed the use of technology to gather intelligence.

57, because of being a modification was not so capable. I stated that, in my opinion, the J-73 (General Electric) would not be good enough to do the job in Johnson's airplane. And further, I overlaid a curve showing that the J-57 (Pratt and Whitney) installed, it would then be competitive with the Bell and Fairchild designs."

This meeting, along with Eisenhower's approval[27] of the CL-282 helped to get the USAF's vote. However, the USAF didn't give up on the Bell X-16 till the Lockheed bird was already airborne.

November 19, 1954, the day following Major Seaberg's assessment and briefing, the decision came in to go with the CL-282 during a USAF luncheon that was hosted by USAF Secretary John Talbot. Some of the other people at the dinner were Dulles from CIA, Trevor Gardener and General Putt from the USAF. From Kelly Johnson to Edwin Land[28], they all came in on the side of the CL-282. All of them agreed that;

"The special item of material described by Lockheed was practical and desirable and would be sought...It was agreed that the Project should be a joint Air Force/CIA one but that regardless of the source of funds, whether CIA or USAF . . ."

However, Lockheed which had initially developed the CL-282 under its own auspices and funding and spent a fortune in trying to promote it, had to literally be forced to accept the new project on the books. In the interim, they had become very busy with other commitments and really didn't have the room. It wasn't until a phone call from Trevor Gardener to Kelly Johnson on November 17, 1954 in which he asked Johnson to

---

[27] Eisenhower strongly locked the decision of the panel's findings and directed government agencies to come on board by June 1954

[28] Edwin Land served as the chairman of the CIA Scientific Advisory Board for the next 10 years and it unofficially became known as the "Land Panel". This panel gave important advice to CIA especially in the field of overhead reconnaissance.

come to Washington to talk about the deal, Johnson's orders from his board of directors was not to commit to anything! Just get the information and get back to California. In his log, Johnson wrote;

"I was impressed with the secrecy aspect and was told by Gardner that I was essentially being drafted for the project. It seemed, in fact, that if I did not talk quietly I might have to take a leave of absence from my job at Lockheed to do this special project."

When Johnson did get back to California, he used the meeting to convince the senior management at Lockheed, it was take it on, or he would have to on his own. No one at Lockheed wanted that.

By November 23rd, the IAC (Intelligence Advisory Committee) approved Allan Dulles' request to move on the CL-282 project. Dulles signed a three page memo asking President Eisenhower to approve the reconnaissance project. By that same afternoon, at a meeting of both secretaries of State and Defense along with top USAF officials, Dulles presented the document to Eisenhower and got a verbal approval to go ahead. Eisenhower then told Dulles that the project would be managed by the CIA and the USAF would give any help that would be needed to get the program operational. Actually, the USAF called the program officially *"Dulles Folly."* Thus began the long, nasty relationship that developed between the CIA and the USAF when it came to aerial reconnaissance. With this one move, Eisenhower basically took the job that the USAF felt it owned and gave it to the CIA. The USAF was now the 'bridesmaid", not the bride and it wasn't making them too pleased about the change in position. This is also how the CIA got into the world of aerial reconnaissance, because of decisions taken outside the CIA, with the USAF's aid to build the CL-282 program. Eisenhower's desire was to have an over flight project worked by a civilian agency, instead of the USAF. The decision of the scientists[29] that the Lockheed design represented the best bid plan for overheard reconnaissance aircraft was solid.

It was on to the construction phase of the project.

U-2 Construction

On November 26, 1954, Allan Dulles told Richard Bissell, his then assistant, that he wanted him to take over a very secret project. Telling Bissell only that and handing him a package of documents with a few days to absorb its content, Dulles then sent Bissell around to the Pentagon on December 2, 1954 where he would now represent the CIA for the very first of a group of organizational meetings concerning the CL-282 or now known as the U-2.

Major Design of the U-2

As was typical for the Skunk Works, design for the U-2 was a deep, dark secret that had no marking of "TOP SECRET CLASSIFIED" on any of the blueprints or paperwork. Kelly Johnson felt that this process did keep the costs down. However, there was also a very small number of engineers and draftsmen that had access to the program. A small group of engineers and workers sat back to back at desks, with no privacy or concern for personal space. Could you see that operation in today's world? There was constant brainstorming, teasing, and harassment going on. The teams Johnson put together was comprised of aerodynamics, propulsion, stability/ control and strength. By assigning engineers to one part of the project, and keeping everyone in the same room, Johnson controlled development aspects of the project by reducing the possibility of anything getting out of that room. The engineers were also about 50

---

[29] Eisenhower also increased the amount and quality of scientists advice he got. In January of 1956 he created the President's Foreign Intelligence Advisory Board in 1961.

feet from the assembly floor, which meant they were right on hand when the metal was being cut. This was a very unique way of building an aircraft. Problems could be addressed immediately, as they were seen, instead of waiting and wading through weeks of drawings and memos. Engineers would make their notes on existing drawings which allowed for keeping things moving. That is why the prototype project could be completed thirty-seven days earlier than was expected. It would take Kelly Johnson a week to get something going, which was really record breaking. Johnson had made it clear that this aircraft would only be able to pull some 2.5gs (gravity) as its limit, which would make the aircraft fragile. He was looking at maximum speed of Mach 0.8, an altitude of 70,600 ft. and a maximum altitude of 73,100 ft. The new December 1954 specifications brought the U-2 up to: takeoff-90kt, landing-76kts, and glide 244 nautical miles at 70,000 ft.

Weight was always an issue and, in this aircraft, it needed to be kept down. The Q-Bay or reconnaissance bay had a weight limit of 450 lbs. Johnson wrote in his report that the first test flight would be completed by August 2, 1955, and four aircraft would be completed by December 1, 1955. That was fairly radical and ambitious for such a new design, but Johnson was sure of himself.

One of the unusual design features of the U-2 was the tail assembly. Weight again was the issue, and the tail was attached to the body of the aircraft with three tension bolts, which was actually part of a sailplane design. The wings of the U-2 were conventional, as the wing passed spars through the fuselage to give wings strength and continuity to the design. The U-2 used separate wing panels attached to the fuselage with tension bolts, again like a sailplane. It was because of this design that Johnson was able to place the Q-Bay camera behind the pilot and ahead of the engine changing the all important center of gravity and a reduction of weight. The biggest problem of the U-2 was the wings, because they were a high aspect ratio and low drag ratio. Basically, that meant, long and narrow wings much like a sail plane or glider.

There were the also the all important fuel tanks. The fuel tanks were incorporated into the wings, making the aircraft a "wet wing". Each wing was divided into two leak proof compartments, and fuel was pumped in, with the outer six feet of the wing dry and not used for fuel storage. The U-2 also had a one-hundred-gallon tank in her nose. Later in 1957, Johnson increased the fuel capacity by adding the one hundred gallon "slipper" tank under each wing projecting slightly ahead of the wing's leading edge. In the U-2 fuel system, the aircraft needed to maintain trim as fuel was used. The aircraft had a very complex system of fuel lines and valves draining into a central sump which made it impossible to provide the pilot with an empty/full type of fuel gauge. None of the first fifty U-2s had a conventional fuel gauge. Instead there were mechanical fuel total/counters. Before a mission, a ground crew would set the counter to indicate the total amount of fuel in the wings and then a flow meter subtracted the gallons of fuel actually used during flight. The pilot kept a log of the fuel consumption shown by the counters and compared it with the estimate made by his mission planners. In an effort to recheck that, the pilots also kept track of the fuel consumption by keeping a keen eye on airspeed and their time in the air. In essence, it wasn't an easy flight it was labor intensive. Most of the pilots got used to this and those few that didn't, usually ended up running short of reaching home base during the twenty years that these U-2s were in service.

Since the tail was only bolted to the fuselage, and the wings were fragile, this made Johnson look for a way to protect the aircraft from a heavy wind gust at 35,000 ft. That could be detrimental to the survival of the aircraft. However, using the sailplane design as a start, Kelly, devised a "gust control" which could set the aileron and horizontal stabilizers in a nose up attitude negating the wind gust. Yet, this still made the U-2 fragile and difficult to fly with massive concentration on the part of the pilots flying her.

The last of the major design factors had to do with the landing gear. The landing gear consisted of tricycle, lightweight bicycle gear. It consisted of a single oleo-strut with two lightweight wheels towards the front of the aircraft. And two small solid mounted wheels under the tail. The total weight was two hundred eight lbs. Due to both sets of the wheels placed beneath the fuselage, the aircraft had detractable pogos (long curved sticks with small wheels on them) on each wing to keep the wings level during takeoff. The pilot would then drop the pogo gear off after takeoff for recovery and reuse. The aircraft landed on its front and back landing gear and then dipped over to one of the wing tips which was also equipped with landing skids.

Money, Money, Money . . .

December 3, 1954, along with a group of USAF officials, a meeting was held at the Pentagon to decide who was going to take what responsibility for the new aircraft program. Both General Putt and Trevor Garner, along with Richard Bissell didn't spend much time worrying about the USAF and CIA jobs in the project. Both were in agreement that the CIA would take care of the security for the project. The basis of the meeting was centered on the aircraft's engines, which could possibly cause security problems for the program. The Air Force was holding the Pratt and Whitney J-57 engines which was being used in many other aircraft like the B-52, F-100 and the RB-57 Canberra. Bissell wanted to know who was paying for the airframe, which Lockheed was building. Naturally everyone in the room just assumed that the CIA would be paying the bill for the aircraft. However, the CIA wasn't quite prepared to accept that honor. Bissell went home to Allen Dulles to figure it out.

Eagle Eyes

The CIA had what was then known as the *"Contingency Reserve Fund"*. They decided to use that funding to get the ball rolling. That money was something the CIA had used to pay for special covert projects, after getting the approval of the president and the budget director. Dulles told Bissell to start writing up a memo to Eisenhower explaining how to fund the new aircraft program and to begin finding people to support the new program. There was also a change in the name of the project. It was now to be known as "AQUATONE."

It took time to put the new staff together and by early 1955 the staff for project AQUATONE started to form. All funding for the new project was also kept separate the other parts of the CIA. Anyone working on this project didn't get their paycheck in the usual form. Richard Bissell now wrote the checks.

By April of 1955, Bissell had his workers set up. The operational part of the project along with the personnel were set up in different areas, Groom Lake in Nevada and Washington D.C. The USAF quota of personnel was much bigger than the CIA but the largest contingent of workers belonged to the contract employees. This included the maintenance and support workers from Lockheed which included five people per aircraft, the pilots (sheep-dipped USAF pilots) and the people that worked with the photographic set up for processing and loading film.

While all this was happening, the money situation was still being worked on. Dulles had approved money for the project but the Lockheed contract was still unsettled. The U-2 work began anyway. Between November and the 3rd of December 1954, forty-five hours a week were spent on the project, but it didn't take long for that to grow to some sixty-five hours a week. Along with that, the CIA had a Public Law passed by Congress that allowed the Director of the Central Intelligence Agency to use federal money without the need of a voucher. By mid-December

1954, Eisenhower approved Dulles' use of the money from the "Contingency Reserve Fund."

The next step was getting a contract that Lockheed was happy with. Finally, on December 22, 1954, the CIA put *Project "OARFISH"* together which gave the contract officially to Lockheed. Here is where some of those little minor details on how things got down started down the road to angst for both the CIA and the USAF. Where the CIA would give out "performance specifications," the USAF would give out "technical specification." The USAF was more of a tight, demanding package where the CIA was looser. However, Johnson of Lockheed agreed that doing it the USAF way would save money because of the tighter specifications. The original proposal from May 1954 that Lockheed gave to the USAF was for twenty airframes along with the trainer which had two seats and spares, using the General Electric J-73 engine which the USAF would supply. While working with the CIA to iron out the details, some of which consisted of the CIA only paying for the cameras, life support equipment for the aircraft both the USAF and CIA finally agreed to a fixed price contract with provisions for three quarters of the way through, to figure out if the balance sheet was working or would they go over cost. The formal contract #SP-1913 was signed on March 2, 1955 and the first U-2 was supposed to hit the flight line by July 1955, and the last to be completed by November 1956. The CIA wrote a check to Kelly Jonson and mailed it to his house on Feb 21, 1955 completing the deal. There was no review needed in three quarter term, to see if things were balancing out. Johnson was right on the mark and delivered the aircraft under budget. This was the way Kelly Johnson worked. His **"Keep it simple, Stupid"** known as the **"KISS"** policy, never failed him.

At least the USAF, CIA and the White House could not complain about the fact the whole U-2 project was completed in time and with money to spare. That was a rarity in any industry, and usually a non-occurring one in Aviation.

Chapter Eleven

Building the U-2—The Angel Who Changed Aerial Reconnaissance

"SKONK WORKS"

When Kelly Johnson brought the U-2 contract home to Lockheed, he already knew that this project must be kept secret. Kelly Johnson put it into the Lockheed Advanced Development facility at the Burbank plant, California. Known as the "Skunk works", the title actually came from an old cartoon written by Al Capp called "Li'L Abner". As we all remember, it was about a hillbilly family and all their moon shining friends. There was a character by the name of Injun Joe who created a brew called "Kickapoo Joy Juice". He had the "Kickapoo Joy Juice Factory" which consisted of a huge black cauldron, constantly boiling. Everything edible and inedible was tossed into this noxious mixture and turned into moonshine. To say the least, it was potent stuff and of course, the still was the best kept secret in the comic strip town. Back to Lockheed, in 1945 when Johnson started work on the P-80 Shooting Star for WWII, he created a very secure area where the engineers could work. He had a problem initially, because of the war effort all the buildings were in use. He needed something private, so true to Kelly Johnson's way of doing things, he rented a circus tent. In addition, Johnson made sure that he set the tent up near a vile smelling plastics factory so that NO ONE wanted to hang around there too long! One day, with the vile smelling plastics factory pumping away, a very disgusted Lockheed engineer came to work wearing a gas mask. His name was Irv Culver. Culver also went down in aviation history as being the man most fired by Kelly Johnson.

SeyMore the Skunk the official Lockheed Skunk Works Logo
(Lockheed)

It wasn't unusual, Johnson fired everyone in the circus tent at least twice a day, anyway. Culver, this particular day, answered the ringing telephone with "Skonk Works" and the name stuck like bubble gum to the sole of a shoe on a hot day in California. Of course, when Johnson got wind of the little joke, Culver was fired and just went back to work like he always did. In 1973, the greatest Black Projects house in the world added a logo to their name. "SeyMore" the Skunk became the official Lockheed Advanced Development Company's mascot.

Johnson only had a handful of engineers working on these projects and those men were told to keep it quiet. They could not speak to anyone, including spouses, about what their day's work was about. Kelly believed in keeping things very simple, no markings of TOP SECRET on documents, no hidden corners, but God help you, if you didn't put your drawings in the safe at night. Johnson had NO patience for anything shabby or poorly done and he made sure that his people understood that the first time around, because there wouldn't be a second chance.

All his engineers worked in one big room where they each looked over the other guy's shoulder. What this did do, was to build a camaraderie, and it also allowed for impromptu brain storming, sometimes saving time and effort in solving problems. It also allowed them to be close to the production floor where the metal was being cut. That was a brilliant idea because it allowed the engineers to see their ideas in three Dimensions, before it went into production, which would allow them to make any changes happen quickly without a lot of red tape and time wasting bureaucracy. During the 1950s, Johnson's new project had to work much the same way, however the circus tent was out. Kelly found some new space in the Lockheed facility. Building 82, an old bomber building facility, Well, it was going to be home, hell or high water.

The space was small. It was loaded with all types of equipment and machinery that wasn't in use at the moment. There was no air, no windows and akin to living in a shoe box. Johnson felt it was perfect. Johnson loved to tell the story of the new "SkonkWorks" home. In his biography *"More than My Share of it all"*, Johnson tells the story of; *" When the hangar doors were opened, the birds would fly up the stairwell and swoop around the drawing boards, and dive bomb the heads of the engineers, knocking themselves silly against the permanently sealed and blacked out windows, which I insisted on for security."*

Basically, this gives you an idea of the eccentric method of secrecy that protected the development of the U-2 Dragon Lady and would be the foundation for later Skunk Work projects.

The U-2 and How to Hide Her

There was still one hell of a hullaballoo going on because of the failed balloon program. Everyone was skittish about what to do with the U-2. How were they going to cover this program, whose basic output would come from over flights? This was still going on while the U-2 was already in her flight readiness tests. The brains of the program at CIA were busy trying to manufacture a story that would be believable.

The only thing that they did have going for them was the fact the new U-2 looked like an innocuous glider aircraft, not a hot jet. She carried no weapons, was light as a feather, and while she was still a curious looking aircraft, you would never consider this aircraft as a reconnaissance genius.

Richard Bissell's idea for the cover story was that the aircraft would be called a high altitude weather research aircraft, and it had to be a reasonable story so that NACA(National Advisory Council on Aeronautics) would also buy the story since the CIA was going to use them as a part of the cover.

The story had to be agreed on by all the parties involved which meant USAF Intelligence, Air Weather Service, the Third Air Force, the 7th Air Division, the SAC U-2 project office, USAF headquarters project office and NACA 's top official Dr. Hugh Dryden. This also included the CIA's Scientific Advisory Committee.

By March 1956, it was agreed on that the final cover plan created by Bissell and shoot down (which was prophetic) over enemy territory. Bissell never left a stone unturned. His staff produced a series of documents for the press and politicians including an operations suspension story, including overall weather research cover.

By June 21, 1956, General Goodpaster, one of Eisenhower's most trusted aides, James Killian and Edwin Land did look at the cover story and weren't too pleased with it. Meanwhile, the U-2 took to the air on its first reconnaissance mission over Eastern Europe. The entire group looked over the story and discussed the upcoming Soviet mission which included the emergency plans. Both Killian and Land didn't agree with Bissell's plan. They were looking for something more comprehensive. These three gentlemen felt that should the U.S. lose a U-2 to enemy fire or otherwise, the U.S. should not deny responsibility but say that the flight was supposed to "guard against surprise attacks". The idea was basically filed under "unwanted" and never saw the light of day again. The weather aircraft concept stayed in place. More plans were written which included pilot capture. That of course, was not supposed to happen as all pilots flew with the "L" pill that would assure no enemy agent could ever interrogate them. However, the pilots were not forced by the CIA to do this, but it was more or less expected of them as a code of honor. However, this entire scenario was actually visionary since by May 1, 1960, it would be a reality.

RAINBOW

In the development of the U-2 a program was created to see if it were possible to reduce the RCS or radar cross section of the U-2 to make her less detectable to enemy radar. This was called project RAINBOW. RAINBOW consisted of a series of wires attached to the leading and trailing edges of the U-2's wings. A pole made out of fiberglass was used to hold the wire to the wings fore and aft. The layout of the wires consisted of trapezoid ferrite beads which were used to manufacture the different frequencies necessary for low reflection. The program was a total failure actually costing one U-2 and pilot. On April 2, 1957 during a test flight from Groom lake in Nevada, a RAINBOW test flight crashed killing the pilot. The RAINBOW program was a failure and the anti-radar mods really didn't pan out the way Lockheed thought they would. The program was shut down in 1958.

As of January 1956, Project AQUATONE was revving up to ship out. All during its flight test phase, the U-2 was almost perfect in every regard. The aircraft range of 2950 miles was enough to do the job and get the U-2 over the Soviet Union and anyplace else that CIA wanted to send her. Flying at 72,000 ft. made her totally out of the reach of any aircraft or missile out there at the time. The U-2 camera was the finest ever made for a mission like this and added to the U-2 assets.

The delivery (in sections) of the U-2 to Groom Lake better known as the "ranch" (Lockheed/USAF)

The First Weather Reconnaissance Squadron Provisional (WRSP-1) the word "provisional" handing the U-2 more security, since provisional Air Force units never had to report to a higher authority. (WRSP-1) in CIA language meant *Detachment A*. This unit started to move out as of April 29, 1956, and by May 4, 1956 the entire detachment, with aircraft, arrived at their Nevada home called Groom Lake, also known as the "Ranch." Johnson gave the name "Ranch" to the Groom Lake facility, to entice the Lockheed employees to sign on for the program he couldn't tell them much about. Not too long after that, on May 7, 1956, NACA sent out a memo on the U-2 cover story which basically said that a new Lockheed aircraft was flying with the USAF Air Weather Service that would be tasked with studying high altitude occurrences like the clouds, jet stream temperature, and winds at jet stream levels including the effect of UV rays up to 55,000 ft in altitude. It was a solid story.

Things internationally were still very touchy about any type of over flight. To get around more problems and to protect England from getting in an uproar with other countries for supporting the U.S., the CIA decided to move operations to Wiesbaden, Germany on June 11, 1956. However, the CIA did not inform the German authorities about the move. Colonel Fred McCoy, who was the Detachment Commander, was "disappointed" that this move to Germany could be done without a lot of attention. However, the uniqueness of the U-2 design and the move to Wiesbaden, was temporary measure. The Air Force started renovating an airfield close to East Germany that was used in World War II and also was a launch site for the GENETRIX balloons.

Dragon Lady

As with all aircraft, weight was the problem that all designers dealt with. Kelly Johnson was no different. Johnson already knew in his own mind that the U-2 was going to be a delicate creature. She would have to stay aloft for at least nine hours per mission, fly some 6,000 miles in range and stay at 70,000 ft altitude. She looked almost like a glider but was in no way considered one. Those beautifully delicate wings, 80 ft. in length would carry 1350 gallons of fuel split between four tanks. The main issue with the weight of the aircraft could be simply worked out to one pound of fuel equaled one foot of altitude. If the U-2 was going to survive, she would need every foot of altitude she could manage.

The U-2 was constructed with weight as the main concern for sure, hence, she needed to remain light, almost ultra-light, so thin aluminum was used and fragile she was. The 50 ft. fuselage was susceptible to any minor ding or hit by a foreign object. Even Lockheed was worried that maybe she was too delicate, but the U-2 would stand up. She wasn't quite as fragile as she looked. The main landing gear was a two-wheel bicycle arrangement with a nose wheel and a second wheel which was carried within the belly of the aircraft. The entire bogey weighed only 200 lbs. It was the first time this was used in any kind of powered aircraft. The tail of the U-2 was very thin. Consider that the tail was literally bolted to the fuselage by three 5/8 of an inch bolts. That really would scare the best of pilots in a heavy crosswind.

As for the equipment, the Q bays carried the eyes of the U-2. Two high resolution cameras were installed. The first carried a long focal length. The camera systems were huge and weighed in at several hundred pounds. The one camera used most frequently was the panoramic camera, which carried a 36-inch focal length lens. This camera would go from one horizon to the next, taking its photos at several different locations. The Trimetragon "A" and "B" cameras carried almost 12,000 ft. of film. After the mission, the film waslater in the month then flown to the United States where it was processed in a couple of days and sent to the photo interpreters at Omaha, Nebraska's facility for SAC, then on to CIA's photo interpretation center for further analysis.

Loading the camera pallet onto the U-2 (Lockheed)

Francis Gary Powers and the U-2 in Jeopardy

The mission was initially called Operation TOUCHDOWN and brought back some really great photos of the Soviet heartland. While this mission flew, another mission was flying what was known as a "ghost" mission. The U-2 flew a diversionary mission over the Soviet-Iran border. On September 12, 1959, the USSR launched the LUNA 2 rocket that impacted the lunar surface west of Mare Serenitatis on the Moon's surface.

Premier Nikita Khrushchev crowed like a rooster over the success. When he arrived in the United States, three days later on a tour, he also made sure that he let President Eisenhower know all about the lunar success. Eisenhower, after the Khrushchev visit was over, could not have been pleased over the Soviet's success. After Khrushchev left the U.S., he went home to push his rocket program, beaming at the success every chance that he got. Khrushchev didn't stop, except now he was crowing about the hydrogen /nuclear warheads he was working on for those rockets.

Eisenhower was not moved by the Soviet success and wanted to keep the over flights down to a minimum. He refused to send any more over flights to the Soviet Union. In 1958 and 59, the intelligence department was literally a barren wasteland when it came to finding out anything about Soviet missile intelligence. By January of 1960, The Senate hearing brought the word to Congress about Soviet successes. Testimonies from various CIA officials, USAF officers and more brought the word on the SS-6 ICBM that the Russians were flying. Director of Central Intelligence, Allen Dulles showed photos to Congress on how these missiles could be moved via railroad track to any launch site the Soviets wanted.

On February 2, 1960 General James Doolittle stepped up to the plate and urged Eisenhower to overfly the Soviet Union. Eisenhower's answer was almost like a premonition. Eisenhower said; *"If one of these aircraft were lost where we engaged in apparently sincere deliberation it could be put on display in Moscow, and ruin the President's effectiveness."*

Eventually, what really worked on Eisenhower was finding out the word on a new Soviet bomber called BACKFIN that appeared out of Kazan. Yet, the fight to fly again still went on. All the agencies involved were fighting with each other on what was the true story. Was there a bomber? Was there is missile? No one knew for sure.

Later in the month of February, Eisenhower approved four additional U-2 flights. One mission to be flown in March 1960, had the main objective of getting missile information. Allowing the new flight, Eisenhower wanted it done from our airfield. Eisenhower agreed to extend the deadline until April 10, 1960. The U-2 took off one day before deadline with a "B" camera and was the last successful flight over the Soviet

Union. Operation SQUARE DEAL was the second U-2 to fly a diversionary path over the Soviet/Iran border for which the U-2 got shots of two new Soviet radars "HEN HOUSE and HEN ROOST" installations. In his memoirs, Khrushchev[30] said U-2 should have been shot down, but the anti-aircraft batteries were caught napping and didn't open fire soon enough. Khrushchev also said that Soviet missile designers had a high altitude, anti-aircraft missile and batteries of that missile were deployed near known targets that the U-2 would have gone for.

The CIA already knew that the Soviets had improved their air defenses system and early in 1960, the Development Project Division had asked the USAF experts at the Air Technical Intelligence Center (ATIC) for an assessment of the Soviet capabilities against the U-2.

On March 14, 1960, Colonel William Burke, acting chief of the DPD (Development Project Division) released the ATC assessments to Richard Bissell of CIA; *"The greatest threat to the U-2 is the Soviet SAM. Although the ATIC analysis concedes that the SAM may be less effective than estimated.*

Their present evaluation is that SAM(Guideline) has a high probability of successful interception at 70,000 ft. providing that detection is made in sufficient time to alert the site."

OPERATION GRAND SLAM— The last flight of the U-2 over Soviet Union. Prior to the April 9th flight, Eisenhower agreed on a March 28th date for an additional over-flight during the month of April. Eisenhower' agreeing to another over-flight felt even better when the Soviet Union didn't protest the April 9th flight, practically wanting the United States to overfly them. The two flights approved would cover a few targets. The

---

[30] Nikita Khrushchev—Khrushchev Remembers—The Last Testament; Little/Brown; Boston, 1974 pgs 444-445

program was called Operation TIMESTEP and the concept was for the U-2 to leave Thule, Greenland, and then overfly Novaya Zemlya and the Ural Mountains.

The other flight GRAND SLAM was the first U-2 mission planned to cross over across the Soviet Union from South to the North. Richard Bissell informed the White House that neither mission could be flown before April 19th. Once the bad weather cleared over the Soviet Union, the flights could happen but the weather was playing hell with the schedule. Bissell asked Eisenhower for a little more time. On April 25th, General Andrew Goodpaster, Eisenhower's aide, let him know about the problem and the fact Bissell wanted more time. Eisenhower responded with; *"One additional operation may be undertaken provided it is carried out prior to May 1. No operation is to be carried out AFTER May 1."*

The president didn't want to fly missions any later than that date because of the upcoming Paris Summit with the Soviets which was scheduled for May 16, 1960. The CIA was already working on GRAND SLAM. The most likely route for the mission, offered the best chance of photographing suspected locations of the Soviet IBM sites. The other flight TIMESTEP, which would fly out of Greenland, was more likely to hit bad weather (affecting photography). A letter dated March 14, 1960, sent to Richard Bissell, said that TIMESTEP was the last choice because it was assumed that 90% probability of being right, and the flight being detected on entry and tracked the four hours in denied territory, would aggravate Soviet PVO (Soviet Air Defense). The flight would allow the SAM sites and prepositioning of missile equipped fighters in the Murmansk area (this would be the U-2 exit) and allowing for a successful intercept. The Soviets would be unable to go after the U-2 and would also allow the Soviets to put in a diplomatic protest.

The issues with TIMESTEP should have been applied to GRAND SLAM as well, but they clearly weren't. If the Soviets could track the U-

2 so early in the flight, there would be more than enough time to mount a defensive flight to intercept the U-2. GRAND SLAM's chosen pilot was Francis Gary Powers was the most experienced pilot in the program. With twenty-seven missions under his belt, including the Soviet Union and China, six Soviet border flights, he was more than well equipped to answer the call.

The U-2 aircraft were kept undercover and ferried to her takeoff point in Peshawar, Pakistan. Once she was refueled and the camera set in place, the U-2 would leave at Daybreak, without the local residents paying one bit of attention to the six hours on the ground the U-2 had spent there. The flight was scheduled for April 28th however, GRAND SLAM was canceled due to bad weather conditions over the Soviet Union.

When this flight was canceled, the U-2 went back to Adana, Turkey before the sun rose for another hot day. That night, the U-2 took a chance at the planned mission, hoping to pull it off on April 29th, but again, the weather was not cooperating and pushed the cancellation of the mission yet again. The U-2 returned to Adana, Turkey with weather still being a main issue. The mission was pushed to April 30th. The U-2 once again, was taken under cover to its launch site. However, all the flight time for the 27th and 28th of April actually pushed her into periodic maintenance. Another U-2 was brought in on April 30th which was Saturday night. The new U-2, Article #360 had a crash landing that previous September and was returned to Lockheed to be rebuilt, including putting the new J-75 Pratt and Whitney engine in which would allow for higher altitude. It seems that many of the U-2 pilots didn't have a lot of faith in #360, they felt she was a "hangar queen", basically not reliable. Francis Gary Powers said in his memoir "Operation Over flight"[31]; *"Its current idio-*

---

[31] Operation Overflight - Potomac Books, Francis Gary Powers with Curt Gentry Dec 31, 2003

syncrasy was one of the fuel tanks which wouldn't feed all its fuel" Carrying the "B" camera and ECM package, she was ready for flight, again. However, Powers wasn't enamored of using the aircraft, obviously. Operation GRAND SLAM #4154, was the twenty fourth deep penetration over flight into the Soviet Union. The mission already had a cloud over it as it started some thirty minutes behind schedule on May 1, 1960. The reason was political not mechanical. As usual, Washington D.C. couldn't make up its mind and was slow in sending the approval for the take off, delaying the flight's critical take off time. The fact that communications were a problem during sunrise and sunset was a factor which was a given. The ionosphere could not support good communications at those times. Since the pre-arranged times and frequencies were not working, an operation started sending a message when it was clear, using one of the ground frequencies in the transition area between the daytime and nighttime frequencies. Radio operators were hearing Morse code as they turned from one frequency to another. One operator used the ground frequency where the transmission was the strongest. The operator could then make out the letters of the code. The Detachment Chief, Colonel William Shelton, who was nervous and waiting for the yes or no answer to finally get the mission off the ground, ran out of the radio room and across the flight line. He told Powers it was a "GO" as Powers sat in his U-2C at the end of the runway, all this time…waiting. His flight would take him from Pakistan to his landing site in Norway and deeper into USSR territory than ever before. Powers started his roll down the runway, releasing his brakes at 015:92Z time on May 1, 1960. After getting airborne, Powers brought the U-2C# 360 into the path for Afghanistan. Since this was standard operating procedure, Powers put his radio on when he reached 66,000 ft, which told those waiting below in Operations that all was well and he was on his way.

After this signal, Powers, like all the U-2 pilots maintained strict radio silence. The first leg of the mission put Powers and the U-2C over Tyuratam Missile test range. Next on the list was Chelyabinsk, just south of Sverdlovsk, which would then take him to Kirov. The route then went north over Yur'ya and Plesetsk, Severodvinsk, and northwest to Kandalaksha. He then traveled north to Murmansk and on to his target. Power's flight started to be tracked by the Soviets when Powers was still fifteen miles south of the Soviet –Afghanistan border and continued to follow him across Central Asia. Powers got to Tashkent and thirteen Soviet interceptor aircraft scrambled in a failed attempt to reach the U-2 high above them. Powers got to Sverdlovsk some four and a half hours into the nine hours flight. It was then that the SA-2 missile rose from its launch site to chase the U-2. The SA-2 did not hit the fragile U-2, but did detonate behind her, causing damage to the aircraft at 70,500 ft. altitude. The aircraft started a downward spiral while Powers tried to find a way out. He couldn't eject due to the centrifugal force that was pulling on the aircraft, which threw Powers up against the closed canopy. Powers released the canopy cover and started to bail out, with the plan to arm the destruct device in the last minutes before he jumped, waiting so it wouldn't go off prematurely while he was still in the aircraft. After releasing his seatbelt, he was literally sucked out of the aircraft, and found himself being held by his oxygen hose which prevented him from hitting the destruct device. The hose finally ripped away and Powers pulled away from the U-2. He fell a few thousand feet when his parachute opened automatically and he landed in a Soviet farm field, surrounded by many very perplexed and eager Soviet citizens, thinking he was one of their pilots. They quickly bundled him into a truck and hauled him off to the local Soviet officials[32]. Since he couldn't hit the destruct button, the aircraft did not destroy itself in the crash and that pleased the Soviets no end, because so many parts were identifiable. The Soviets gladly picked up the many pieces of the aircraft and prepared a lovely display for Soviet T.V. some days later to show the world how the U.S. was abusing the Soviet Union with their spy planes. If Powers could have thrown the switch, it would have only destroyed the camera.

There was lots of speculation around if Powers was flying too low via a mechanical error. Powers swore he was at the assigned altitude and was brought down by the SA-2 going off behind him. In March of 1963, the U.S. Air Force attaché investigating the *"Moscow Feb 13, 1962 Board of Inquiry on Conduct of FG Powers,"* found that Sverdlovsk SA-2 Missile battery had fired a three missile salvo that not only took Powers out, but also made a direct hit on a Soviet fighter sent to intercept Powers[33]. The Soviets could not have been too pleased about that. It was later found out that the SAM site was not located by flights prior to GRAND SLAM.

---

[32] Operation Overflight-Powers/Gentry Pgs. 82-84: Beschloss; Mayday! Pgs. 26-28. Transcript of debriefing–FG Powers
[33] Oct 4, 1963 Cunningham interview (TS Codeword) OSA History Chapter 14 pg. 55

Soviet Premier Khrushchev
viewing the remains of the U-2 downed over Sverdlovsk
(CIA Public Domain)

Chapter Twelve

Eisenhower's Nightmare or How to be Embarrassed Before a Major Paris Summit with the Soviet Union

The first idea that something was wrong with the Powers mission was that he was overdue at his next check-in. The CIA Operations Center on May 1, 1960 at 3:30 hours Washington time, realized the Soviets had stopped tracking the Power's flight some two hours earlier and south west of Sverdlovsk. There was nothing from the Soviet Union on the shoot down, and CIA personnel tried to discuss what to do next. They did come up with a new program to figure out what to do with the U-2. Richard Bissell and the rest of the CIA didn't know if Powers was dead or alive or captured, if the plane and camera were intact or destroyed, but they believed no one could survive a explosion from 70,500 ft.

They decided to stay with the weather reconnaissance flight story, staged by NASA (then NACA, which was renamed when NASA was created in 1958). Eisenhower approved the cover story years before in 1956. Later in the day, a story was approved to fill the available information on Powers flight and to show Adana, Turkey as the aircraft's base of operations in order to cover Pakistan's part of the mission. The "new" story along with a new flight plan was sent to the mission commander to replace the original cover story that was sent out in advance of the Mission to back it up.

NASA, sent out a statement May 3rd, that a high altitude weather reconnaissance plane had gone missing on a flight from Turkey. It was supposed to be an explanation for the U-2 parts that were spread out all over Sverdlovsk. They also noted that the "pilot reported over the emergency frequency that he was "experiencing oxygen difficulties." So, should the Soviets protest (and they would), NASA could claim the pilot lost consciousness and the aircraft untended, crossed over to the Soviet border before crashing. This would be a perfect excuse, if the film and camera were not intact. But, sadly, that wasn't what happened. The small explosive package that was supposed to destroy the camera and film wasn't enough to do the job. With the film spooled so tight, it would give away all the secrets on it even if the pilot, and the aircraft didn't make it. Even Kelly Johnson proved the film would survive in an experiment showing a totally burned out aircraft with the camera film still viable.

There was another issue that was really not thought about. The fact the MAYDAY was a huge political holiday in the USSR. It was loaded with parades of the military, political leaders and all the rest. Apparently, no one on the United States side of the fence took the day too seriously, or really thought about the implications. There wasn't much air traffic in the Soviet Union that day since all were partying, literally. However, there were military on duty and the radar operators, who were having an easy day, were just ripe to pick up a slow moving, high altitude, aircraft like the U-2. With a total of four years of successful missions flown, Richard Bissell and the CIA were most definitely overconfident and not ready to face a "worst case scenario." This gave Khrushchev and the USSR a step up in the Cold War game. Khrushchev knew how to use the CIA's story of the weather reconnaissance aircraft and throw it right back at Eisenhower by not telling the White House and CIA that they pilot was alive. The Soviet Union waited till May 5, 1960 to announce at a meeting of the "Supreme Soviet", sort of the U.S. Congress body of government, that a U.S. spylane was "brought down newer Sverdlovsk." There was no mention of Powers at all. Of course, Khrushchev just played this up as both the State department and NASA put out another statement that continued the "weather plan" cover story that the pilot was lost during routine mission near the Caucasus Mountains. It was right after this disclosure that the U.S. Ambassador to Moscow called a report in to the State department indicating that the pilot might still be alive and in Soviet hands.

On May 7, 1960, two days after Khrushchev confirmed this report by revealing to the entire world that the U-2 pilot from the crash was in fact, alive and did admit he was spying on the Soviet Union flying a U. S. spy plane. This little disclosure blew the United States cover story right out the proverbial window. Allan Dulles, the CIA Director, offered to take the heat for it and to resign, but Eisenhower didn't want to show that he wasn't in control of his administration, so he refused Dulles' offer. By May 11, 1960, Eisenhower was choking on the press release he read to the nation that he was fully responsible for the U-2 Mission. But, he left open the question of future over flights. This was regardless that four days prior he had approved the recommendation of his foreign relations policy advisors to end all provocative intelligence operations against the Soviet Union.

The U-2 disaster brought up the greatest of problems when the long-awaited Paris Summit meeting on May 16th convened. Khrushchev was to be the first speaker and made sure he took up enough time in an elongated protest about the U-2 over flight over his nation and demanded an apology from Eisenhower at the end of the diatribe. In Eisenhower's reply, he stated the over flights were stopped and would not be resumed, but still was adamant about the apology to the Soviet Union. The Summit ended abruptly and Eisenhower canceled his trip to the Soviet Union.

The U-2s Come Home

With the loss of the U-2, the "B" Detachment of U-2s in Turkey was closed down. Once the Development Projects Division heard that Powers was still alive, but in a Soviet Prison, they abandoned their secret base to protect their involvement in Turkey. The Project officials had hoped to continue flights from Adana, but Eisenhower's order which ended the USSR over flights made this virtually impossible.

Four weeks later, a coup ousted the Turkish Premier, Adnan Menderes on May 27, 1960 and since the new government had no idea of the U-2s presence, it would not allow any flights from Adana, including any maintenance flights to keep the U-2s in shape and air worthy. Because of this problem, no more U-2s left Adana. Instead of being ferried home, three of the four aircraft that were left were disassembled and packed for a C-124 cargo aircraft and flown home to the United States and Groom Lake, the Nevada desert home of the U-2s. The fourth aircraft remained inside a hangar at Incirlik airbase for many years. The lone U-2 was looked after by a skeleton crew with the hope that just on the off chance, the Turkish government would relent and allow the U-2 to fly from Adana.[34]

With Detachment "B" came forty-four months of active service, twenty-one pilots that had flown the U-2 with great success. There were three pilots that were transferred to the defunct Detachment "A", fourteen Detachment "B" pilots were reassigned to other U-2 Detachments.

With the loss of the U-2, the Paris Summit was a total debacle. The end of the U-2 in Turkey was the start of many more setbacks for the U-2 program. By July 8, 1960, the Japanese government was also facing the anti-U.S. sentiment regarding the presence of the "spy planes" on Japan's homeland. The United States was asked to remove the U-2s from the Japanese mainland. The very next day the "Detachment "C" U-2s were disassembled and packed onto a C-124 for a ride home to the United States. The U-2 program was really being kicked to the curb by the countries that agreed to have them clandestinely on their homeland. By

---

[34] OSA history Chapter 12 pg. 46-47

July 1, 1960, in the middle of the Japanese turmoil and six weeks after the botched Paris Summit, a Soviet aircraft shot down an RB-47[35] spy plane that was on an "ELINT" (electronic intelligence) mission over international waters near the Kola Peninsula of the Soviet Union. The two airmen that were rescued were caught by the Soviets. The USSR claimed that the aircraft had violated Soviet airspace, while the United States denounced the Soviet Union for the shoot down over international waters. The atmosphere of the Cold War was quickly heating up.

The hits just kept coming for the U-2 program in the summer of 1960. NASA was deeply concerned about the damage that was done to its reputation with the association in the U-2 affairs. The agency was trying to hold onto its international cooperation for the space program and decided to opt out of the "support cover story" that the U-2s used for flying weather reconnaissance under NASA's name. With the Mercury and Gemini programs in full swing, NASA did not want to lose that goodwill. At a meeting of high level CIA and NASA officials, including the State department on May 31, 1960, NASA said that they were willing to continue its association with the U-2 fights for the time being, but the new administrator for NASA, T. Keith Glennan believed that his agency "would be well advised to disengage from the U-2 program as rapidly as possible."[36]

All of this resulted in a shutdown of the U-2 operations overseas for more than six months. Pilots and aircraft from both Detachment and B and C were consolidated into "Detachment G" which incorporated the

---

[35] Mystery of the RB-47 Newsweek July 25, 1960; pg. 36-37; Nikita and the RB-47 Time-July 25, 1960 pgs. 30-31
[36] James Cunningham Memo for record "Telephone Conn. Dr. Hugh Dryden Deputy Director NASA, June 1, 1960.

eight pilots from "B" and "C" brought three pilots in. Because of Powers being held by the Soviets and Project "CHALICE" had been so compromised, the CIA assigned a new name to the U-2 project. It was now called "IDEALIST."

How Powers Survived Soviet Russia and the Effect on the Reconnaissance world of the U.S.

Francis Gary Powers went through an extensive interrogation by the Soviets. Extensive is mild. One can only imagine how he was treated by the KGB. Powers had instructions from the CIA on what to do in the event of a capture and that was not well advanced. The CIA really expected their pilots to do the honorable thing, and use the needle in the coin they carried which was loaded with a quick acting poison. While the CIA never explicitly said that to their pilots, it was "understood" though never expressed. It really made no difference what Powers told the Soviets because since they had the aircraft, camera and film, they had all they needed to know. However, Powers did try to conceal as much classified information as possible while giving the appearance of cooperating with the KGB.

To get the most out of the propaganda, the Soviets made sure that there was a "showboat" of Soviet justice. The Soviets produced the most grandiose trial that they could come up with for Powers which began on August 17, 1960. Powers did try to conceal as much as he could in the information department from the Soviet Defense Council. He apologized for his over flight into Soviet territory. It didn't help because the Soviets judged and sentenced him to ten years "deprivation of liberty" with the first three to be spent in prison. One can only imagine what that meant. It was not the well planned, easy life of Guantanamo bay which the ISIS/Al-Qaeda prisoners "suffer through", with as much Oreo cookies and T.V. sitcoms that they can take. No, Soviet prison was a level of hell in the finest form. During the next eighteen months there were high level, confidential negations that went on between the Soviet Union and with the Rudolph Abel spy trial completed in the U.S., his sentencing was the next phase. Donovan[37] was the one who placed the suggestion to the judge in the case, not to give him the death penalty, explaining with insight that you would never know if you needed to "trade" someone. He reminded the judge that a Cold War was on and that just as we got Abel, the Soviets could get one of our people. Who would we use as a bargaining chip, if you killed Abel?

The judge obviously thought about it and gave Abel 30 years in prison. The rest was history as Rudolph Abel did become that chip to bargain out both Powers, in the Soviet Union and Fredric Pryor, the U.S. student caught in East Germany. By November of 1961, the acting director of the CIA, Pearre Cabell put a memo out to Secretary of State Dean Rusk, which supported a trade of the two prisoners that would take place on February 10, 1961 on the Glienecke Bridge connecting East and West Berlin. This exchange was portrayed in the 2015 movie *"Bridge of Spies*[TM38] with good accuracy. As part of the exchange of Abel for Powers, the United States also got back U.S. graduate student Fredric Pryor, who was picked up in East Germany for espionage(of which he was totally innocent) and released in another location, "Checkpoint Charlie" that separated East and West Germany. After Powers returned to the United States, he went through the most callous, severe debriefing that the CIA could come up with. The CIA had their damage assessment

---

[37] Donovan was a U. S. Naval officer in the office of Science research and development in WWII working in the old OSS, precursor of the CIA. He went on to become general counsel for the OSS. When he retired from the OSS, he moved to an insurance law firm in Brooklyn New York, where he was chosen by the CIA to help Rudolph Abel.
[38] Bridge of Spies-DreamWorks, 20th Century Fox. 2015

team, which spent two months of the summer of 1960 to figure out just how much Powers really knew about the program and how much he could have told interrogators. Given that Powers had a long association with the U-2 program, the team figured out that his amount of knowledge was extensive and that he most likely told the Soviets all of it. After the two weeks of hell debriefing by the CIA in February of 1962, this same team found that "damage" was much less than initially had been estimated and they were satisfied with Powers behavior under their scrutiny[39]. Allan Dulles read the report and expressed support of Powers and told him "We are proud of what you have done". Dulles had already resigned his office as Director in November of 1961, for all that was worth. The new Director of the CIA, John McCone, wasn't so generous with his sentiments. He demanded a closer look at what Powers had done and set up yet another board of inquiry to be headed by retired federal Judge E. Barret Prettyman. After a total of eight days of hearings and deliberations, the panel and Judge agreed that Powers acted in accordance with his instructions and "complied" with his obligations as an American citizen during this period." The Board did recommend that Powers receive his back pay. Judge Prettyman's Board was based on a superior body of evidence which showed Powers was telling the truth about the events of May 1, 1960. The testimony of the experts who debriefed Powers after his return to the United States was a completely thorough investigation of Powers. With this, they based the doctors, psychiatrists and former Commander at Adana, along with Powers own testimony under a polygraph test, for which he volunteered. Kelly Johnson of Lockheed, who built the U-2, examined the wreckage of the U-2 aircraft and concurred with Powers version of what happened. The new director

---

[39] The Unmasking of a Hero 1960-65 Francis Gary Powers (CIA History draft-Staff 1974-pg. 19)

of the CIA was not satisfied and still basically skeptical of the whole story. John McCone asked the USAF to convene its own panel of experts to check Powers story out. Kelly Johnson's assessment of the aircraft seemed not to be enough. The USAF asked again and once again, Kelly Johnson told them the same evaluation he had from before. The USAF concurred with it. McCone was still hesitant and went to one piece of evidence that contradicted Powers. This was a report by National Security Agency (NSA) that suggested Powers may have possibly gone to a lower altitude and turned back in a broad curve towards Sverdlovsk before being shot downed. McCone turned right around himself and ordered Judge Prettyman's Board to reconvene on March 1st, for yet another look at all of Powers evidence. However, the Board was not convened by the National Security Agency and the evidence was not reviewed. The Board stayed with its original findings. Even though all of this found Powers acted properly, the CIA did not release many of the favorable things about Powers trials and tribulations to the general public, which had gotten a rather dim and negative story of what Powers actually went through and what happened. The press, based on this effort by the CIA and McCone had a negative image of Powers and it was sensationalized for the general public, along with some public/political figures who spoke about it and hadn't a clue of what they were talking about. Powers didn't stand a chance as there was nothing like a tweet back in the 60's. The press was powerful and was not questioned.

The Senate Foreign Relations Committee member, Senator John J. Williams was very concerned about how this "silence" on Power's actions would impact Powers. The senator questioned McCone on March 6, 1962: *"Don't you think he is being left with just a little bit of a cloud hanging over him? If he did everything he is supposed to do, why leave it hanging?*[40]*"* It was an excellent question considering the fact that it was obvious McCone most definitely had a problem with Powers and his story. There were many in the public sector that really saw Powers as questionable because he received no recognition in public for his efforts to hold information back from the Soviets. It was confirmed by his son, Francis Gary Powers Jr., his dad was ostracized by President Kennedy, who just one year prior so warmly greeted and received two RB-47 USAF airmen, who were shot down by the Soviets and released by them. That was unconscionable! McCone never reversed the very low opinion he had of Powers. Francis Gary Powers Jr., also confirmed that his father did not receive the Intelligence Star that was awarded to all U-2 pilots, except Powers, back in April 1963. Powers did not receive his till McCone left office on April 25, 1965. Powers then received his Intelligence Star from the CIA, which was dated April 1963 (shown in a photo in his son's possession) from the deputy Director of the CIA Marshall S. Carter.[41] This was despicable treatment for a man who was a USAF pilot, flew for his country for many years and served this nation. Powers started out as a F-84 Thunderjet pilot for the 468th Strategic Fighter Squadron based at Turner Air Force Base in Georgia. Powers left the Air Force in 1956, and signed on for the U-2 program as a civilian pilot. The CIA's treatment was low, vicious and unnecessary. The treatment of Powers by the president of the United States, JFK was plainly cruel. Powers followed the rule book, the USAF and CIA rule book. He did nothing wrong. What happened was part of a very dangerous job and he should

---

[40] 11 US Congress Senate Foreign Relations Committee (Vol 12 86th Congress 2nd session) Report on the U-2 incident" March 6, 1962 pg. 265 (Declassified Historical Series)
[41] OSA History Chapter 14, pg. 54 (TS Codeword) Beschloss MAYDAY, pg. 37

have been recognized for his valor under fire. He did not deserve to be treated like a pariah. After the shoot down, Powers and life in the civilian world was not much better.

A point needs to be made here regarding the type of work these" sheep dipped pilots" and other "Ferret" crews did in the name of intelligence/reconnaissance. This was not by any standard an easy job. Falling into the hands of the enemy while on a spy mission came with the job. It was a known factor albeit, they all tried to avoid it. As we look further into what happened to Francis Gary Powers, it is necessary to look hard at the spy business and what was expected of these "Cold War Silent Warriors". They flew in silence, worked in silence, kept the work they did from their families and anyone else they knew. They suffered in silence when shot down either being caught by the enemy or dying from the crash of their aircraft. No one really can say, with the exception of the men and women who survived the Cold War, what these feelings were like, going out every day to do a job and possibly not coming back. The notice their families would get was they were either killed in action or missing in action, with no other explanation. It would be literal years before family members found out, if they ever did find out. Many never did, as they waited for the declassification of the mission that just never came. We are looking at Powers situation closely so that the reader can understand and hopefully, get a feeling of what happened to these men and women in the Cold War. As for Powers, his homecoming was not what he expected. His return was already decided the prior year. Colonel Leo Geary (USAF Project officer), the USAF, and the rest of the State/CIA bureaucracy were desperately worried. Even with a "black mark" against Powers, the USAF agreed on April 4, 1962 to reinstate Powers and that would be in force on July 1, 1962. This reinstatement was also approved by the CIA, State Department and the White House. Sadly though, Powers had family issues. His wife was divorcing him, which again put the USAF into a tizzy, worrying about the bad publicity and what would come out in the divorce proceedings. The USAF did what it does best, it covers its political butt. The reinstatement for Powers was withheld until the divorce proceeding were completed. The humanity displayed by the USAF and the government in general towards Powers was pathetic and schizophrenic. Knowing schizophrenic is a strong word in relation to the discussion, it is still hard to comprehend how the president of the United States could greet and embrace two RB-47 pilots and yet shun Powers. Yes, its politics, but humanity should have played a part here.

Kelly Johnson at Lockheed showed more humanity to Powers than the entire U.S. government. He gave Powers a job flying the U-2 in test for Lockheed. In March of 1963, Powers did meet up with Colonel Leo Geary to talk about his future and Powers decided to stay with Lockheed and the commercial world. The generosity of Johnson could only go so far, sadly. According to Kelly Johnson's "U-2 log" dated September 25, 1969 he says[42]; *"We have no flight test activity at all. I must let Gary Powers go. Have protected him for about seven years, but he doesn't have an ATC (air transport rating) so we have no other jobs for him, even flying the Beechcraft jet[43]."*

Powers left Lockheed in September of 1969. He finally did get to publish his side of the story in a book called *"Operation Overflight"* with a co-author Curt Gentry. Powers came down from the lofty heights of flying the U-2 to flying a light plane as a traffic reporter for a Los Angeles TV station. On August 1, 1977, Powers died in a helicopter accident

---

[42] OSA History, chapter 14, Pg. 52(TS Codeword)
[43] Beechcraft jet was the house jet that Lockheed officials used to travel around the country on business

along with his cameraman, when it crashed on the way to a TV assignment. It was a very sad ending to a career that should have been treated with more respect.

Reconnaissance Changes after the U-2 Incident—the COLD WAR Moves On

There were many changes after the U-2 incident of May 1, 1960. The basic change was how missions would be approved. It would now be in a more formalized manner and not so clandestine. That meant more people to sign off on it and more ways to cover any eventualities that should arise. In the first four years of the U-2's service, there weren't many people involved with the program from the Eisenhower administration, that had anything to do with decisions on making flights over the Soviet Union or anywhere else for that matter. Eisenhower personally authorized every flight over the Soviet Union and this also included Richard Bissell of CIA, along with the deputy director of the CIA. This went along with a discussion with Eisenhower about each mission or the program in general. That discussion included the Secretary of State or the Under Secretary of State, the chairman of the Joint Chiefs of Staff, the Secretary of Defense or his deputy and the President's secretary, General Goodpaster. The process for approving the mission for the U-2 under Eisenhower was totally unstructured. There was no formal group that oversaw any of the overflight proposals and Eisenhower made sure that the power /authority remained solely in his hands. With the loss of the U-2 on Mayday, 1960, this all came to screeching halt.

The National Security Council was now involved in the decision making process. All missions were now filtered through the NSC. A special group in the NSC would make the approval. The group now consisted of the Director of the CIA, Deputy Secretary of Defense, the Under Secretary of State and the President's military advisors.

When requesting permission for a U-2 flight over denied territory, the CIA made a detailed plan which would give credence to the missions, and maps showing what areas needed to be photographed, flight time and an emergency landing site. These program plans now came in loose leaf binders made of black plastic and became known as the "Black Book." After the discussion the group presented it to the president for a signature. This new process didn't come into play immediately as there was the stand down of U-2 flights directly after the incident.

The new plan for missions started to come into effect in October, 1960 when the Cuban Missile Crisis reared its ugly Soviet head. The full procedure was duly established and put into place. The process established requirement for any overhead reconnaissance as it became more formal. In August of 1960, the U.S. Intelligence Board took over the AdHoc Requirement Committee and merged it with the Satellite Intelligence Requirements Committee to form the new *"Committee on Overhead Reconnaissance"*. The Director of the CIA sent out a directive, which gave COMOR (the acronym for Committee on Overhead Reconnaissance) with the *"coordinated development of foreign Intelligence requirements for overhead reconnaissance projects over denied areas"*. The CIA director defined "overhead reconnaissance" to include "all reconnaissance for foreign intelligence purposes by satellite or any other vehicle over a denied area, whether it be by photographic means, ELINT[44], or other means". The only exception for COMOR's area of responsibility was reconnaissance and aerial surveillance in direct support of actively combatant fares.

---

[44] ELINT-electronic intelligence; COMINT' Communication Intelligence; RADINT; Radar intelligence, infrared RADINT

The Special Group created by the NSC Intelligence Document (5412/2) created in 1955, was to oversee covert activities and was known as the 5412 Committee. Later on, the Special Group was now known as the 303 Committee (which you will hear more about in the Black Shield Program and the A-12) and after that the 40 Committee.

By this time, the USAF had developed a large overhead reconnaissance plan of its own. It was not letting the grass grow under its feet. This included the U-2s and when there were conflicts between who's area of responsibility COMOR or the USAF/military services for collection requirements. The USAF won a large agreement in 1958, when it claimed the White House had given the responsibility of peripheral reconnaissance of the Soviet Union to the military. The CIA and Allan Dulles, who was always against getting involved in the areas that were the military's domain, didn't fight the USAF statement and the *Ad Hoc Requirements Committee* ceased making requirements for peripheral flights. This ended a major requirement study which estimated the gain of flying a U-2 over the Soviet Union borders and using oblique photography. On June 22, 1958, the last of the CIA/ Soviet Union over flights, which were only peripheral missions were flown. Not till the spring 1961 was there any coordination of military reconnaissance activity even within the separate military services. Each commander of a theater of operations or unified and specialized command held his own independent reconnaissance activities. The Joint Chiefs of Staff came up with the "Joint Reconnaissance Center" (JRC) under the J-3 Operations of the Joint Staff. What that all means is the JRC[45] began to coordinate and obtain approval for

---

[45] The U.S. Congress Senate Committee to Study Governmental Operations with respect to Intelligence Activities Foreign and Military Intelligence Book I—US Govt. Printing Office 1976 pg. 45-53

approximately five hundred missions per month, assigning each a risk factor which ranged from "Critical, Sensitive, Unique or Routine". The Joint Reconnaissance Center then prepared a monthly book of activities which gave details of proposed missions. The CIA received a copy of this book. Most of the military missions were approved or not approved at JCS level but sensitive missions went through Secretary of Defense and Special Group approval. The Department of Defense then stepped in to approve it. Hence, we went from the small, concise presidential control to this massive dichotomy in overhead reconnaissance. The military could also submit a plan through the head of the CIA, using their representatives on COMOR.

Basically, the military services had four channels for submitting reconnaissance missions to the special group while the CIA had only one channel. The biggest part of the conflict in requirement committees and military services started with the Far East missions that added up to the Vietnam War, North Korea and China.

Picking the New Targets

In the early 1960s Vietnam was designated a denied area by the U.S. Intelligence Board (USIB). Hence, the military services could plan their missions without consulting COMOR. Such missions did come close to China, which also was a denied area and under COMOR responsibility. When the Vietnam War broke in 1964, the military services received a responsibility for the entire area. To cut down the number of flights between CIA and the USAF, which were competing on reconnaissance projects, and managing the growing satellite program, an agreement was made between both organizations to provide overall coordination for reconnaissance activities at the national level. The first of the interagency agreement came in the Fall of 1961 and it was followed by three additional agreements during the next four years.

Photo Interpretation, the New Art form

With the coordination of the reconnaissance efforts, both the CIA and the Military were also affected the field of photo interpretation. After the May 1, 1960 U-2 incident, the President's Board of Consultants on Foreign Intelligence Activities (PFIAB) had urged the establishment of an interagency group to study ways to improve the entire U.S. intelligence community. The Group of Foreign Intelligence met for the first time on May 6,1960. For the next seven months, led by Lynn Kirkpatrick, the CIA Inspector General, one of the study group's key recommendations in the report that was issued December 1960. It was the creation of the National Photo-Interpretation Center (NPIC) that would bring together photo interpreters from the CIA and the Military services. The report further recommended that the CIA be placed in charge of the new center. Ignoring Air Force claims that CIA should not head such a center, President Eisenhower approved the report's recommendations, and on January 18,1961, the National Security Council Intelligence Directive (NSCID) #8 established National Photographic Interpretation Center (NPIC).

was designated by the Director of the CIA and approved by the Secretary of Defense. The Deputy Director would come from one of the military services. The first director of NPIC was Arthur S. Lundahl, head of the CIA's photo-intelligence division.

Arthur Lundahl—the Master of Photo Interpretation

Arthur "Art" Lundahl was a former naval intelligence officer, who was brought back to the CIA in 1952 in hopes he would be the master key in developing the Photo Interpretation Section for the CIA. It would be the first time this type of group was set up for CIA. The new department was called "Photo Intelligence Division" or PID which would be the mother of the Office of Imagery Analysis later on down the line.

Lundahl already had the Photo Interpretation Center (PIC) and had prepared them to handle the work that would be coming in. The PIC was housed in the old Steuart building which resided in the rather derelict section of Washington D.C. The address was on the corner of 5th and K street, not exactly the most prestigious of addresses. Lundahl was responsible for producing the photographs that put the literal nail in the coffin of the Soviets and their ICBM project in Cuba. It was already well known in the heat of the Cuban Missile Crisis that the photo interpreters and image analysts were at the forefront of the delivery of the final word which was the damning images of the Soviet buildup of ICBMs on Cuba's shores. President John F. Kennedy never doubted the importance of the photo intelligence and how it helped to solve the Crisis. JFK personally presented the 363rd Tactical Reconnaissance Wing with the USAF's Outstanding Unit Award and to each of the sixteen pilots that flew the missions over Cuba, the Distinguished Flying Cross. Special praise was given to Art Lundahl and the NPIC, along with DCI John McCone and brought back the prestige the CIA once enjoyed before the Bay of Pigs fiasco.

Politics and the Imagery Analysts

In a final note to the Cuban Missile Crisis and a very important item for the imagery analyst in general, is the position of the photo interpreter in the line of political power. The Imagery Analyst/Photo interpreter's job is to monitor certain activities of foreign nations and to assess if there are violations to treaties, certain troop movements, and anything that might smack of trouble or be out of the ordinary.

Their job is to "MONITOR NOT TO VERIFY". This is an absolute critical point. To do any sort of verification would be to violate an arms control agreement. For example, information is given to the National Security Council where the decision would be made as to whether the activity could equal a conscious violation to deceive; or the existence of the violation could be protested and received in private by the offending group. It could also be totally ignored. Should the violation become public knowledge, the intelligence community, imagery analysts in particular, would be held responsible for missing any part of whatever was going on or releasing the information. There is also the problem of the photo interpreter/imagery analyst monitoring for months a situation, with no interest from the intelligence community, when BANG! something happens and it becomes a major political nightmare that could be blasted worldwide by some journalist, or given to someone who is running for a political office using it for their purpose or to cause a major National Security problem.

Something just like this occurred with the SALT II treaty. President Jimmy Carter did not ratify the SALT II treaty because of a retired USAF General who came upon some information regarding the USSR and Cuba. As it turned out, the Soviet were building fallout shelters along the coast of Cuba. There was the main question of "why didn't the intelligence community know about this?" (all of this occurred in the 1970s)

This USAF retired general saw it as the Soviet Union was getting ready for a first strike against the United States, when it fact, this activity was "well monitored" but no one in the "front office" of Washington, D.C. felt it was worth the effort. It all fell apart after literal thousands of hours of imagery analysts time documenting this activity. In this case, the imagery analyst was in the middle of this miasma of "who wants to know what and can they use it and make it relevant". Of course, Carter never signed the SALT II treaty. Another incident in the summer of 1970, President Nixon, sent Henry Kissinger to warn the Soviets to stop constructing what looked to be submarine tender bases at the Cienfuegos port in Cuba. The Soviets claimed they had no plans for building any bases but construction stopped. Once again, image analysts stopped what could have been another Soviet problem.

As the Cold War ended, and overhead reconnaissance lost its primary mission for which it was created, Congress decided to consolidate most of the imagery resources into a single new organization called. NIMA (National Imagery and Mapping Agency). By 1995, President Bill Clinton put in the Declassification Executive Order 25, which released images from the early satellite days. Of course, these photos were from the CORONA project which did have coverage over Communist China, the Soviet Union and other "denied "territory. The Photo Interpreter/ Imaging Analyst does walk a tightrope of politics and National Security.

Richard Bissell Departs the Scene

One major change in the U-2 program follows the 1960 shoot down, although not directly related to Powers and the U-2. What occurred was Richard Bissell's leaving the CIA and the re-organization of the CIA's reconnaissance and scientific activities. The basis of Bissell's ouster went back to January 1959, when he became the Deputy Director of Plans and made the decision to put all CIA's air assets in the DDP, in order to maintain control of overhead reconnaissance projects like the U-2, the later A-12 Blackbird and the DISCOVERER satellite system.

Before the *Independent Development Projects* Staff became *the Development Project Division* of the DDP and now controlled all the CIA's air operations, including air support for covert operations, the U-2 were used for gathering intelligence to support DP operations in addition to their primary mission of gathering strategic and tactical intelligence. This re-organization helped with increasing the efficiency of CIA air operations, the use of the U-2 support covert action and disturbed Bissell's backing advisors which were the renowned Edwin Land and James Killian. They were worried that Bissell was getting too involved in covert action and had not devoted sufficient time to overhead reconnaissance programs. Of course, there was the Bay of Pigs fiasco in April of 1961.

That certainly didn't help Bissell's situation. It destroyed his credibility with President John F. Kennedy and his advisors. Later in the year 1961, Bissell's last and most important backer dropped out of his CIA position, Allan Dulles, the CIA boss resigned in November of 1961. In his last months as deputy director of plans, Bissell found himself in a major struggle with Killian and Land who were working in JFK's Foreign Intelligence Advisory Board. Both of JFK's influential advisors were working hard to get the CIA out of the overhead reconnaissance business. Given the disaster with Bay of Pigs, JFK was not enamored of the CIA and would love any reason to cut them out. He wanted to take overhead reconnaissance out of the DDP and put in into the newly formed "Science Directorate". Bissell fought this proposal tooth and nail, only deciding to get out while he could retain something of his legacy. Hence, on February 17, 1962, after turning down an offer from the new Director of the CIA John McCone, to become the CIA's first Deputy Director of Research[46] and two days from Bissell's retirement, the new Directorate came into being (New Science Directorate). It took with it all the Development Projects Division's special reconnaissance projects. Only the conventional air support for the clandestine services remained in the DPD's bag, now called the Special Operations Division. The U-2 program was no longer the connector with the covert operations.

The first half of 1962 was a mess for the Development Projects Division. After losing the individual who had created, supervised the program for seven long years, the DPD also was no longer autonomous when it was transferred from its own building to the new CIA Langley, Virginia headquarters. Colonel Stanley W. Beerli who was in charge of DPD since 1960, went back to the USAF. On July 30, 1962, the overhead

---

[46] Killian's interview (SS) Land interview (TS Codeword) Bissell to McCone Feb 7, 1962 (DCI Records)

reconnaissance projects had a re-organization to the new *Office of Special Activities*.

In essence, the USAF would now replace the DPD. The Organization of the OSA, with ten divisions or staff heads reporting to the director of the Office of Special Activities proved to be too weighty. On September 30,1962, another re-organization divided most of these offices between two major sections—the *Deputy for Technology* and the *Deputy for Field Activities*. The **Office of Special Activities** (OSA) continued to control reconnaissance activities and the related research and development after the directorate of research was expanded and renamed the *"Deputy Directorate for Science and Technology (DDS&T)*. This change went on the books on August 5, 1963. Along with the other Directorates, DDS&T dropped the deputy in 1965 and became the Directorate of Science and Technology. In 1965, the head of the OSA got yet another new title, "Directorate of Special Activities." This title held until 1974 when the CIA totally gave up their involvement with manned reconnaissance aircraft.

After the MAYDAY Affair—What Happened to Aerial Reconnaissance and the CIA?

After the May 1, 1960 debacle that turned the CIA's aerial reconnaissance dreams on their proverbial head, Eisenhower ordered a total stand down of all U-2 flights over the Soviet Union, they were not resumed even when John F. Kennedy took office in January 25, 1961. In a quote from JFK; *"I have ordered that the flights not be resumed which is a continuation of the order given by President Eisenhower in May of last year."*

While not set in stone, Director of the CIA, John McCone, who took the DCI position in November of 1961. Kennedy was assassinated in November of 1963. McCone pointed out to JFK's successor, Lyndon

Baines Johnson, on January 15, 1964 in request from LBJ for information on the U-2 overflight policies; *"Contrary to popular assumptions, President Kennedy did not make any pledge or give any assurance at least publicly that there would be no further over flights. He limited his response to a statement that he had ordered that the flights not be resumed. An order, obviously, is valid only until countermanded."*

There were several proposals to resume over flights on the USSR in the following years, but none reached the mission planning level. The Kennedy Administration came the closest to resuming over flights over the USSR during the Berlin Crisis in the summer and fall of 1964. Kelly Johnson of Lockheed noted in his personal **"Project Log"**: *"Have request from Mr. Bissell to propose ways and means for increasing safety of the U-2 on probable over flights. It seems President Kennedy, who publicly stated that no U-2s would ever be over Russia while he was president has requested additional flights. Some poetic justice is this."*

Johnson also continued in his Project Log further ideas about a resumption of U-2 flights. In preparation for the possible resumption of over flights, Johnson began thinking about what to do in a worst case scenario like that of May 1, 1960. He noted in a September 21, 1961 entry: *One of the greatest technological problems and of course a great moral one, is how we insure destroying the aircraft and the pilot should the mission fail. I have proposed a time-altitude fusing set-up for multitude bombs, that looks like it should do the trick. Beerli (Col. Stanley Beerli, USAF director of the Office of Special Activities) doesn't want anything to do with this, but we will go ahead and develop it in case someone decides it's necessary."*

On September 25, 1961, the "Committee on Overhead Reconnaissance", wrote a detailed report called *"Justification for U-2 Photography over the USSR."* This was in favor of the U-2 flying over selected high priority targets like the ICBM missile sites.

The COMOR report also said satellite photography did not provide sufficient detail to answer many critical questions about the Soviet Union's ICBM missile program. The report showed a U-2 and satellite photography of a USSR target, side by side. The U-2 photos showed the higher resolution and better quality than the satellite images. Yet, not all of the COMOR members were quite happy about the thought of over flying the Soviet Union again. When COMOR requested for the over flights, the USIB on October 1, 1961, the State department and the CIA's members dissented and found *"insufficient justification for resuming the U-2 flights over the Soviet Union at this time"* The proposal was negative on resuming the over flights in the Fall of 1961. Both the USIB and the Special Group were completely against it and as long and the U-2 photos were showing technically more precise images that the satellites, the idea of the U-2 overflying the Soviet Union was still a juicy one.

In February of 1962, the USIB (U.S. Intelligence Board) considered the COMOR (Committee on Overheard Reconnaissance) idea to send a U-2 over Kamchatka to check out the Soviet Union's antiballistic missile sites but put a hold on it since the USAF was already working on a mission, and finally decided to go with satellite coverage as suggested by Director McCone.

Both the CIA and State Department decided to hold on using the U-2 over the Soviet Union unless there was some compelling situation, which would be worth the gamble of again risking a shoot down. The U-2 was used very successfully in many other areas where the tracking technology was weak, like the areas of Latin America and of course, Vietnam where the CIA was very active between 1958 and 1974, until CIA was finally divested of doing any manned reconnaissance flying.

The U-2 and the Cuban Missile Crisis

It was in the summer of 1960 that the Directorate of Plans was setting up a counter-revolutionary invasion of Cuba for 1961. The CIA had asked the National Security Council and the Special Group to approve some over flights of Cuba. In one mission, Operation *KICK OFF*, the flights were to get intelligence to see just what the Cubans had in the line of "Order of Battle".[47] Only two flights were permitted for this mission and the Detachment "G" would fly from McLaughlin AFB, in Texas, which was a base used by the USAF U-2s. The CIA photo interpreters would travel to Del Rio, near the base in Texas, to read the "take", the photography the U-2 would deliver. Both flights took place on October 26 and 27, 1960. The missions covered 3500 miles and were nine hours long, which played severe hell on the pilots. The clouds decided to roll over Cuba and the mission "take" was poor. More missions were asked for by the CIA, by the Special Group.

The Detachment "G" received the okay to go for three more missions now called "Operation "*GREEN EYES*" to take place on November 27, and December 5th and 11, 1960. These flights got good results.

The necessity of these long missions brought up the question of fueling the U-2 in flight. In May of 1961, Lockheed started to adapt the CIA's U-2s so that they could refuel in the air, which would expand the U-2s flight range. Six of the U-2s that got this new refueling capability, were now called U-2F. All of the CIA's pilots were retrained for the new refueling technique and to be sure, it was a graceful and precise maneuver. Matching the speed of the KC-135 to the very delicate U-2 with that long wingspan, was a dance to behold! The KC-135 tanker had to reduce

---

[47] Order of Battle—formation, units and equipment of a military force

their airspeed to 200 kts. to be slow enough for the U-2 to catch up. The U-2 was always in a critical position due to those wings, which couldn't handle stress. Again, there were the vortices[48] that were created by the KC-135's wingtips. With the long wings of the U-2, the pilots had to position themselves almost in between the wings of the KC-135 tanker and the four jet engines she carried, as to not allow the U-2 wings to slip out into those vortices. There were accidents in the first few years of working this maneuver out, one pilot died and two U-2s were destroyed when their wing tips slipped into those vortices. There were some good things about the aerial refueling and that was it allowed for a longer range, yet it still prevented any mission from going past the 10-hour mark. Pilot fatigue was a huge issue and one that could not be remedied quite so easily.

CUBA Becomes Hot

Cuba was still a very hot topic since the failure of the Bay of Pigs invasion in April of 1961. President Kennedy took the blame for the fiasco, yet he still did look for other ways of getting his intelligence. Kennedy was still interested in finding out what Castro was up to. While the U-2 had altitude, she did not have great range. That was a point that was found out as the U-2 was now being used over Latin America and Vietnam. The Kennedy Administration also had a deep "curiosity" of what was going on in Cuba. "Detachment "G" was flying a monthly mission over Cuba called NIMBUS, which came out of Edwards AFB in California. Through the technological breakthrough of in-flight refueling, the

---

[48] A wingtip vortice is a spherical pattern of air the rotates behind the wingtips of an aircraft as it generates lift. Being caught in a vortices can cause another aircraft to become unstable and possibly fly into the other aircraft or go out of control.

mission was getting ready to handle the its operation from Laughlin AFB in Texas. There were some missions flown over Cuba under Operation *LONG GREEN* on March 19 and 21, 1961, to photograph Cuba and help in plans for a final invasion of Cuba. In the spring of 1962, it was obvious something was up in Cuba, there was a lot of activity showing up in the photography. The Soviets were quietly running rampant all over the island. The CIA asked to send for more photo coverage of Cuba. The Special Group agreed to "increasing more flights over Cuba starting with two a month in May of 1962. The National Photographic Interpretation Center (NPIC), right about the same time started to publish the *"Photographic Evaluation on Cuba* "series of documents and photos. Early on in August of 1962, the CIA saw an increase in Soviet armament on the island. In a U-2 flight from August 5th, mission#3086, that was flown too soon to detect all the construction the Soviets were doing, as it was just starting up in different parts of the Cuban island. Mission #3038 that was supposed to fly August 8th, was canceled due to poor weather and was continuously postponed till August 29th. Mission #3038 did fly and it brought back the first true evidence of exactly what was going on with the Soviets and Cuba. A couple of days after that mission flew, the CIA put on a report *"President's Intelligence Checklist"*. In that report at least eight surface to air missiles (SA-2) sites were seen in the west side of Cuba. On a September 5th mission #3089, the U-2 brought home some more evidence that the Soviet were most definitely up to something. Three more SAM missiles sites were found, along with a MiG21, which was the newest of the Soviet jet fighters, that was found in the Santa Clara airfield.

Finding the SAM sites was a shock to the Kennedy administration and had a major effect on the entire reconnaissance picture of Cuba. It did add meat to the bone for John McCone's CIA worries concerning Cuba's becoming an operating base for Soviet medium MCBMs, which were literally ninety miles off the coast of Florida. The CIA felt that these SAM sites would have only been set up to protect a high priority facility like a missile base. However, there were more urgent issues of the SAM sites discovery and that was to make the Kennedy Administration more aware of the U-2's use for overhead flights on Cuba. As shown by the MAYDAY Affair, the U-2 didn't have a high tolerance for SAM SA-2 missiles being shot at her.

In the Kennedy Oval Office concerns were starting to catch on cornering the Soviet missile rolling into Cuba right under the Kennedy Administration's nose. Flying the U-2 over Cuba with a shoot down possibility by a SAM missile was a very risky business. It would cause a major showdown with the Soviet Union, but that would come anyway, without the shootdown's help. As it was, the Soviet's feathers were ruffled by an August 30,1962 USAF U-2 mission that was flying along the border over Sakhalin Island in the far east, which brought a lot of protest from the Soviet Union.

On September 4, 1962, the United States officially apologized for the flight. On September 10, 1962, Secretary of State Dean Rusk, called a meeting of all the advisers including McGeorge Bundy, Deputy Director of the CIA, Marshall Carter and other National Security advisors. The Secretary of State was the first to object to the two extended over flights on the uncovered areas of Cuba. Dean Rusk wanted flights only on the outside and over international waters of Cuban territory. Rusk felt the loss of an aircraft on a mission with either type of flight would make it hard to protect U.S. rights over international waters. McGeorge Bundy and Carter both felt that the flights had to be split into four mission; two over flights and two border flights, making them a fast "in and out" operation across the narrow width of Cuba, instead of flying the whole length of Cuba like before. The September 5th mission was the last. Just to be on the safe side, all SAM sites would be avoided. It did limit the mission in getting the information needed but it was better safe than sorry. Weather proved to be a total issue along with the limited flight path. It did ground all aircraft for a while. On September 17th, on mission #3093, the weather again turned foul and held on till the 26th of September when mission #3093 finally flew, covering the eastern part of Cuba and collected more information on an additional three SAM sites. September 29th brought mission #3095 and covered the "Isle of Pines" and the Bay of Pigs area including a flight over the coast where the defensive missile sites were being installed. The U-2, even on the cautious side, did turn up more SAM sites but nothing that proved surface to surface MRBMs.

The CIA was worrying about the lack of evidence. John McCone, the DCI in an October 4, 1962 meeting of the "Special Group" said the policies of not flying over SAM sites was holding back on finding the information needed that was on the south-eastern side of Cuba. McCone said; *"Whether this was a reasonable restriction at this time, particularly since the SAM's were almost certainly not operational."*

The CIA U-2s continued the reconnaissance program the Special Group had approved in September of 1962. In early August, two border missions, #3098-south east coast, and October 5th and 7th, additional SAM sites, totaling five were found and that brought the amount up to nineteen, but not an MRBM to be found. There was more evidence that areas of Cuba in the September and early October missions, missed or avoided picking up what was in the area where the MRBMs were holding out. On October 6, 1962 the "Committee on Overhead Reconnaissance" recommended frequent and regular coverage of Cuba pointing in particular to the need for renewal coverage in western Cuba: *"The absence of coverage of the western end since August 29th, coupled with the rate of constriction, we have observed means that there may well be many more sites now being built of which we are unaware. Ground observers have in several recent instances, reported sightings of what they believe to be the SS-4 SHYSTER MRBM in Cuba. These reports must be confirmed or denied by photo coverage."* Attached to this memo was a list of the targets with the area around San Cristobal at the top. It was a critical location. The Special Group met on October 9th to discuss the COMOR's recommendations, with the most important of which was a U-2 flight over the suspected "MRBM "sites as soon as the weather permitted. This flight was to pass over the SA-2 site that was thought to be most nearly operational, in order to determine the status of SA-2 defenses of Cuba. Hopefully, over flight was not going to cause a SA-2 reaction stating a *"Maximum coverage of the western end of the island by multiple U-2s simultaneously."* Due to the dangerous nature of the SA-2 sites, this area is one of urgent importance.

In the minutes of the Special Group meeting, a memo for John McCone was received from J.S. Carmen, the inspector general; *"Handling raw intelligence information during the Cuban Arms buildup Nov 20, 1962.*[49] John McCone, director of the CIA, who was the head of the "Special Activities," presented a vulnerability analysis that estimated the odds of losing the U-2 over Cuba, was one to six. The Deputy Secretary of Defense, Roswell Gilpatric and the USAF representatives questioned the adequacy of the CIA's cover story that the pilots were actually Lockheed employees on a ferry flight to Puerto Rico.

The USAF and the Department of Defense representatives argued that it would be better to use USAF pilots, and in the event of a failure or mishap, it could be said that the overflight, was a routine USAF peripheral surveillance mission that had gone off course. DCI McCone asked

---

[49] Lehman Report Pg. 30 (TS Codeword)

Colonel Jack Ledford, who was the head of the Special Activities, his opinion of the idea. Ledford felt that the Department of Defense cover was a good plan. However, he did point out that the Strategic Air Command's (USAF) U-2s were more open to problems than those of the CIA's birds, which had the better electronic countermeasure (ECM) equipment, a higher maximum altitude. Ledford suggested that the USAF pilots use the CIA's aircraft instead of the SAC U-2s after a total retraining program.

McCone met with President John F. Kennedy, who then approved the San Cristobal mission and the use of USAF pilots in CIA aircraft. On October 1st, the USAF and the CIA representatives met to discuss the new "arrangement" for the cover stories. The CIA went along with the story, but the USAF cover story was the best and emphasized that a USAF pilot should not be used until he had received adequate training. The conversation went to the issue of who would run the next mission, the CIA or the USAF. With the USAF very much in favor of the USAF control of the U-2 missions over Cuba, the Department of Defense representatives called McCone at the CIA and got his approval. Right after that, McCone left Washington D.C. for California and was gone till October 14th. The USAF control of the Cuban flights became official on October 12th, when control was transferred and the "responsibilities" were to include command control and operational decisions with regard to the U-2s reconnaissance flight of Cuba from the CIA to the Department of Defense. The CIA was not pleased. In a memo from DCI McCone to McGeorge Bundy, *"Reconnaissance Over flights of Cuba"* dated October 12, 1962, the DCI showed his disapproval: *"Lt. General Marshall S. Carter, (Army), the acting DCI had a very strong reaction to the USAF takeover of a major CIA operation. He said:" I think it's a hell of a way to run a railroad. It's perfectly obvious it was a geared operation to get SAC into the ACT.[50]"*

In many of the conversations that went back and forth between the USAF upper echelon and the Kennedy administration, Carter fought against a change in command and control of flight at such a dangerous time for the country. The CIA operation, Carter said, was working perfectly where the USAF just didn't have the experience in controlling U-2 flights, especially the U-2C, and that aircraft was not part of the USAF inventory. Carter also brought out the fact that the USAF pilots had virtually no experience with the new J-75 Pratt and Whitney engine that flew in the U-2. Carter told Ross Gilpatric; *"To put in a brand new green pilot just because he happened to have on a blue suit and to completely disrupt command and control an communications and ground support system on 72 hour notice, to me, does not make a goddamn bit of sense, Mr. Secretary![51]"*

You don't need much imagination to understand the frustration and aggravation that was running through the CIA with this change of the U-2 reconnaissance missions. This is one of the reasons for the bad blood between the USAF and the CIA in this time frame. Even though Carter knew the pilot would come from the USAF, he worked on convincing the Department of Defense and the Kennedy Administration for allowing the CIA to continue operations for a few weeks, using a USAF pilot and gradually allowing the USAF to take over command and control. However, it just didn't work between Kennedy's hatred of the CIA and the USAF's gloating over getting one up on the CIA, there was no hope for a getting a stay of command. The USAF insisted upon immediate control of the operations and the Kennedy administration was not prepared to get

---

[50] Telephone conversation between DDCI- Carter and McGeorge Bundy Oct 13, 1962
[51] Telephone conversation between DDCI Carter and Gilpatric Oct 12, 1962

into an argument between both services about jurisdiction. To further put consistency of the agreements between the USAF and the CIA, this puts the icing on the cake. A presidential assistant to the National Security Agency, McGeorge Bundy told DCI Carter; *"The whole thing looks to me like two quarreling children.*[51-A] No one cared to challenge the President on his decision. It is interesting to note that this is almost true to form for the Kennedy administration. As we all know, after the Bay of Pigs fiasco, it was a well known fact that Kennedy had no fond feelings for the CIA. JFK as much as broadcasted it he was going to close the agency down. Given this sudden change to remove the CIA from the U2's main function is just further proof of JFK's intentions to tear the CIA up from the inside out. Once JFK said it, it was final, there was no going back. The CIA gave its complete total support to the USAF to plan the next mission. At the CIA's Detachment for the U-2 at Edwards Air Force Base, California, a USAF pilot showed up unannounced on October 11, 1962. The CIA ran him through the fast course on the U-2C. On that Sunday, October 14, 1962, the weather finally cleared over Cuba and the first of the USAF/SAC missions took off. After the flight, the film pallet was removed from the U-2C and sent to NPIC. By October 15, 1962, photo interpreters at the NPIC found the evidence of the MRBMs in the San Cristobal area. The NPIC director, Arthur Lundahl called the DDI Ray Clive, who then called the DDCI Carter. This sounded like the game of "telephone", the old kid's game that one child whispers a message to one kid and passes down the line to find out if the message comes out right. Calls proceeded down this line. The National Security Advisor, McGeorge Bundy and Roger Hilsman of the State Department Bureau of Intelligence and Research called the Secretary of State, Dean

---

[51-A] Telephone conversation between Carte and McGeorge Bundy Oct 12, 1962 DCI records.

Rusk. On October 16th, the DDCI, Marshall Carter briefed the president on the results of the October 14th mission.

It was now known the Soviets had placed MRBMs in Cuba's mainland. It was solidly confirmed. The U-2 rules for the mission approval changed yet again. SAC now had a total approval to fly whatever and how many missions were needed to cover Cuba totally. This was done without consulting the "Special Group". A week after the MRBMs were found, SAC's U-2s were racking up lots of missions each day. The U-2 photographs were backed up by low level photography taken by Navy and USAF aircraft. Through what was left of the Cuban Missile Crisis, the CIA-s U-2 pilots sat waiting, with nothing to do along with their hours and hours of training. The USAF and JFK had usurped the reconnaissance mission from the CIA. The NPIC photo interpreters did "yeoman service" in studying the thousands of feet of film that came back from the USAF and Navy reconnaissance aircraft. JFK used the NPIC photos to show the Soviet missile build up in Cuba on October 22, 1962. JFK then declared the "Naval Quarantine" to stop the shipment of nuclear weapons to Cuba.

By October 27th, at the height of the Cuban Crisis, one of the U-2Cs that the CIA had loaned out to the USAF, was shot down and the pilot USAF Major Rudolph Anderson was killed. Again, this shoot down showed how fragile and vulnerable the U-2 really was.

Altitude was a great thing to have, but without speed, it really wasn't worth all that much as far as safety was concerned. The SAC U-2s over flights continued both during and after the Cuban Missile Crisis and the USAF held the responsibility for the work, leaving the CIA totally out of the picture. The CIA pilots never flew any of the Cuban missions.

While SAC carried out the work, during the Crisis, the CIA's U-2s made the vital contributions at the beginning of the showdown. Project IDEALIST pilots had 459 hours in the air over Cuba during 1961-62.

These pilots from the CIA got and gave the basic evidence that the Soviets were clearly up to something. The over flight was the only way to get the information. Even with the CIA Discoverer Satellites imaging, the photos were just not of the quality the U-2 produced. All attempts made with satellites were not adequate, usually because the orbits of the satellites never placed them over Cuba at the right time of day to get the evidence needed.

Where It Really Started

The U-2s history with the CIA started in 1958 with a problem in the People's Republic of China and Nationalist China (Taiwan). Things were getting hot. On June 18, 1958 Detachment "C" set up a U-2 mission to get photos of the Chinese coast and some of the adjoining islands of Quemoy and Little Quemoy where the nationalists had put large amounts of troops to stop any invasion. On August 23, 1958, the Communist Chinese started to shell the islands heavily for five days nonstop. This made getting supplies to the islands virtually impossible. The head of the Nationalist troops were ordered to surrender intimating that an invasion was imminent. The Nationalists refused to surrender and received support from the U.S. in the form of warships from the 7th Fleet, which started to escort the Nationalist ships which brought supplies to the hard hit troops on both islands. Detachment "C" U-2s flew four missions over the mainland looking for any troop movement that would show the Communists were pushing to take over the islands While photos showed no troop movement, it didn't help cooling things down between the two warring factors.

Two more flights came out of "Detachment "C" on September 9 and October 22 to track the communists but found nothing. This very heated period soon started to cool down when the Communist Chinese found out that they would get no help from Mother Russia and if this "argument' got into a hotter phase, the United States might have something to say.[52]

To make sure that the NASA cover story for the U-2 would look "legal", in July 14, 15 and 16 of 1958 "Detachment "C" flew high over Typhoon Winnie which was beating the stuffing out of Taiwan, causing mass destruction. It really was the first time the weather reconnaissance story actually held up to the light of day. The photos actually made a weather magazine called "Weather-Wise" and the July 21st edition of Aviation Week magazine. There were twelve of more typhoons that were photographed by Detachment "C" in September 1958.

Upgrades for the U-2

Lockheed started the upgrade of the thirteen U-2s that the CIA held by putting the new Pratt and Whitney J-75-P13 jet engines in. The first three of the U-2Cs made it to Detachment "C" in the summer of 1959.

On September 24, 1959, using U-2C #360, the pilot decided to try for a new altitude record. The flight went up with a camera, but no film and without a full tank of fuel, which obviously made it much lighter than the U-2C used in a mission. During this U-2 flight, the aircraft used up more fuel than anticipated for a test flight, which caused the engine to flame out when she lined up to return to base. The pilot made a wheels up landing at a local glider club strip near the Okinawa base. While nothing and no one was damaged, what did happen is the U-2 got more publicity than it really wanted. Most of it came from the unit's security team, who

---

[52] Mission folder 17739June 10, 1958) OSA Chapter 15 history pgs. 25-26 (TS Codeword)

wore loud Hawaiian shirts and carried large, heavy guns. That would attract anyone's attention and definitely got the Japanese reporters who were hanging around to wake up. One reporter got a helicopter to overfly the Kadena base on Okinawa and take photos of the U-2, which ended up in a Japanese magazine and newspaper. That did not make the CIA and USAF terribly pleased.

U-2 Crashes

The loss of two U-2Cs was painful to all. The one U-2 over Cuba, #349 used in Operation TOPPER, April 5, 1960 occurred due to a failure in the landing gear doors closing properly, which caused a higher fuel consumption. The pilot crashed into a rice paddy. Since the aircraft could not be recovered fully, it was cut into pieces and carried out of the rice paddy by the local villagers and put into a C-124 under cover. As a thank you to the village, a school was built with funds given to the village leader. This left Detachment "C", with two aircraft out of the three that they had. The workload was light since they were not overflying the Soviet Union anymore.

More Headaches and the Vietnam War Creeps Up

There was only one important mission left to fly and that was Operation HASP in which a specially equipped U-2C that took high altitude air samples trying to look for Soviet Union nuclear testing. The pervading wind direction made it perfect to track this phenomenon.

It started in 1958 and ran through 1960. Detachment "C" was about to do that when the Powers incident occurred, stopping all U-2 action. Again, with all the Japanese coverage of the U-2, in June 6, 1960, headquarters decided to draw down Detachment "C" between July 15 and September 1st and this was pushed up when the Japanese government formally requested the removal of the U-2s by July 8. With the loss of

Powers, the two overseas U-2 detachments went back home to the United States with the personnel and aircraft, mixed into "Detachment G" which stayed at Edwards AFB, California. This detachment was now responsible for providing coverage over Asia and the first mission over Laos in Southeast Asia. When the Laotian government collapsed in December of 1960, there were reports that a leftist government were using Soviet armament. On December 30, a new Laotian government asked the United Nations for help against the North Vietnamese and maybe Communist China. Worried by the concept of a civil war getting out of control because of the addition of foreign troops, the outgoing Eisenhower Administration ordered Detachment "G" to gather more information on what was going on is Southeast Asia.

Five of the Detachment "G" pilots were sent to the Philippines. During January 3 thru 18, 1961, these U-2s made seven flights over Laos, North Vietnam and China. In addition to the foreign troops that were suspected, all these flights worked on the lines of communication that led into Laos from Vietnam and China. The U-2s scanned the North Vietnam airfields for any Soviet aircraft to determine the magnitude of the airdrop supporting the Pathet Lao troops. NPIC photo interpreters were brought in to get a fast look at the Laotian claims from the photos. However, the photos showed nothing and on January 26th, the Laos government withdrew all charges of a foreign invasion. Detachment "G" returned to Edwards AFB on February 1961.

There was one large glitch during all of this and it was a complete security issue. The film from the January 16 thru 18 flights were sent to the United States for duplicate processing. After the film was loaded on a CIA C-47 on March 14th and sent to Washington D.C. during the flight, an engine failure occurred which forced the crew to drop forty three boxes of the highly classified film over the mountains around the Williamsport, Pennsylvania area to keep the C-47 in the air. The C-47 made an emergency landing at Scranton- Wilkes-Barre Pennsylvania airport. The pilots went immediately to CIA headquarters and told them of the drop of the film. State police sealed off the wooded area as per CIA instructions and CIA security quickly began to search for the boxes. All forty-three were recovered and not a one was damaged. Detachment "G" worked on only one lonely mission over North Vietnam during the 1961 summer. This was called Operation EBONY on August 13, 1961. Two days later the flights were successful and Detachment "G" was returned to the U.S. this Detachment provided aircraft for pilots who flew over parts of Asia and Indochina, which was an area of particular interest as the United States got deeper into Vietnam and the War.

The U-2 and Vietnam Continues . . .

In between 1962 and 1964, the CIA had thirty-six flights with photo missions over North and South Vietnam. Photo requirements were changing just about every day from strategic to tactical reconnaissance and back again as the Viet Cong started infiltration into the South Vietnam, due to the weaknesses in the government and the coup that tossed out President Ngo Dinh Diem in 1963. More coups followed from various military officers as the instability grabbed on.

South Vietnam, as a strategic holdout, was slowly breaking down and the Viet Cong were just getting stronger in their attacks. Because of the combat level stepping up, the USIB gave responsibility for the aerial reconnaissance of the areas where fighting was strongest to SAC. The USAF was in control again. SAC U-2s were used over South Vietnam and part of Cambodia and all of Laos including all of North Vietnam within thirty miles of South Vietnam on the coast.

What was left of Indochina remained the responsibility of the CIA's U-2s. On August 1964, following the Gulf of Tonkin resolution, the USAF resumed responsibility for the reconnaissance of all of Indochina.

The CIA remained active in Asia. In March/April 1963, the USIB met to reconsider if COMOR's intelligence requirements could be met by the U-2s because of heavy cloud cover, which made it rough for satellites to photograph areas needed. On May 28, 1963 the meeting of the "Special Group", DCI McCone requested authorization for overflight to meet the requirements needed for additional support. The Special Group established a "bank" of four over flights subject to a monthly review. However, because of the increasing intelligence community interest in the Far East, both CIA's U-2s became very active in the region. The increased lead of U-2 activity in the Far East during Spring of 1963, showed some serious weakness in PROJECT IDEALIST and a shortage of aircraft.

The CIA had only a total of seven aircraft available to fly. After the Mayday debacle and the lost aircraft over Cuba, McCone asked the Secretary of Defense McNamara, the Joint Chiefs of Staff, on June 10, 1963 to transfer two U-2s from the USAF to the CIA. The Defense Department quickly approved the transfer. Before the two USAF U-2s were placed in service, the CIA had them upgraded with the J-75/P-13A Pratt and Whitney engine and various electronic devices which took a total of four months. President Johnson ordered a stand down of over flights. It was welcomed to allow time to pass before more over flights were done. It turned out that they only qualified U-2 Pilot "disqualified "himself due to severe nervousness. No one could be gotten up to speed before the August deadline. The time had come for a faster high flying aircraft. The request brought the CIA to suspect that either the USAF or someone had learned of the very dark, secret Project *OXCART*, the U-2's successor, which was still in the testing phase. The U-2 was still having pilot shortage problems. McCone was still looking for a way to fix the U-2 pilot shortage. The Special Group agreed, that President Johnson should know but McGeorge Bundy (Nat'l Security Advisor) told McCone that because the Secretary of State Dean Rusk and Secretary of Defense McNamara didn't like the idea. Johnson was not going to hear about it[53]

It didn't take long, only seven days, for Colonel Leo Geary to call Lockheed and tell them to upgrade six of the older U-2s into U-2Cs, using the Pratt and Whitney J-57 engine with priority basis. This meant taking crews off the upcoming A-12 OXCART to help speed the conversions.

All the demand for overhead reconnaissance was still strong and growing. This was pushed on by the success of the U-2 missions, which now brought the Soviet MiG 21s into the literal picture. There were more issues at stake, showing that possibly SAMs were being produced where they were not thought to be. The other issue was the A-12 OXCART. She was almost ready to fly at the Area 51 Nevada test site. Meanwhile, the nightmare of the Tet Offensive in South Vietnam and the 303 Committee (the new name for the "Special Group") decided on February 1, 1968 to hold a group of over flights which were scheduled for February and called for mission by mission approval during this period of tension. The 303 Committee approved one more overflight, which was flown on March 16, 1968 and two over flights on Cambodia, carried out on March 27 and April 3, 1968, by the first operations since early 1966. By this time, the U-2 flights became so dangerous that the State department opposed further over flights and on April 10, 1968, the 303 Committee decided not to approve any mission that could fly any closer.

Over flights were stopped. There was a steady increase in ability to track and engage the U-2, as seen by its success in downing 5 U-2s. By

---

[53] 26 OSA History chapter 17 pg. 58-59 TS (Codeword)

1968, they were watching U-2s detailing and tracking them, soon as they let the ground on takeoff. The U-2 had to face a more vicious Vietcong defense system that not only consisted of SAMs SA-2 missiles but also the fast and high flying MiG 21s. Mig21 pilots had become adept at the power zoom technology and were threatening almost every U-2 mission. The risks to U-2 now seemed too great to deal with.

The decision to end the Asian over flights was also rooted in President Johnson's change in his whole approach to the war in Vietnam, in the spring of 1968. On March 31, 1968, LBJ limited the bombing of the North Vietcong to improve cooperation in the peace talks. Operation *SCOPE SHIELD* was put together to gather intelligence on activities in North Vietnam, and North Vietnamese were the USAF's responsibility since 1964. However, under the terms of the cease fire agreement negotiated with North Vietnam in January of 1973, the U.S. flights in the area by military were forbidden. The newly elected President, Richard Nixon told the CIA that they would watch North Vietnam for compliance with the cease-fire accords.

A very sensitive mission stayed 15 miles from North Vietnam coast and it initially flew a low altitude flight, in a deceptive direction to avoid Communist China radars. Constraints made missions difficult because of the low altitude, especially for the U-2, which consumed more fuel and also encountered more turbulence. The pilots pressure suits tended to overheat. The first mission on March 30, 1973 was marginally successful because of cloud cover and haze, which prevented it from photographing most of the targets. The second mission the next day, had somewhat better luck with the weather but the problem with the film processing reduced the mission's coverage. Afterwards, the monsoon season literally blew in and prevented any further missions until July 21, 1973.

The mission obtained useable photography of SAM sites and North Vietnamese supply operations, although the resolution of the images was not as high as it should have been because the camera had not been properly focused. The *SCOPE SHIELD* mission on Jan 6, 1974, finally succeeded in obtaining high-quality photography. The mission provided total coverage. The images of the Haiphong Harbor, SAM defenses and North Vietnamese Naval Order of Battle were just what was needed to tie up this mission.

The U-2 Developments and a Whale of a Tale

There were many developments in the growth of the U-2 Dragon Lady. In the middle of 1963, the Office of Special Activities put into motion "*PROJECT WHALE TALE*" which would look at the feasibility of adapting the U-2 aircraft for operations in the Navy, basically to fly off the deck of an aircraft carrier. The CIA planners felt that if the U-2 could be modified so that it could operate from the deck of a carrier, the United States could avoid the political problems of trying to ask a host country for the rights to use an airbase for operations. It would open up a lot of new territory. The equipment, formations, amount of troops of a military unit, for the CIA, mission wise would really use the U-2's potential. However, there was one thing that could hold it back, and that was the fragility of the U-2 itself. Kelly Johnson started working on the changes to the aircraft. If anyone knows anything about flying off the deck of an aircraft carrier or landing on one, you have to build the keel of the aircraft like it was made out of solid steel. The torture of a "trap", which is landing on the carrier deck and hooking the wire extended across the carrier deck and to be pulled back after landing, is brutal on the underside of an aircraft. This is the reason the Naval aircraft are built to take it. Fragile birds like the U-2 could never handle it without some sort of refit. With the help of CIA's Office of Special Activities Deputy Director, James A. Cunningham Jr, a former Marine Corp aviator, Kelly Johnson started to refit the U-2 for just that sort of operation. The first test of the

U-2's ability for aircraft carrier operation took place in August 1963 on the deck of the USS Kitty Hawk which operated in the Pacific Ocean off San Diego, California.

A U-2C, which had been loaded aboard the carrier in North Island Naval Base, took off from the flight deck with a full load of fuel and was airborne within 321 feet. No assistance from the catapult was needed. Although the takeoff was very successful, the attempted landing was not. The aircraft bounced, hit hard on one wing tip and then just barely managed to become airborne again, before reaching the end of the deck. It didn't take Kelly Johnson long to realize that the airframe would have to be altered in order to make carrier landings a reality. These alterations involved strengthening the landing gear, installing an arresting hook at the rear of the fuselage and fitting spoilers on the wing that would cancel the aerodynamic forces that were left once the aircraft was over the flight deck. These modifications were designated the U-2G. While several aircraft underwent these modifications at Area 51, the pilots started training with landing on the aircraft carrier. The first successful carrier landing took place March 2, 1964. There was never a CIA, U-2 mission from an aircraft carrier. Although the idea of using a floating airbase to avoid political wrangling proved feasible, the cost of it did not. Aircraft carriers are costly to operate and require an entire flotilla of vessels to support them and protect them. The movement of large numbers of big ships is a difficult process to hide and can't be quickly accomplished, while deployment of a single U-2 to a remote airfield can take place literally overnight.

The U-2 Changes . . . yet Again

The number of viable U-2s in the CIA inventory had dropped from six to two. There were three at Lockheed that were in for repair. The CIA order for twenty U-2s in 1954-55 with the thirty one that the USAF had ordered made a tidy sum of fifty one U-2s. The Skunk Works of Lockheed and the inimitable Kelly Johnson put together four extra aircraft from spare parts and usable sections of aircraft that crashed. The total number of aircraft that the CIA actually managed to get was twenty-four.

As the U-2s changed and reformed itself into various different configurations, there was something else going on at its creator, Lockheed. Kelly Johnson was working on the U-2 successor. Not only would she have altitude, but she would have speed and stealth. This aircraft was something that no one had seen ever before. She was a nightmare to build and an archangel to fly. She was known as the A-12 Blackbird, also known as OXCART or Cygnus. If she was known for anything, it was the Mach 3 speed she could attain and sustain at heights never before known. Johnson had worked a miracle yet again at the Skunk Works and it would take some forty years before anyone really knew or understood exactly what magic Johnson had created.

Even before the loss of the U-2 on May 1, 1960, there was a program in the pipeline. It was a dark pipeline and only the CIA knew about it. The program called GUSTO would determine the successor of the U-2. On November 5, 1954, Edwin Land, (of Polaroid and optics fame) was chairman of the *"Project 3 Panel"*. This was also known as the *"Technological Capabilities Panel"*. Edwin Land wrote to CIA director Allan Dulles and suggested reconnaissance flights over the Soviet Union and also asked that the USAF begin to work on this concept also. Land's proposal brought up the point of *"a unique opportunity for comprehensive intelligence"* and brought the risk of provocation of war that any overflight could produce.

On August 5, 1955, a memo was put out by the *"Technological Capabilities Panel"*. It was called *"Organizational Risk and Delineation of Responsibilities"*. This was a directive for project control to both the CIA Director and the Chief of Staff of the USAF. The CIA went about picking project directors while the USAF picked deputy project directors. The holding of direct responsibility for the "project" attitude throughout would be subject to a higher command authority. Colonel Russell Berg headed the strategic role as he was the Chief of Staff for the USAF and Strategic Air Command or SAC. He would be in charge of support for any operations the CIA instituted. The plan was to have the project operate so that *"it would be a clandestine intelligence gathering operation, to be conducted in such a way as to minimize the risk of detection"*. It became known much later that the upper echelon of the USAF command was not truly interested in the subject of reconnaissance. The USAF had considered the RAND Corporation, which the USAF used to help them figure the best solutions to different problems. RAND looked at a different form of aerial reconnaissance. The USAF wasn't completely assured that real time reconnaissance was all that necessary as the CIA did. It really was a matter of both time and speed.

RAND decided to explore the concept of the "electro-optical" satellite. This concept used a television camera to send radio images down from the satellites. The concept on paper was good, but there was a hitch, the ground resolution was 144 ft., hardly acceptable for a good image. With a ground resolution of 144ft., you would not be able to pick out details like aircraft on the ground or discern bridges and trucks. RAND[54] suggested to the USAF that the other contractors be invited in to develop a higher resolution television system for satellites. In the time frame, television was still evolving for just everyday TV viewing, it would be a

---

[54] Rand Corp was formed May 14, 1948 which was an organization to connect military planning with research and development decisions it was part of the Douglas Aircraft Co. and evolved into an independent, nonprofit organization that took its name from the Research and Development Contraction R and D.

tough order to come up with an image that would be acceptable beaming down from a satellite in orbit. It was a huge waste of time and money, but the USAF went ahead with the plan anyway, soon to find out the technology just wasn't ready yet.

In March 1958, RAND came up with a new method of collecting aerial intelligence. This method had to do with using standard photos from satellites and then dropping the film in canisters from orbit to be collected via parachute. This plan was developed by a RAND physicist Richard C. Raymond. Raymond wrote a twenty page report titled: *"Photographic Reconnaissance Satellites"*. However, as the report was sent around and read, the USAF pulled the idea that "near time" TV solutions was the way to go, even though the quality was less than acceptable. The USAF dropped the idea of the capsule recovery containing regular film and felt it was archaic. It proved out the USAF was all wrong and would later return to this method.

While CIA and USAF were never on the best of terms, the CIA felt it should control the missions and the aircraft while the USAF felt that they should be doing it. The jealousy and infighting between the two services would be the lynch pin between then the conflict between the CIA and USAF, even much later would be responsible for the loss of one of the most sophisticated aerial reconnaissance systems the world had ever seen.

While the CIA and the USAF were still working on hating one another, there was another program in the works, the RB-57D Canberra program. These modifications were already in the works and it was positive that this program would help the USAF intelligence need in Europe.

The Lockheed tailless G2A GUSTO model part of the package that Johnson showed the USAF (Lockheed)

Chapter Thirteen

Vietnam, the Blackbirds—the Answer to Overhead Reconnaissance—Stealth Speed and Altitude

The U-2 and the CORONA satellite program were successes, regardless of the loss of the U-2 lost over Soviet Russia. That was part of the business of overhead reconnaissance and had been for some time. The word "calculated risk" could not have been more correct when applied to any overhead reconnaissance project, be it U-2, RB-50, RB-29, or the new kid on the block, the A-12. The Cold War was in a very precarious stage, it was dangerous as always and with the loss of the U-2, it was obvious that the successor would need to arrive on the scene very soon.

Kelly Johnson, of Lockheed, had been called on once again by Richard Bissell and the CIA, for his expertise on how to get this job done. Bissell, then special assistant to the DCI for special projects decided to appoint a panel of the finest minds of the time and start the process for creating the fastest aircraft the world had seen, or not seen in this case. It has already been mentioned that the CIA and the USAF had no great love for each other and this would really drive the wedge between them, regardless of the fact that both would have to work together. With the name *OXCART*, the A-12 would have been thought to have been some slow, ponderous aircraft with not much to offer. That was dead wrong, the A-12 was before her time, she would be relevant in the 21st century aviation world, while being produced in the mid part of the 20th century. Created from an exotic metal that could not even be produced here in the United States in sufficient quantity to build the aircraft, Johnson and the CIA, in their best spy fashion, went to their adversaries, the Soviet Union to obtain the high quality titanium needed to produce the A-12 airframe.

The Cold War Starts to Warm Up

Both the CIA and the USAF had to reinvent themselves when it came to the art of collecting intelligence in the early 1950s. Technology had finally started to catch up and with all the extra research done during the second World War, much of that along with the many German scientists brought over to the United States and the Soviet Union after the war, suffice to say aerial reconnaissance was now open for business.

The USAF left WWII as a new service that was autonomous and no longer part of the Army. Yet, the new USAF was not willing to give up its "turf" of being in charge of aerial reconnaissance for the United States. The CIA was also a brand new service and they also were trying out their "wings" and trying to find their place in aerial reconnaissance also. Of course, by the late 1950s the CIA was clearly in the lead and already encroaching on the sacred sky that for so long belonged to the USAF. The CIA had come up with the U-2 Dragon Lady, a magnificent creation from Kelly Johnson of the Lockheed Skunk Works. Even though she was compromised with the May Day affair, the U-2 was still a viable reconnaissance asset to the CIA. The USAF was still working with recycled aircraft from WWII like the RB-29, RB-47 and the RB-57D Canberra along with some others. While these were sufficient early on, as the Cold War started to heat up, the Soviets were not tolerating anything in their airspace. They were hungry for anything that was flying their way and loved nothing more than to take down an RB-47 with a Soviet MiG 17 Fresco. Altitude and speed were becoming critical issues when it came to aerial reconnaissance. The days of recycling aircraft and hoping to continue with "Ferret" missions was just becoming too costly in lives and hardware. This is where the CIA made the difference.

The RCS model being constructed of the
A-12 for testing on the RCS pole at Area51
(Lockheed)

The Blackbirds.

It was obvious that the year to year budgets for the USAF were showing that the USAF was already overstuffing their Congressional budgets to meet the inflated needs of both the "missile gap" and the "bomber gap", both of which proved out to be a fish story to increase the USAF's wallet and ego . However, the new founded jealousy between the USAF and the CIA would get worse with the coming years. The CIA was proving they could do the job with both the U-2 and the CORONA Satellites, while the USAF was busy trying to find something that they could call their own.

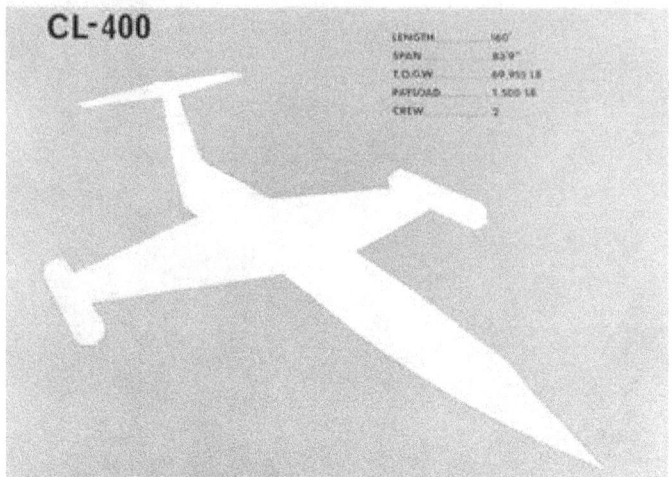
The CL-400—the start of the A-12's concept
(Lockheed)

SUNTAN and GUSTO . . .

Both Kelly Johnson and Lockheed were working on a project for the USAF called *SUNTAN*. *SUNTAN* or the CL-400 as it was named and developed by Johnson was to be a high altitude, high speed, hydrogen fed aircraft. *SUNTAN* ran into a multitude of issues with the main problem being the hydrogen itself. Johnson, who already had the feeling this was not the way to go, had named the aircraft the "flying vacuum bottle" as in the old picnic basket thermos bottles. The aircraft had severe weight and fuel issues. The plan was for two prototypes and one static test aircraft that would use the Pratt and Whitney 304 engine. The aircraft carried two engines weighing 6,270 lbs. and provided 9,450 lbs. of thrust at sea level. Johnson was looking for 5940 lbs. of thrust at 100,000 ft. altitude using conventional intakes, a very dicey deal. The CL-400 for the first time actually did define the characteristics of the Mach 3 aircraft. The CL-400 planform used the long, sleek missile type fuselage/nose of the F-104 Starfighter, with a deeply swept wing. Here was the gleam in the father's (Johnson's) eye, this was the start of the A-12 Blackbird. However, Kelly

Johnson knew he had a loser with the CL-400 and actually told the USAF just that. The only good thing that came out of this project was the 304 engine went on to power the Centaur rocket and the CL-400 did give Johnson the impetus for the A-12 Blackbird. In an April 21,1958 diary entry, the word *ARCHANGEL* was first used in Kelly's log; *"I drew up the first Archangel proposal for a Mach 3 cruise airplane having a 4,000 nautical mile range at 90,000 to 95,000 ft"*

Three months later, in another diary entry, Johnson continued with," *I presented this airplane along with GUSTO Model G2A to the program office. It was well received. The Navy mentioned a study they had been asking on the slower, high altitude airplane, on which the program office wanted my comments.*

The next meeting with the "Land Commission "on August 14, 1958 in which Kelly Johnson presented the commission with a layout of the Navy plan. The Navy really did propose to use a very unique inflatable airplane. It would be ramjet powered with a cruise altitude of 150,000 ft. The airplane would be carried by balloon to the prescribed altitude. Johnson did some quick calculations and found that the balloon would be a mile in diameter, hardly a workable solution.

By August 25, 1958, Johnson and the Skunk Works were still working on the **Archangel**, Johnson wrote in his diary; *"Have contacted Marquardt and Pratt and Whitney and gotten some ram jet data. Have reconfigured the Archangel to include wing tip ramjets as per our proposal on the F-104 to the Air Force in 1954. This appears to give us an airplane, which would cruise at Mach 3.2 at 95,000 to 110,000 feet for the full distance. As of today, it looks like the rubber blimp would have a radius of operation of 52 miles "*. The Lockheed crew and Johnson spent the next eight days from September 17 through the 24th, burning up the drawing boards working on this proposal. Another entry into Johnson's diary: *"Spent considerable time in Washington and ended up in*

Boston September 22, and 23rd to review Archangel Project. I presented a report on evaluation of Navy inflatable airplane design and also a revised version of the Archangel design for higher altitude performance, for our particular mission. Convair proposed a Super Hustler which apparently was a Mach 4 ramjet, piloted turbojet, assisted on landing, to be launched from a B-58 to do the mission." Johnson, as always true to form had already analyzed the whole scenario and continued in his diary:*" I presented GUSTO 2A which was well received and* **Archangel II**. *This airplane was 135,000 pound gross weight. Powered by two J-58 turbojets and two 75 inch ramjets, it could do a 100,000 foot mission and a 4,000 mile range. This airplane was not accepted because of its dependence on perta-borane for the ramjet and the over all cost of the system. We left Cambridge (Massachusetts) rather discouraged with everything".* However, on the way back from Boston, Johnson had already planned that he would attempt to break one of the ground rules that was part of the competition. Johnson wanted to use the engines "in being" which meant that he wanted the use the Pratt and Whitney J-58s. This was the same Pratt and Whitney engines the company was have a tough time trying to tame. One of the reasons the *Archangel II* was so big, was the fact that the weight of these engines installed was 15,000 to 18,000 lbs. Johnson had already scaled them down and *Archangel II* was also down to 17,000 from 20,000 pounds gross weight, using the JT12A turbojet engines. He felt it was a good solution.

While the development went on between CIA, Johnson and the Skunk Works, Richard Bissell went ahead with his plan. August 13, 1958 had Bissell sent the first of many top secret memos to his boss, CIA director Allan Dulles. In these memos he named: *CHALICE*—(which was *AQUATONE* renamed); *RAINBOW* (which was the U-2 Radar project: *GUSTO* (the soon to be A-12) *KINGFISH* (competition-Convair Proposal against A-12) *CORONA* (new reconnaissance satellite program)

This would be the new CIA line up for all of its effective reconnaissance tools.

The parasite KINGFISH mounted on the
B-58 Hustler on this wind tunnel model (Convair)

KINGFISH vs. ARCHANGEL.

Johnson and the Skunk Works were hard at work with the *Archangel*, while over at General Dynamics, Convair division, they were busy with the *KINGFISH*. The differences in the planforms were radical, one was a parasite, that was the *KINGFISH* and the other was so very unique, no one had ever seen anything like her, the *Archangel*. The dollar amount for the competition contract was $4.5 million. This covered the dates from September 1, 1959 to January 1, 1960. In September of 1959, the CIA gave Johnson permission to start on the anti-radar structural tests along with other functional modifications. The aircraft went through many different versions from the *Archangel II* through and on up to the *A-11A*. Johnson's team started with plans to build a full-scale mock up of the *A-11* to hang on the RCS pole for radar testing. EG&G (Edgerton, Germeshausen and Grier) would run the radar cross section testing for radar reflection. Johnson was not pleased with the original site chosen for the pylon to hold the mockups. It was too close and viewable from a local highway. The site was moved to Area 51 which was behind the atomic testing grounds and adjacent to Groom Lake, in Nevada. There was a larger pylon built at Area 51 to allow the A-11 model to be hauled up there. It was brought up from the Lockheed Burbank plant in a specially designed trailer.

The mockup would verify that the A-11's planform would have a good RCS signature, meaning a small one. Later on fuel additive and composite parts would be added some eighteen months later. Johnson was still not happy with the numbers he was getting from the radar testing. It was here that Johnson said those famous words, *". . . aircraft that looked like a snake that had swallowed three mice."*. The theory of the chines and the curved airframe used to deflect radar was verified and the new planform showed that radar could not catch on to the rounded edges of the chines. It was also the first time the word "Stealth" was used to describe an aircraft.

Line drawing of the A-11A. Note the lack of the nacelles.
That would soon change (Lockheed

A-11 and Almost There . . .

The testing was ongoing at Lockheed and moving fast. Johnson had come up with the latest version of the A-11 with a smaller wing and tail than the previous design. Along with all the theoretical ideas, Johnson had decided that he wanted yet another change. The North American XB-70 Valkyrie was being built the same time as the A-12 was being created. The XB-70 was also a Mach 3 aircraft that was to be a bomber and the replacement for the B-52 Stratofortress. The difference here was while Johnson's aircraft was totally unknown by the public, the XB-70 was on the cover of LIFE magazine. She was incredibly unique and was facing many of the same Mach 3 issues that Johnson was facing. The XB-70 also had a unique feature. Her engines were laid out side by side at her tail. This was known as the "6 pack". Her General Electric YJ-93A engines were made exclusively for the XB-70 and were powerhouses. Since Pratt and Whitney was still having a lot of production issues with their J-58 engine, the YJ-93 was starting to look good the Johnson. The YJ-93 was still not totally what Johnson needed, but it might be a suitable replacement till they were ready. There were two versions of the YJ-93; the -5 version used JP-150 fuel in the primary stage of the engine and HEF (high energy fuel) in the afterburner. The second was the -3 engine, which used all JP-150. The XB-70 as we know was using JP-6 fuel a highly volatile fuel with a high flash point, while the J-58 by Pratt and Whitney, used the JP-7 low flash point fuel and needed the TEB (Tri-ethylborane) as a starter. Because of the low flash point of the TEB it basically combusted when exposed to air. Johnson still ran into a wall however, the General Electric engines would not be ready until September 1961, which was almost two years later than the first A-12 flight.

Johnson was still fighting a number of other issues with the A-11. He had added the "chines" rounded edges to the airframe and the engine housings, leading edges and trailing edges of the wings. With this addition, the RCS issue was finally resolved. Another of the problems had to do with the titanium used to build the aircraft. The finished A-12 would be 93% titanium. It was not an easy metal to deal with. Many of the issues had to do with how to manipulate the titanium into the curved airframe. Johnson solved the problem by using "fillets" in triangular shapes. These triangular shapes were epoxy glued onto the airframe. The upcoming A-12 would have electrically resistant, honeycomb plastic composite with a fiberglass surface that would resist the high heat temperatures during flight. It would also reflect radar instead of absorbing it.

As the problems of the A-11 got solved, Johnson got closer to the finished version of the A-11. She would be the A-12 OXCART.

OXCART

On January 26, 1960, Richard Bissell approved the many changes that Johnson had made to the A-11 and authorized the building of the aircraft. It was the twelfth version of the aircraft, hence the name A-12. The original quote of $96.6 million for the twelve aircraft would cover about one third of a F-22 Raptor of today. Yet this would be the most phenomenal aircraft ever created. The CIA realized then that the building of this aircraft with the exotic titanium and composite parts would be in cost overruns for sure. A clause was placed in the contract to cover this. Project GUSTO had just turned to Project OXCART and she was the final product. Never had anything so fast been named for something so horribly slow! Johnson had proven his theory and now on to building the new aircraft. It was realized that there would have to be a place to test this new wonder. You certainly could not do it a Burbank airport. Johnson and Bissell along with Colonel Ozzie Ritland of the USAF, went to look for a place to roost this new bird.

Area 51 ... the Place That Doesn't Exist

The Atomic Energy Commission was responsible for all the nuclear testing of the various hydrogen and atomic bombs that went on in the Nevada desert and various other places, like the Bikini Atoll in the Marshall Islands. The particular area in question in the Nevada desert was contaminated by radio activity after the many test blasts that occurred there. It was also adjacent to Groom lake which was the secret home of the U-2. Well, there was going to be new neighbor in Nevada's Lincoln county. The enigma of Area 51 actually began much earlier, even as far back as the "Manhattan Project" that created the first atomic bombs that were used to finish the Japanese part of WWII. The area was chosen with great care and great security surrounded it. Compartmentalization was the technique that was used to ensure that there would be no leaking of information or product out of that area. This was done to maintain secrecy at highest levels possible and also allowed the project to support itself independently away from the constant annoyance of Congressional committees and nosey bureaucrats. Since WWII, the CIA and the military did work feverishly to protect the locations of their secret projects. It did cost tons of taxpayer dollars, but as always, the taxpayers along with the members of Congress did not know and what they didn't know couldn't hurt them, in fact it was to protect the security of the nation.

The Dragon Lady, also known as the U-2, took up residence in Groom lake at the start of her operations. The A-12 was now ready to be tested and needed to find a safe, secure place to do that. It was a logical step although not the one that Kelly Johnson initially wanted. Early in 1955, Richard Bissell of CIA , Johnson, his senior test pilot for Lockheed, Tony LeVier, Dorsey Kamerer, Skunk Works foreman and Colonel Ozzie Ritland, liaison of the USAF, all intrinsically tied to the OXCART project took a Lockheed Beechcraft airplane and flew looking for a place to hide their new creation. After looking at deserted air bases, other parts of the California, Arizona and Nevada desert, they came upon the place that they would call home. It took looking at some fifty different areas that finally brought them to the perfect place for the A-12. It was Colonel Ritland who remembered a very remote lakebed that he himself had flown over many times while he was working on the nuclear test program for the USAF. It was called actually adjacent to the U-2's home at Groom Lake and right behind the nuclear atomic testing grounds. Ah, what a place! It would keep many prying eyes thinking twice before even going near the desolate place that would soon not exist on any geodetic survey map.

Off the team went to take a look at this desolated place. It was far from perfect for testing and Johnson made that known right away. It was too far away from the Burbank plant, where the aircraft was being built and literally adjacent to the AEC nuclear test site. It also lacked any type of the amenities, there was nothing but a bunch of rocks, lizards and dried up brush. It was loaded with tons of old armament gunnery shells from the testing the Army did there. All of that had to be cleaned up before anyone could move in. After many disagreements, Johnson finally gave in and accepted the site. There was one good thing if you could call it that, no one in their right mind would be stalking around trying it find out what was going on there in that radiation infested wasteland. There were days during the program, according to Frank Murray, A-12 pilot and historian/archivist for the Roadrunners Internationale Association (the workers ,pilots officers of the OXCART/U-2 programs) that work would be curtailed at the A-12 side of the base because of the winds blowing radioactive dust up towards the A-12 hangers. One of the members of the OXCART officer team would go down to Command Post 1 which handled these nuclear shots, by special pass, and see what was happening so as to keep the OXCART team safe.

Eagle Eyes

With some $830,000 in "black" money construction was started at this site for the A-12. Bissell then thought of something more, he requested a presidential action to add "AREA 51" to the AEC list of properties. From this point on, Colonel Ritland wrote three more memos which went to the USAF, the AEC and the other training command that ran a gunnery range on the site. These memos were then endorsed by Trevor Gardner the AEC secretary for research and development which now ensured that this new area would not be tampered with by the AEC at any cost. In April of 1955, Johnson and the CIA sat down to discuss the new home for the A-12. There have been many nomenclatures put to this wasted bunch of desert and rocks; Johnson initially called it "Paradise Ranch" during the U-2 days, in a tongue in cheek manner, to entice some of the Lockheed workers to sign up and come out to this godforsaken place and also not to let them know what they would be working on. However, as things progressed, in May of 1955, the three-mile-long runways that would be needed for the A-12 were also marked out on the hard dry, clay surface of the ground. The "Silas Mason Company" which was a bogus set up, got the license for construction while Johnson and Lockheed hid the rest of the goings on behind the *CLJ Organization* which could receive the black money that could not be traced.

In July of 1955, the CIA, USAF and Lockheed employees started arriving at the newly opened basically bare base with only recycled Navy Quonset huts to greet them. On August 10, 1955 President Eisenhower signed Executive order 10633, formally nautical miles. In June 1958, another 38,400 acres were set side and withdrawn from public access under the Public Land Order 1662. This rectangular parcel of land next to the Nevada test site would become the place that "officially did not exist" and was in the AEC map This was **AREA 51**.

Area 51 and the redevelopment of the site was called "PROJECT 51." From 1960 through 1964, new runways sufficient to manage the high speed A-12 were put into place, the old U-2 hangars were rebuilt to support the new bird. The airspace above the old dry lake bed was modified and became another restricted area known a R4084-N. Flight was prohibited below 60,000 ft. The FAA later joined in by adding more restricted airspace and creating the "no fly zone" over four hundred and forty square miles of the nearby Nellis Air Force Base range. The politics surrounding the OXCART program was busy unveiling itself to the many CIA people involved with the money/security end of the project.

The concrete runways that were the bone of contention at Area 51 being readied for the A-12 (Lockheed)

A-12 packed and on the road to Area 51 taking a "pit stop" on the two-day journey to Nevada from California. (Lockheed)

There were situations that came up during the initial reconstruction of the Area. In 1960, the construction workers that came to work at Area 51, had quarters that were your basic trailers, surplus at that. However, Nevada had some laws on construction sites that needed the names of all the personnel and companies working on a site. It said that anyone outside the state that resided in Nevada for more that forty-eight hours had to sign in with the state officials. Obviously, this was not good for the "black project" security maintained for OXCART, and could really compromise the entire project. However, the CIA's attorney general found a way to deal with it. It said that government employees were not liable under this law, giving all the contractors "appointments as government consultants, who received no payment for their services, and this solved the problem. This allowed for no reports to be written and if anything was questioned, they would fall back on the fact all the guys working were "government employees."

September of 1960 saw construction extremely intense on Area 51. It continued at a frantic pace with double shifts until the middle of 1964. One of the largest problems faced were the runways for the new bird. The A-12 needed a runway length of 8,500 ft. The existing tarmac runway left over from the U-2 was only 5,000ft. and could not support the weight of the A-12. There is an existing memo which showed just how tough something like this could be. On November 13, 1961, a memo written by James Cunningham, assistant chief of development projects division, stated; *"I would agree that if in the last analysis we must increase the length of the bloody thing that we should do it sooner than later, I believe that to do it now might well be premature."* Cunningham went on to say; *"At last in the testing of the J-75 version (engine), and presumably even during a portion of the testing on the qualified engine, reduced vehicle loads will compensate for the increase in design weight."* Cunningham basically suggested that if the flights were made in the night hours with ambient temperatures within reason, it would solve a multitude of problems. To say it gently, Kelly Johnson really didn't' t think so. The war on the runway went on, with Cunningham stating that he was waiting for the Kelly Johnson "blast" regarding the suggestions made. To say the least, Kelly Johnson suffered no fools and he also had no patience for bureaucrats telling him how to build his airplane. Another issue had to do with fuel storage. 500,000 gallons of fuel were needed to support the new aircraft. Many things needed to be considered, that being pipelines, transport by trucks and airlift. Truck transport was an early solution, and it did help that eighteen miles of roadway was resurfaced to facilitate the arrival of the aircraft via truck and trailer.

By 1962, a new tank farm sprung up, which could hold 1,320,000 gallons of JP-7 fuel. There were fuel deposits set around the country and in Europe: California, Eielson AFB, Alaska, Thule Air Base Greenland, Kadena Air Base Okinawa and Adan in Turkey.

The new home of the A-12 Blackbird was almost ready and it was time to move the new bird to her home in the desert. By February of 1962, Johnson and the CIA, along with the USAF devised a plan to move the aircraft overland by truck and trailer to Area 51, out in the Nevada desert. The first of the A-12's, CIA article #121 or tail number 606924, arrived at Area 51 on February 28, 1962, after leaving Lockheed's Burbank plant on February 26, 1962, via a specially built trailer.

The A-12 and the trailer that she will travel in being prepared at the Lockheed plant in Burbank California and travel overland to Area 51 in Nevada (Lockheed)

Arrival and Test Flights

The arrival and start of the test flights for the A-12 OXCART began with a flush of activity. First, the aircraft had to be reassembled at the Area 51 site and readied for the runway. There was still building going on and of course, the usual chaos of a new program. The A-12 made her first" unofficial test flight" on April 25, 1962, with test pilot from Lockheed, Lou Schalk. Schalk took the first of the A-12s #121, on her first flight which was less than two miles at twenty to thirty feet altitude.

Lockheed OXCART test pilot Lou Schalk being congratulated after the first test first with the A-12 (Lockheed)

During that very short hop, Schalk had found that the control linkages were not correctly installed and needed to be repaired. The official maiden flight took place on April 22, 1962 with a small group of VIPs from the CIA, Air Force, and various others "in the know" officials in attendance. This flight lasted fifty-nine minutes with Lou Schalk once again at the yoke of the A-12. The A-12 took off from the Area 51 runway at 170 knots, climbed to 30,000 ft. and attained a top speed of 340 knots. The A-12 went supersonic for the first time on her second flight on May 2, 1962. The Archangel had been officially "delivered" and a stunner she was! Sadly, on November 22, 1963, the national nightmare of the assassination of President John F. Kennedy took place in Dallas, Texas. Out in the Nevada desert, the A-12 had met her speed goals reaching Mach 32.2 at 78,000 feet. Kelly Johnson wrote in his diary; *"The time has come for the bird to leave the nest"* It had been a literal three years and seven months since the contract had been signed to put OXCART on the CIA books, clandestine as it was. JFK had become our lost president representing youth and vitality, yet the A-12 was here to protect the legacy and the country he loved. On February 3, 1964, the A-12 made its longest flight above Mach 3. She had hit Mach 3.2 at 83,000 ft., for ten minutes.

The rest of the A-12 fleet had started to arrive at Area 51. Four of the aircraft had arrived, one of them being the two-seat trainer. Even though the aircraft had started to arrive, the J-58 Pratt and Whitney engines were still having problems getting up to speed. Many of the early test flights were done with the J-75 engines. As the J-58s began to show up, the two-seat trainer, flew with one J-75 and one J-58. The first of the A-12s to be equipped with two J-59s was flown on January 15, 1963. The rest of the performance test flights started in earnest in 1963 and by July 20, 1963, the A-12 had flown to Mach 3. Before this year was out, the nine A-12s that were now in inventory would make 573 flights for a total of 765 flight hours.

The A-12's Camera Systems

For all the altitude and speed, the A-12 would have been just a test aircraft if not for the superior camera systems she would carry. That concept brought with it many problems since you had to be able to get a good photo when traveling at Mach 3 and 85,000 ft. The creation of camera systems that could deliver that were just as urgent as the A-12 herself. There were several prominent people in both the optics and photography world that added their expertise to this problem. Dr. Edwin Land (Polaroid fame) had dedicated much of his working life and effort to the United States government in World War II. Land worked in the radiation labs of the Army and later was part of the Air Force's advisory panels. Land also served as head of the "Technological Capabilities Panel". This group investigated how the United States was comprising its intelligence gathering abilities. Edwin Land was one of the first professionals that encouraged the development of a high altitude reconnaissance aircraft, which later became the U-2. He would later go on to develop a polarizing filter and of course, the instant Polaroid camera all of us enjoyed in the 60s and 70s. A fellow scientist, Dr. James Baker, who was an astrophysicist from Harvard was interested in optics and contributed to this project. During WWII, he worked for the Army as an optical designer for the Army's newly formed aerial reconnaissance department along with Colonel George Goddard. After the War, Baker went on to advise the U. S Air Force Photographic Lab in their work. Both Edwin Land and James Baker were instrumental in convincing President Dwight D Eisenhower that the U-2 was an aircraft that was badly needed. Both Baker and Dr. James Killian,[55] worked together when it came to getting an idea that would later become the CORONA satellite project. There were others that were stepping up to help devise this new high speed camera system. Richard Perkin and Charles Elmer of the Perkin-Elmer Company also contributed many of their designs for improved cameras, periscopes, rangefinders and bombsights, along with other optical apparatus for the Army Air Force in WWII.

Both Perkin and Elmer were constantly redesigning and modernizing, and developing the art of developing high altitude reconnaissance cameras and lenses. Some of the A-12's cameras actually came from Richard Perkin love of astronomy and his building of a telescope and camera that could photograph celestial objects from altitudes above the earth's atmosphere. Perkin-Elmer were responsible for sending a telescopic instrument aloft in an unmanned balloon that was filled with helium and allowed to drift some fifteen miles high above Minnesota, in September

---

[55] Chairman of the President's Science Advisory Council and aide to President Eisenhower in helping Eisenhower improve the nation's defenses.

of 1957. The balloon eventually came down in Iowa, some two hundred thirty miles away, which brought back some of the most clear and distinct celestial photographs ever gotten.

The photos had no atmospheric encumbrance whatsoever, no dust, smog haze or clouds. Think of what that could mean to a reconnaissance photograph. The newspapers, of course, had the story on the front page *"Perkin-Elmer telescope takes Photos at an altitude of 81,500 ft!"* It would be part of the A-12's camera history as well.

The Perkin-Elmer Type 1 camera used in the A-12 (Lockheed)

The A-12 carried several different photographic systems:

Type I Camera-built by Perkin-Elmer used a f/4.0 18 inch lens and a 6.6 inch wide, 5,000 ft. supply of film. It could resolve 140 lines per millimeter and had a ground resolution of 12 inches. The film transport used a concentric supply and take up system to keep the weight of the film centralized, minimizing and shift in the A-12's CG (center of gravity), as the film was advanced upon exposure. A rotating cube mirror replaced a prism for the scanner. The TYPE I camera covered a ground swath of seventy-one miles wide and produced images with a thirty percent stereo overlap. A thermal barrier between the film and the lenses was used because of the high heat encountered in flight. The majority of lenses were made to compensate for high temperatures of 90 degrees Fahrenheit. The A-12 in flight temperatures could range from -60 degrees to +550 degrees Fahrenheit, making an isothermal window an absolute necessity. The TYPE I cameras was literally sealed to the glass and a pump was used to create a vacuum between the camera base and the glass.

The A-12 required a special "clean room" hangar for its film processing needs. The A-12 photo shop had doors that fit tightly around the aircraft so that all dust could be kept out while the film pallets were loaded and unloaded. Before entering the photo shop, the technicians were required to wear clean room overalls and go through a high velocity air wash. This procedure was also followed when the A-12 left Area 51 for duty in Kadena Air Base, in Okinawa. A new facility was built so film could be swapped out overnight. During the OXCART program, there were a total of five TYPE I cameras in inventory. By the time OXCART was phased down, two for the TYPE I cameras "A" series were placed in storage.

The Eastman Kodak type II Camera used in the A-12 (Lockheed)

TYPE II CAMERA: out and given to the Eastman Kodak Company, in hopes of development of a less complex system. The Eastman Kodak TYPE II camera had two separate panoramic cameras that had convergent, overlapping stereo coverage, which was an advantage in photographing areas that were partially obscured by cloud cover. Using a refractor lens and two rolls of the SO-132 film, the camera was simple in style and in maintenance. However, the ground resolution was nowhere as good as the TYPE I camera. The TYPE II camera used a 21 inch lens and a 8,400 ft, 8 inch wide film supply.

This produced photographic pairs covering a sixty-mile-wide ground swath, with a stereo overlap of about thirty percent. It could resolve 105 lines per millimeter and had a ground resolution of 17 inches. While the TYPE II camera was designed to run at very high temperatures, it hs too many operational issues to deal with. The TYPE II was given a marginal focal length lens for higher resolution and better stereo coverage. It didn't help the problem one bit. Another camera would have to be developed.

TYPE III: The HYCON B camera was a modified version of the one that the U-2 used. This was a 36 inch focal length camera, developed because the first two versions were not giving the type of ground resolution needed. The problem with this camera was that is was not made for high speed flight the A-12 was made for. The problem was not solely the designers. They were never given the correct design requirements because the A-12 was top secret, so in essence they designed a camera for the XB-70 instead of the A-12. HYCON Corp. never really knew who or what they were designing for.

TYPE IV: The TYPE IV Baker designed camera was known as the "Hammer". This was an advanced version of the Hycon B camera. This one used a 48inch f/5.6 lens and a 12,000 ft and a 9.5inch wide film, for extremely high resolution spotting. It could resolve 100 lines per millimeter and produced a ground resolution of eight inches. It covered a forty-one-mile ground swath, with half of that in stereo overlap. This camera was difficult for photo analysts, as they had to rotate two huge 6,000 ft long rolls of film in opposite directions. The photo analysts had learned to do this because of the extensive experience with the Hycon B camera. Inside the camera, the images rotated as oblique angle increased. This camera was the one that was deployed when the OXCART moved operations to Okinawa and Kadena Air Base. It was also the last camera the A-12 would see, it was with the program when it was canceled. The TYPE IV camera did not require special conditions of extreme cleanliness for processing, which made it much more suitable for operational work and advance deployment.

There was no long axis camera ever developed for the A-12, as their size caused too many installation problems. The aerial film used for these cameras was the Kodak Type 3414, with an ASA speed of 6. That very slow film speed was needed to achieve the high resolution needed for reconnaissance work. With film in general, the slower the speed, the greater the resolution. Because of the slow film speed and the high speed attained by the aircraft, image stabilizers were built into each camera head.

The OXCART Inventory

The Hycon Corp was also responsible for the more compact camera that the D-21 drone carried. We will discuss the D-21 shortly. There were three of the TYPE IV cameras, two of which had been test flown and were operational. The third was scheduled for test flight validation around January 1968. In the first summation which included test flights at Mach 3 and 80,000 ft. and 22 operational missions since the beginning of the OXCART program. As of December 31, 1967, the test flight times at Mach 3 and 80,000 ft were;

TYPE IA: 980 minutes
TYPE1C: 5, 667 minutes
TYPE IV: 1,903 minutes.

Total flight times for the cameras were:
TYPE IA 98 FLIGHTS   75 HOURS   6 FAILURES
TYPE1C 64 FLIGHTS   119 HOURS   9 FAILURES
TYPE IV 67 FLIGHTS   37 HOURS   11 FAILURES

In a February 19, 1964 CIA report, the TYPE1A and 1B camera systems were being used for flight test and were showing gradual improvement. The improvement was due to retrofits that had been brought in later in the A-12's program. The TYPE 1C camera was delivered to Area 51, on February 15, 1964. Two of the TYPE II camera systems were also in flight test having shown that they could handle the design goals within speed and altitude limits that were being flown, yet proof of the camera's utility at higher speed and altitude had to wait until the *PROJECT SKYLARK* program came into plan. The *SCOPE CROWN E* package was developed for an evaluation route. The test resolution targets were in Phoenix, Arizona and Area51.

These covered the route and also had an overwater air refueling area 450 nautical miles off the California coast. That route was flown June 1967. Later on, in the A-12'shistory, with the start of *BLACK SHIELD*, the TYPE 1camera was used for all twenty-two missions in the *BLACK SHIELD* mission, all results bordering on good to excellent.

There was one important limitation to the camera's quality. That was the quartz window through which the camera was aimed. This window had to manufactured so that there were no uneven temperatures throughout, and it needed to be tolerant of the high Mach temperatures generated by the A-12. It took close to three years and about $2 million to find an effective method of making the glass window. The glass was used on the TYPE IV camera and sourced from West Germany, after many failed attempts to make the glass of adequate quality in the USA. This glass was fused to its metal frame by a process that used high frequency sound waves.

With all the high tech cameras, the A-12 produced some of the finest aircraft reconnaissance photos ever taken. It could cover three times more area that the later SR-71. The A-12 also performed marginally better, flying 2,000 to 3,000 ft higher and with a speed that approached Mach 3.3 compared the SR-71's Mach 3.1.

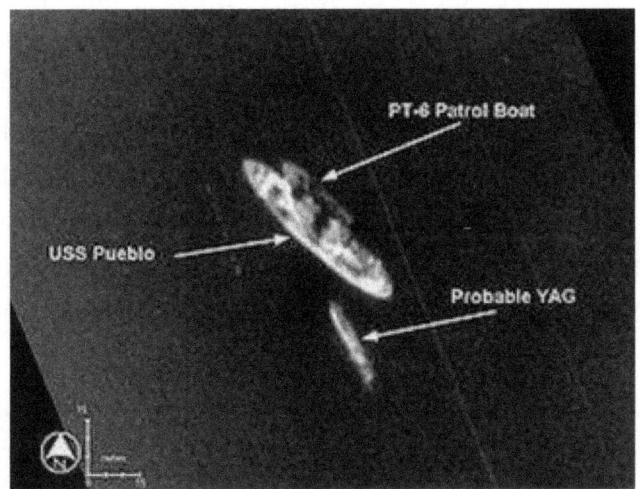

Photo taken from the A-12 on Black Shield Mission #BX6847, the USS PUEBLO in Wonson Harbor after capture by North Koreans. (Global I)

The A-12 and the Black Shield Missions

Before the A-12 began her career for real in Southeast Asia, there were two programs that the A-12 underwent: the *SKYLARK* program and *SILVER JAVELIN*. The *SKYLARK* program brought huge changes to the aircraft itself, with many of the upgrades modifying the aircraft for the installation of additional ECM gear and the strengthening of the fuselage, due to the extra gear which would cause a bending moment. There was also the inclusion of being able to sustain a three aerial refueling missions, adding the ARC -50[56] to the nose of the A-12.

SKYLARK also allowed TACAN (tactical air navigation) for system wide operational suitability. Much of this took place in 1965. SILVER JAVELIN on January 25, 1965, A-12 CIA Article #129, completed the

---

[56] The ARC-50 radio used standard UHF frequencies that allowed for secure communications between the tankers which were the KC-135 tanker and the A-12

first of a series of long range, high speed flights. The flights were allowing for longer sustained flight times. It also allowed for the installation of new air inlet ducts seals to improve the inlet efficiency and strengthen the rudder. The ARC-50 radio used standard UHF frequencies that allowed for secure communications between the KC-135 tankers, and the A-12. It also supported linkage, and rescheduling the fuel management system to keep the aircraft balanced and reduce drag. Another item that was tried out and would have been added, had the program not been canceled was *KEMPSTER*. *KEMPSTER* used an electron gun that could be added to the front of the aircraft and project an ion cloud ahead of the aircraft that would reduce its radar cross section. *EMERALD* was another part of this ECM program, using the same principal but was not successful. While KEMPSTER was thought to be the best of the lot, it was only tested on the #122[57] aircraft, which would have been the "production" aircraft had the program not been canceled. Given all the new bells and whistles installed due to *SKYLARK* and SILVER JAVELIN, these really improved the A-12. She was now ready to see operational action.

By 1965 the United States started to move troops to Southeast Asia and South Vietnam. President John F. Kennedy had already committed four hundred troops and one hundred military advisors to South Vietnam on May 11, 1961. That very same day, he also ordered the beginning of a secret war against North Vietnam. The South Vietnamese were supposed to head this operation to infiltrate Laos and do anything they could to

---

[57] The author while working on the restoration of this aircraft on the Intrepid Sea Air Space Museum, actually found those holes in the forward chines as they were being replaced. At that time in the 1990s we had no idea what this was as there was no CIA material available on what we were looking at, let alone the airframe itself. The beam would have been sent from the side of the chine which would have allowed ionized air to reach the inlet and be ingested by the engine. However, the system was taxing on the aircraft because of its energy requirements.

upset the local communist forces that had taken hold there, by destroying their lines of supply and their bases. The outgoing President Eisenhower had already warned Kennedy that he would have to commit some forces to South East Asia, if they were going to keep it from turning communist. By 1965, things had already started to heat up all over Southeast Asia.

OPERATION BLACKSHIELD

The A-12 was finally going to see some action and that action would be unbeknownst to many in the military and in the political arena. *PROJECT SKYLARK* and *SILVER JAVELIN* had given the A-12 a lot more in the line of clout and pulling off the mission that was assigned to her. June of 1965 found the United States paying a lot more attention what was going on in China, due to the fact of their increased defensive abilities. The Chinese were working hard at it. The CIA felt the time was right to release the U-2 mission, and the use of the Ryan FIREBEE drones that were being used for intelligence gathering. On June 11, 1965, the CIA director William Raborn sent a letter to Secretary of Defense Cyrus Vance to look at the plans for moving the A-12 out to Okinawa's Kadena Air Base. Kadena was often used for clandestine type missions or critical ones. Of course, that move was going to take money. With the provision of a much earlier CIA/USAF agreement on OXCART which was dated February 18, 1961, along with the National Reconnaissance Office (NRO) the arrangements for the funding and the planning of the move was already on the books, albeit, black books.

With troops now arriving in South Vietnam, Defense Secretary Robert McNamara wanted to know if it was feasible to move the A-12 in place of the U-2 which was becoming increasingly more vulnerable to SAM missiles which abounded in South Vietnam. The CIA director, William Raborn, new to his office said the A-12 could operate in the area as soon as she was past her final operational readiness test. That took no time at all to accomplish.

U.S. Navy BQM Firebee Drone (U.S. Navy)

In late November 1965, the Defense Department officially asked the *"303 Committee"* which had been created by the National Security Council (NSC) to take over the covert operations, and make up a proposal for deploying the A-12 to Southeast Asia. The proposal was turned down, due to the committee's objections starting from a concern that the Japanese might find out about it and object which was not something that the U.S. wanted at the time. However, on August 12, 1966 President Lyndon Johnson decided to uphold the *303 Committee* decision. The CIA stepped in and put up their proposal that the A-12 should overfly Cuba in a test flight. Again, the *303 Committee* decided against it, feeling it might upset a very, very fragile peace in the area. It was finally decided that the A-12 would be used to find SAM sites that had gone undetected in North Vietnam.

Operation CAROUSEL

On May 11, 1967, the first airlift for the crews of Black Shield were starting out for Kadena Air Base. On May 22, 1967, the first of the A-

12s, CIA Article #131 flew nonstop to Kadena in six hours and six minutes. By May 24th, the second A-12 #127 left her home at Area 51 and flew out to Kadena in five hours and fifty-five minutes. Those were fairly heady records already. On May 26th, the third aircraft #129 left the Area 51 desert in Nevada and was in a normal flight till she developed problems with her inertial navigation and communication systems that forced the flight down on Wake island in the North Pacific Ocean. A pre-positioned emergency response team secured the aircraft without any issues and when repaired, the aircraft and pilot flew on to Kadena the next day. There were many clandestine arrangements ambassadors to the Philippines, Formosa, Thailand and South Vietnam along with Japan and the high commissioner of Okinawa. Both the prime ministers of Japan and Thailand were told of the move, as was the defense minister of China, and chief of the Thailand air force. All parties were in agreement. There is a small story about the A-12's landing in Okinawa. All involved thought that it was a deep, dark, secret. Well, not really. Apparently, some very enterprising photographer got a photo of the first A-12 landing in what was supposed to be critical secrecy. However, the photo appeared on the front page of the Okinawa newspaper! So much for the secrecy of *BLACK SHIELD*. The whole island knew something was afoot. On May 29, 1967 the A-12 unit at Kadena Air Base was ready to go to work, under the command of Colonel Hugh" Slip" Slater, along with his two hundred sixty personnel. They were ready to make BLACK SHIELD happen. Thirteen days after leaving Area 51 in the Nevada desert, the newest aircraft in the aerial reconnaissance world was ready to show her stuff.

May 31, 1967, the first of the *BLACK SHIELD* missions was on the boards. The way these missions were set up was with a minimal of information. Two pilots were briefed and suited up. The A-12 pilots flew in pressure suits. The lead pilot's aircraft was the first up on the runway, while the second was prepped and waiting nearby. The second pilot waited in the suit up room, in case on the runway something happened to the first aircraft or the first aircraft could not make the first tanker refueling. It was only after the first pilot made that tanker refueling and was on his way to the first target, that the second pilot waiting in the room designated for suiting up, was allowed to disrobe and was released from the mission. The only time this didn't happen was with the North Korea mission. Only ONE pilot was briefed and only ONE pilot made the flight. There was no back up on the runway.

These Are Some of the Missions That Were Flown over North Vietnam

BX001—flown May 31, 1967 at Mach 3.1 and 80,000 ft. for 3:45 hours. This mission searched the Lao Cao area for SAM missile sites, along with Dien Bien Phu. Hanoi were four possible missiles and a guidance radar site. The Hai Phong SAM support site consisted of one drive through building, and two support buildings. No missile sites or missile related activities were found. Another Hanoi SAM site was found to SONG radar and at least two support vans in the near vicinity. This was the first of the *BLACK SHIELD* missions. The photographic images were considered to be good.

BX003—was flown June 1967, at Mach 3.1 at an altitude of 81,000 ft. for a 4:30 hour mission. This mission covered a total of 97 SAM sites. Of the 97 sites found 4 were status. Of the seven, major airfields that were covered, five provided an order of battle for the NVA. The large area of unidentified rail service activity was shown 8 photographic images were good.

BX6705—was flown June 20, 1967. The mission as flown at Mach 3.1 and 82,000ft. altitude, for 5:30 hours. The mission did produce a total of 133 SAM sites identifiable. Consider what this information would mean to the troops and all the pilots that were flying over South Vietnam. Of the seven major airfields that were photographed, four gave more Order of Battle information. The Viet-Tri railroad numerous bomb craters. At least twenty pieces of rolling seven in the rail yard, were overturned and derailed. The imagery was considered excellent.

BX-6706—Flown on June 30, 1967, at Mach 3.1 and 81,000ft. 5:00 hours. The mission produced imagery showing yet another 109 SAM SA-2 sites that were identified. Three were newly identified with occupation of one and 10 were for identification only. The photo take was considered good. There were twenty-nine operational missions flown in *BLACK SHIELD*, with three missions flown over North Korea. One mission in particular was a very special mission.

RF-4C Phantom taking off from Udon Air Base 11
Tactical Reconnaissance Wing (wikkipedia.org/USAF)

Vietnam…the War from hell

Some of the other aircraft that were used in Vietnam reconnaissance need to be mentioned. In 1968, there were five companies in Vietnam that used an aircraft called MOHAWK. There were three versions of the Mohawk produced, the OV-1A basic visual photographic aircraft, the OV-1B a visual photographic aircraft with side looking radar and the OV-1C which carried visual photographic aircraft with infrared cameras.

The most sophisticated part of the Mohawk would have been the side looking radar, which created a permanent film record of fixed and moving target from a single roll of 9-inch film that was auto processed. The processed film was put on a light table for immediate interpretation. The system could transmit "radar to photo to ground status 50 to 100 miles away."

The North American RA-5C Vigilante taking off from a carrier
USS CONSTELLATION (US Navy/FLIKR.Com)

There was an operation called RED HAZE which was an airborne scanning device that allowed the cockpit display to make a permanent film record of the ground using small differences in visual light emissions. Night photo missions used stroboscopic light flashes systems that took photos every three seconds.

The MOHAWK missions were highly classified. It was revealed that electronics sensor devices dropped by the aircraft and monitored by aircraft had been keeping track of NVA troops infiltrating the South. Sensing devices were part of "McNamara's Fence", an electronic barrier approved for construction one mile from DMZ to South Vietnam. Much of "fence" was airborne and involved the MOHAWK. The MOHAWK had a two-man crew, pilot and sensor operator who got signals from black boxes seeded in the ground. It was effective at Khe Sanh where 6,000 Marines and South Vietnam Rangers were besieged by 20,000 North Vietnamese troops. Using more than six hundred sensing devices, electronic acoustic pressure and others reports on almost 1800 enemy troop movements in the area, two thirds of the reports were used and accounted for bombing raids. One enemy den was hit so bad at Khe Sanh by U.S. aircraft, it was ordered back to regroup in Laos. The information was important to the military after the bombing halt in 1968 and the start of the Paris peace talks.

    Another aircraft used was the RA-5C Vigilante, built by North American Aviation. The Vigilante was the only Mach 2 aircraft that ever flew off the deck of an aircraft carrier. On December 3, 1968, a RA-5C Vigilante took off from the deck of the USS Ranger on a reconnaissance mission in North Vietnam. A SA-2 SAM missile was fired at the Vigilante and exploded nearby the aircraft, giving her fifteen holes in her fuselage. No one was hurt and she returned to the USS Ranger. This was during the halt in the fighting, and indicated the dangers faced by the U.S. Navy reconnaissance crews on their missions. They and their brothers in the Air Force faced the same foe.

The RB-66 Destroyer at Takhli Royal Thai Air Force Base
(Natl Museum of the USAF)

The OV-1A MOHAWK being prepped for flight in Vietnam
(USAF/ Pinterest.com)

The *Integrated Operational Intelligence System (IOIS)* a multi-sensor reconnaissance system and modifications of the RA-5C aircraft to carry it, along with development of associated carried based intelligence processing center known as *Integrated Operational Intelligence Center*

(IOIC) was a major modification for the Vigilante used in this new concept. The Vigilante used a "canoe" to carry its reconnaissance system, which was a AN/ASB12 Bomb/Navigation system with inertial reference platform and digital data system that imprinted a code matrix block giving location, time, altitude and other parameters for imaging forming sensors. The pilot and the reconnaissance navigator handled radar, which was an inertial television viewfinder. Almost all the reconnaissance missions flown over North Vietnam in Vigilantes were from Yankee Station at the 17th parallel, where the South China Sea joined the Gulf of Tonkin. The 7th Fleet Task Force 77 operated twenty-four hours a day, seven days a week from this point. RA-5C Vigilantes using the carrier decks had six hours preflight, before a mission and speed was, of course, its best defense.

The greatest threat to any reconnaissance aircraft was the SAM-SA-2 missile. The RA-5C flew off the aircraft carriers USS Enterprise, Kitty Hawk, America, Saratoga and the USS Forrestal.

The Integrated Operational Intelligence Center was responsible for four main functions:

a. photo processing
b. electronic data processing
c. storage and retrieval
d. multi-sensors interpretation.

All information was sent to Fleet Intelligence Center and various national agencies. The US Navy was vitally important to reconnaissance in South east Asia.

The RF-4C Phantom, built by McDonnell Douglas Aircraft Corp, is one of the best known aircraft in the world. The Phantom was comparable to the Vigilante as they carried the KS-72 panoramic cameras in a three camera fan: side, oblique and split vertical configuration. The Phantom had integrated sensor control and automatic in-flight film processing ejection and camera station. The in-flight processing allowed for film to be jettisoned in a canister during flight with all frames marked. The rear cockpit of the RF-4C was filled with many of the up to date sensors that were operated by the navigator in the tandem two seat aircraft.

The 432nd Tactical Reconnaissance Wing and the 460th Tactical Reconnaissance Wing flew the RF-4Cs on a twenty-four-hour, seven day a week basis. During the initial three-year period in which the USAF conducted air operations over North Vietnam, reconnaissance units had a much higher loss percentage than the fighter bombers. Loss rates for the Voodoos became so high that the RF-101s were withdrawn completely from parts and sectors of the North Vietnam flight plan. By 1968, the introduction of new equipment aided in shocking the enemy radar and directed guns on the ground into misses galore. The odds did improve for the USAF flights and six out of seven reconnaissance crews could survive to a one hundred mission tour. That was a record, indeed!

During the daylight hours, the RF-4Cs operated in pairs while at night, they flew alone. New methods were added to flights over North Vietnam:

1. plan to be above the highest terrain in the area at all times
2. watch for the hills by the given moonlight, (which was treacherous during a new moon) so that they could avoid hitting them.
3. Use of terrain following radar (TFR). This turned out not to be the most reliable of equipment.

Voodoos and Phantoms accomplished most of the Vietnam reconnaissance missions.

A new aircraft was added, that being the RB-66 Destroyer built by Douglas Aircraft Co. It was a beauty of an aircraft. The three seat version of the RB-66 was used mostly for night photography, while the "C" model was used for "COMINT" communications intelligence. The RB-

66 flew from 1,550 ft to 35,000 ft altitudes, whatever the mission required. The RB-66C version of the aircraft carried a four man electronic warfare team for ELINT snooping. The RB-66s were stationed at Detachment 1 of the 432nd Tactical Reconnaissance Wing, at the Takhli Royal AFB in Thailand for all of 1967. By June of 1967 they had already put in 1,819 hours of flight time doing ELINT work which equaled out to 200 hours a month.

Another acronym used in the Vietnam war aerial reconnaissance workings was the CETF (College EYE Task Force) which used a modified EC-121 Lockheed Constellation. The Constellation carried a literal ton of electronic devices and computers. She also was manned by a thirty-one-man crew. The CETF was part of *Aerospace Defense Command* and flew out of the 552nd Airborne Early Warning and Control Wing at McClellan AFB, in California. A normal crew complement for the EC-121 was usually eighteen, but it would change with the mission. The main job of the CETF in Vietnam, which flew out of Tan Son Nhut Air Base, Saigon, provided airborne intelligence in places where there was no ground radar and that was usually a good portion of Southeast Asia. They were the "BIG EYE" of the fighter /bombers that would be on a strike mission, and were responsible for many MiG kills. Without them, it would have been much tougher on the pilots of the fighter/bombers that were trying to do their job and get the targets prescribed in Vietnam.

Because of the "guerilla warfare" in Southeast Asia, Operation "BLIND BAT" used Lockheed's C-130 Hercules aircraft which carried two hundred fifty of the two million candlepower flares. The C-130s were the hunters while the fighter/bombers were the killers. The C-130s lit up the area for the fighters/bombers to strike and that was usually during that seven-hour time slot between dusk and dawn. "BLIND BAT" teams went out over pre- determined areas to find the enemy in the dark of night. The 315th Air Division, out of Ubon Royal AFB in Thailand, felt the mission was simple enough, dropping flares into the dark jungle and when finding a suitable target, they called in the fighters/bombers which aided in the demise of many Vietcong in the process.

During the siege of Plei Mei by the Vietcong, illumination by the "BLIND BAT" crews so bugged the enemy that they finally just left. For the Vietcong to just hear a C-130 in the air above was enough to scare them right out of attacking anything!

The C-130 Hercules from OPERATION BLIND BAT complete with bat logo. (Scott Pederson)

The "take" from BX6847 and the North Korean mission flown by CIA pilot Jack Weeks and the A-12 OXCART (CNES/SPOT)

The PUEBLO Incident and the A-12 OXCART

Reconnaissance in the skies or on the sea is not for the faint hearted. While most times it can be quiet and almost routine, although that is not often if truly ever, it is dangerous and deadly. The USS PUEBLO found that out on a reconnaissance mission that should have been "routine" in the sense that they were in international waters and should not have been challenged. However, the North Koreans had another idea about that.

On January 11, 1968, the USS PUEBLO set sail from Sasebo, Japan. She was an AGER2 (Auxiliary General Environmental Research 2) class ship that was outfitted for surveillance. No one, not even the Navy really knew what an AGER class ship was and due to her position in the reconnaissance world, she was "of the Navy" not "in the Navy". The USS PUEBLO was a "broker" much like the CIA's A-12 Blackbird. The "mission" for the PUEBLO was listed as mapping the sea bottom, but she was actually spying on the North Korean's Wonson Harbor. Albeit she was still in international waters, when she was seized by the North Korean patrol boats taking eighty-two of her crew prisoner.

PUEBLO was instructed to stay 13 miles off shore of North Korea at all times and to maintain radio silence. She was supposed to be at her post some twenty-two days but eleven days into that mission, she was captured on January 22, 1968. On January 21, there had been two North Korean fishing boats, one coming almost 100 yards near the PUEBLO, but they withdrew and came back later and bolder closing in at 30 yards. Then, they abruptly left. There was no reason to break PUEBLO's radio silence, but the encounter was noted. PUEBLO notified CINCFLT (Commander in charge of fleet) on January 23, at 10:30 hours. The fishing boat encounter turned out to be the beginning of the end for the PUEBLO. Just an hour later, the ship was being challenged by North Korean patrol boats.

It was noon on January 23, 1968. PUEBLO had reported she was again challenged by the North Koreans. However, this time it was a North Korean sub chaser which sent a message to PUEBLO *"Heave to or I will fire."* PUEBLO sent out a fast position notice, off the Korean coast at approximately 12 miles. PUEBLO replied with *"I am in international waters."* PUEBLO reported this information by radio to command in Japan, some 52 minutes after the sub chaser's threat message. PUEBLO also hoisted an international flag signal. The word went out to CINCPAC (Commander in Chief, Pacific), who in turn notified CINCPACFLT. The Pacific fleet commander notified the USS Enterprise aircraft carrier and her sister ships, the TRUXTON and the destroyer HIGHBE, but it was too late. By 12:10 hours, the North Korean sub chaser had radioed into home; *"The name of target is GER-1-2. I judge it to be a reconnaissance ship. It is American guys. It does not appear that there are weapons and it is a hydrographic mapping ship."* 13:00 hours, the sub chaser had company, three North Korean patrol boats showed up, along with two

MiG aircraft flying overhead. The sub chaser was backing towards PUEBLO with intentions of boarding her. PUEBLO turned aside and signaled her intentions to leave. That was approximately 13:15 hours. By 13:27 hours the sub chaser called the patrol boats away because he was set to fire on PUEBLO.

PUEBLO called urgently to CINCPACFLT with an SOS. Commander Lloyd Bucher's message was, *"We are being boarded. Initiating emergency destruction of classified equipment. Request help. SOS."* There was no one to help PUEBLO. Here is where the reconnaissance game gets really dangerous. It doesn't matter whether you are in the air or on a ship. It's a deadly game and PUEBLO serves as the perfect example of just how deadly this game is. The PUEBLO was caught out and what was going on, she was too far away for the U.S. Navy in Japan to launch any sort of intervention. The USS Enterprise was the nearest aircraft carrier, and she was 450 miles from the site of the North Korean capture. There was supposed to be what was known as "critical support"; basically, the Fifth Air Force was supposed to be on "strip alert" but for some reason, it was not available. The PUEBLO was alone and helpless. At 13:45 hours PUEBLO was being fired on. She now had three crew wounded, while the rest of the crew could not uncover the .50 caliber machine guns on deck. PUEBLO was boarded by the North Koreans at 14:32 hours, as the ship made her last call for any kind of help.

Back in the States, CIA director, Richard Helms notified the A-12 OXCART forces at Kadena Air Base to be ready to take off at 21:00 hours on January 25th and to return four hours later. The film from the mission would be offloaded and airlifted immediately to a classified location, which was actually Yokota, Japan for processing and evaluation by the 67th Technical Reconnaissance Squadron who were in residence there. No later than 04:30 EST January 27th. Helms made it clear that there would be no other additional resources to support the A-12 on her mission with the exception of her tankers. Usually when a mission was on the boards, one pilot was briefed on the mission, while a back up pilot was in the dressing room, being suited up and his aircraft being prepared on the runway.

ONE pilot and ONE aircraft was readied for the flight. There was NO backup for this mission. Total time over the denied territory, North Korea would be 17 minutes. CIA pilot Jack Weeks was suited and ready to take off on mission BX 6847. His aircraft was CIA Article #131. Actual time of takeoff was 0:11 Zulu time. The time planned enroute was 4:01 Zulu hours. Actual time elapsed was 04:00 Zulu. Weeks was back in Okinawa by 05:11Z. Weeks' first refueling was completed and that left his aircraft, #131 with 7500lbs of fuel. Weeks proceeded to target. He started to have problems over Hungnam, North Korea. Week's right inlet failed to retract all the way and the aircraft went into what was known as an "unstart". Very basically, that means the air was not accepted by the duct and kicked out. This causes the aircraft to shake violently. Weeks fought the aircraft and managed her back into a straight and level flight at Mach 3.19. He started to make his right turn heading southwest. Weeks had to operate the inlet manually and had a bad spike actuation, which also gave him some grief, but he managed to calm the aircraft down and exited denied territory at 80,000 ft. for the last time over Hungnam. It was a very tough route to fly with both the climb and cruise temperatures way above normal. For Weeks, to have to make his first two passes, both altitude and speed he had to trim the engines to 820 degrees F. for a total of twenty minutes. This put #131 up for an engine inspection later on.

According to a cable sent by Major General Paul Bacalis (USAF), who was in charge; *Weeks had to use some skill and cunning to make this mission good and he did."* Another flash message was sent to John Parangosky, chief of the OXCART Program for CIA. This message was sent after the film had been read, PUEBLO had been sighted in Wonson

Harbor, frozen and trapped by ice. However, she was in one piece and that meant something. The North Koreans had not destroyed the ship. This news was in addition to the reason that the 8th Army had requested information and to prove that the North Koreans were not staging further troop movement. Sadly the crew of the PUEBLO spent the next eighteen months in hell, being tortured incessantly by the North Koreans before they were finally released. Their condition was horrendous, the types of torture they endured was of the cruelest kind: physically starved, beaten daily, interrogated unremittingly, and that was not the worst of it. There were things done to these men that was so horrific it is hard to explain it, yet it should be explained because it defines just what it meant to be a silent warrior. In an excerpt from the **Naval History and Heritage Command section on PUEBLO**[58], this section is offered:

"The prisoner was forced to sit on the floor with his legs straightened out in from of him and an iron bar was secured to the ankles. Arms, straightened and behind the prisoner, were secured by ropes or straps which had been laced tightly from the armpits to just below the elbows. The prisoner's head was then pushed down towards his feet, producing not only severe pain but also causing difficulty with respiration and, in many, a feeling of claustrophobia. If a prisoner failed to respond, an interrogator would slowly tighten the ropes while standing on the prisoner's back. This procedure, which cut off the circulation in the arms, resulted in swelling and excruciating pain."

This is only a small part of the report but enough to make the message loud and clear, that we owe these and all silent warriors a debt of gratitude that we can never satisfy.

---

[58] www.history.navy.mil/research/library/online-reading-room/title-list-alphabetically/s/some-experiences-reported-crew-uss-pueblo-american-prisoners-war-vietnam.html

Jack Weeks and the A-12 he flew was in just as much danger as the PUEBLO crew. If his flight went down, recovery was not possible. The reasons really don't need to be spelled out. Flying an aircraft at 80,000+ft. at Mach 3.19 over hostile territory was not conducive to being at ease. Perilous is a better description of what his chances were in case of a problem and Weeks actually had two serious ones But due to his skill in flying the A-12, Weeks fixed the problems and the job was completed.

BLACK SHIELD flew the last mission ***BX 6858*** over North Korea on May 8, 1968, with CIA pilot Ronald "Jack" Layton. Layton returned filming two fifths of Southern North Korea, lasting 3:30 hours.

After this flight, the OXCART would be heading home, to be replaced by the SR-71 Blackbird, which was the USAF's version of the A-12.

On June 21, 1968, CIA Pilot, Frank Murray brought the last of the A-12s home from Kadena Air Base, Okinawa to Area 51, where for the very first time, the widows and the wives of the OXCART pilots saw what had taken over and shaped their lives for 10 years. From there the aircraft were put into storage at the Palmdale facility Pilots Jack Weeks, Walt Ray were lost in tragic accidents. In a closing ceremony, the pilots were awarded the CIA Intelligence Star for Valor. There is a star on the wall of CIA headquarters at Langley Virginia for Weeks and Ray. However, you will not see a name attached to any of the stars on that wall . . . they are a reminder of those men and women we have lost in the line of reconnaissance and intelligence work for the U.S. silently.

The SR-71—Reconnaissance and More

The A-12 was released from service with **BLACK SHIELD** and returned from Kadena, Okinawa. The A-12s went into storage at Palmdale,

California along with the D-21 drone (we will discuss shortly) and they were held until they were sent to various museums many years later.

Sept 29, 1966, Department of Defense head, Paul Nitze, held a meeting and conferred with the executive committee on the phase out of the OXCART. The DOD felt that there was no need for two high powered reconnaissance aircraft and it was one too many. The United States could not afford both. The National Reconnaissance Office had their ideas, too. Dr. Alex Flax who was the director, was passing around information showing the SR-71 was ready to take over the role in North Vietnam from the OXCART, remember this was 1966 and *BLACK SHIELD* was still in force. As early as December 1, 1967, the Joint Chiefs of Staff were ready to concur on the idea. But there was one person who really didn't agree and that was Dr. Donald F. Hornig, who was a special assistant to President Lyndon Johnson, for science and technology. Hornig's work was based on the equipment lists, statistics and performance curves which showed the SR-71 was two times to four times more vulnerable than the A-12. That was a shock to many people. There were other factors too, which included operational technologies and very critical ECM systems and abilities, the very activity in North Vietnam and any future operations would depend on. Hornig felt the committee was a bit too quick to put the SR-71 into operation. Flax also pointed out that if there were no economic restraints he would hold onto the entire force. Yet, money was always the driving force. Dr. Alex Flax felt that to keep both programs up would only cost $32million. The plan of storage for the A-12, and later retrieval would cost $300,000 to $500,000 per bird to reactive to flight status for the A-12. Truthfully, the cost activation was relevant to being done the first year of storage. The financial plan that was in place would find the A-12 within three to six months of shutting down the OXCART program. It was felt that it would be more than enough time. Even Dr. Flax suggested that the delay would allow for a higher degree of confidence that the SR-71 would be able to carry out its role in the face the newly upgraded North Vietnamese defense improvements. Flax felt the SR-71 should be delayed for three months and the deployment should be scheduled for February of 1968.

This meeting set the stage for the shutting down of OXCART. Truly, not a great and the A-12 did have different missions. The A-12's mission was photography, one man in and out fast as that Blackbird could carry him. The SR-71's mission was more complex because the USAF added in ELINT work, other sensory programs and photography. She took longer to get off the ground. And did not have real time data link up, at least not then. But, the SR-71 thanks to the USAF, was going to come on board.

The A-12 was still at that time, the fastest aircraft, carried the best ECM packages and was already a well proven item. However, those little details didn't seem to matter much. There were 12 single seat aircraft, along with the trainer. The program had accumulated 3,727 hours in flight time, during which there had been 2,189 flights.

The two-seat trainer added another 1,067 hours in 614 flights. There has been thirteen A-12s, five were lost in accidents, leaving the eight that remained. The A-12 had never been touched by an enemy SAM missile. It was the politics that would ultimately bring this fine program to an untimely end. Bowing to intense pressure, on December 29, 1966, the CIA and the Pentagon decided to close OXCART on December 31, 1967.

Research has shown that the SR-71 did not reach operational ready status at the time that was expected. OXCART had to be extended to protect the void that would be created in the A-12s demise. Subsequently, the December 27, 1967 date was extended to June 30, 1968, which would give the SR-71 and the A-12 a one month overlap to still allow for the photographic coverage of Southeast Asia. The SR-71 assumed some responsibility for the missions, which had now changed its name to

SENIOR CROWN on March 15, 1968. The A-12 remained on the line for thirty days to allow the transitions to happen effectively. The OXCART remained on operational readiness throughout June 20, 1968. While winding down its status, the A-12 still remained in top form. On December 21, 1966 Lockheed test pilot, Bill Parks made an extraordinary demonstration flight to prove the readiness of the A-12. Possibly shutting this program down was not the smartest thing to do. Parks flew the A-12 ten thousand one hundred ninety-eight statue miles in just six hours! The A-12 left AREA51, flew over Yellowstone National Park, then east to Bismarck, onto North Dakota, Duluth Minnesota, then Parks turned south and flew over Atlanta, Georgia, then to Tampa Florida. Parks turned northwest and flew over Portland Oregon, and back south home to Nevada. Parks then turned east and passed over Denver, Colorado, and over to St. Louis, Missouri. Towards the end of this odyssey, Park turned the A-12 around at Knoxville, Tennessee, passed Memphis and headed back to Area 51, Nevada. To this very day, no one can touch this flight with any other aircraft. There were no complaints of sonic booms except that a few of the residents in a town some thirty miles west of Area 51 were "boomed" while the A-12 was climbing for altitude.

This was a big reason of conjecture with Secretary of Defense McNamara, who so   rumble like a thunderstorm on the ground below. Since no one could see the A-12 no one could pick her out in the sky.

In a total last ditch effort to save the A-12 program, on November 3, 1967, and to put some sort of reasoning to the A-12/SR-71 issue, there was a fly off between the two aircraft. The code name was NICE GIRL. Both aircraft flew over the Mississippi Valley just about one hour apart. The results of the test were totally inconclusive, making the fly off indecisive. It was fairly obvious that the USAF was determined to have the CIA out of its "sacred airspace "and reclaim its part in aerial reconnaissance for the United States. However, it wasn't just the USAF that wanted the CIA out of the aircraft business, there were many political leanings to this thought. It was a case of soothing the battered ego of the USAF, due to all that had occurred, along the incessant infighting that has arisen during the building of the A-12 and the concept of the SR-71. Would it have been better to keep the A-12 hidden under the cloak of the CIA, along with the SR-71 instead of turning the SR-71 out into "gray world" and allowing the scrutiny of the Congress and other political figures? It would be found out later in the SR-71 program that there were many who didn't know and didn't care what the SR-71 did, and looked to strike her down for political reasons as well.

In any case, the NICE GIRL demonstration did nothing to change the minds of the people involved. While the A-12 was more than available, the will to keep her afloat was not. The USAF had been supporting the A-12 in a "hand maiden" role all through out her mission span. Without the support of the USAF, with tankers, sheep dipped "civilian" pilots, and other support facilities, the A-12 would not have been the success that she was. However, that was not enough for the USAF. It was not getting the glory of performing the mission. In essence, the USAF was not happy being a support team for a CIA Black Project.

With the overlapping capabilities, the purchase of the SR-71s by the USAF effectively took the A-12 off the flight line. As always, there was another political gain to be made by the USAF. The purchase of the SR-71 gave the USAF the lead in aerial reconnaissance once more. The The Bureau of Budget had for many years been deeply concerned over the fact that the A-12 and the two seat USAF version of the SR-71 did not have the same missions and the same type of crew. The most important difference between them was the civilian flying the A-12 NOT a uniformed USAF officer as the case with the SR-71. The SR-71 did carry that liability.

The Last Blackbird

The SR-71 quickly took the spotlight that the A-12 avoided, most intensely. The Air Force was bringing the SR-71 towards the light to carry on in a "gray world" neither a black program or a totally white program. Some things did remain classified, much like the OXCART program, that was not to be opened for the next forty or so years. To the credit of the SR-71, she did have a remarkable twenty-five-year career, that was nearly flawless. To the very casual observers, the difference between an A-12 and a SR-71 is not discernable. Much of the SR-71's experience and knowledge did come from the A-12's very successful program. The A-12 and the SR-71 grew from the same seed. The amazing thing about both aircraft was the life that was still left in them at the end of their programs. When the A-12 was put into storage, many hoped she would be brought back into service. Twenty years later, in the last desperate days of the SR-71, studies showed that the airframe could be supported and fit for flight indefinitely. So, it leaves one to wonder just how much was wasted in retiring both these aircraft.

One of the major differences in the A-12 and the SR-71 was that the A-12 carried one pilot and the SR-71 carried a pilot and an RSO. The position of the second cockpit was held by the RSO, or the Reconnaissance System Officer. The A-12 pilots used a periscope in the cockpit for navigation fixes. The periscope in the SR-71, which was in the forward cockpit, was also used for navigation, but in addition allowed the pilot to have a rear view, so he could look at the top of the fuselage, wings and nacelles. This was something the A-12 pilot did not have at his command. The SR-71 was 105 ft. 5 inches long, compared to the A-12's 99 ft. The main difference was the longer "stinger" of tail cone on the SR-71. The nose of the SR-71 was removable and allowed for many different components to be applied like the Advanced Synthetic Aperture Radar System (ASARS) and the Optical Bar camera (OBC). On Inlet Control

System (AFICS). This meant the SR-71 was not troubled by the inlet "unstarts' that plagued the A-12. This system gave the SR-71 better flight performance at certain regimes via electronic control of elevons and rudder servos. The SR-71 carried a MRS (Mission Recorder System) which was an upgrade from the A-12's "Birdwatcher" system. The MRS was an integrated mission and maintenance data recording system that monitored the aircraft and rest of the internal systems.

In the 1970s, the SR-71 was moved from the "black" list to the "white" list of the budget which allowed congressional oversight. While the SR-71 had much in its favor, it was going to lose the "protection" of being in the black and later on, that is an eye on U.S. adversaries. As the USAF shifted the aircraft's focus towards more mundane things like bomb damage assessment, the spy aspect was de-emphasized. When the SR-71 was finally brought out of the black, no one really in the "white program world" knew just what is was that she did, or what the original program was really about.

More SR-71 Sorties and the Vietnam War

The SR-71 was just starting to feel its oats for missions a little earlier. She would be going to that humid, hot place called Kadena AB in Okinawa, Japan to do some work during the Vietnam War. The first of the combat sorties for the SR-71 didn't happen. It was canceled by bad weather. That was March 16, 1968 and not unusual for the area or climate. However, Sr-71 #978 picked up the slack and left the runway on her first operational mission but was diverted to Ching Chuan Kang in Taiwan, again bad weather. #978 finally got home and returned to Detachment 1 on March 23, 1968. March 21, 1968, hoping for better luck SR-71 #974, flew the first sortie over Vietnam with pilot Jerry O'Malley and his RSO Ed Paine. When they came back home to Kadena they found that their base had been fogged in and were again diverted back to Ching Chuan Kang better known as CCK.

The "photo take" from this mission showed that the NVA enemy had dug in around Khe Sanh, Vietnam which had not been detected prior to this flight. Two weeks after this sortie, the battle of Khe Sanh ended.

SR-71 #976 took the second operational sortie flown by O'Malley and Paine. As they were at 80,000 ft. and descending both of their engines flamed out. Colonel O'Malley brought the aircraft down to 20,000 ft in the hopes of an engine restart, which he got and after refueling the flight went home to Kadena. While the SR-71 had the nickname 'Habu" for the poisonous pit viper that lived on one of the islands surrounding Kadena, it also acquired another name after this mission, "Lead Sled." It took a week, but the flights continued. Another operational sortie went out and took the third mission into North Vietnam. Again, after descent from altitude, the left generator went out and again both engines flamed out. There was a restart at a lower altitude but the aircraft was diverted to Takhli RFB in Thailand. Pilot Buddy Brown and his RSO Dave Jensen were met by Kadena's maintenance crews and after some work, the aircraft was returned to Kadena with no issues.

The fourth mission was flown by Brown and Jensen. It happened again. As they descended from altitude, there was another generator failure followed by a "double looper" or two engine flameout. Once they got the engines restarted it was back to Takhli where, Brown made a joke about enjoying the CIA 's hospitality. That statement came from the fact the CIA had an ops base there for the U-2 and secure hangars that the SR-71 could hide and be repaired in. After repairs, the aircraft and crew returned to Kadena. On April 19, 1968, SR-71 #974 flown by pilot Jim Watkins the same problem descending from altitude and ending up in an engine shutdown. However, Watkins figured out what was going on. He held the RPM's on the engines a couple of hundred revs higher than the check list recommended as he brought the aircraft out of afterburner. That seemed to do the trick. However, back at the base there was an assistant crew chief of #974, by the name of M/Sgt Ronald De Lozier, that figured out the problem really had to do with fuel control scheduling. Flameouts happened because of the outside ambient temperatures which were not normal for that part of the world. Rescheduling the fuel controls fixed the problem for good. Oh! how those crew chiefs knew their "girls"! May 25, 1968, SR-71 #978 was ready to pull chocks and head out on another operational sortie with pilot Don Walbrecht and his RSO Phil Loignon. This was this crew's first combat mission over Vietnam. While not exactly an easy ride, they made it home to Kadena and flew another eight sorties together.

On July 26, 1968, there was a mission to remember. While no A-12 had ever been touched by an enemy missile, the SR-71 was about the prove the same trick. SR-71 #978 was piloted by Major Tony Bevacqua and his RSO Jerry Crew. This mission would take them over Hanoi, North Vietnam. It was not exactly the friendliest of places, and loaded with SAM sites. Sure enough, #976 was fired on by the NVA and an SA-2 missile locked onto the SR-71. Never before had a Blackbird been fired on. Not that it mattered much, the crew was already aware that there were two SAMS fired at them. The crew did a return track around the same area and nothing was coming at them. They headed home to a peaceful landing at Kadena. The terrain tracking camera showed the SA-2 launches and that the one missile actually exploded almost a mile behind the SR-71. In all of Detachment 1's sorties, SAMS were desperately fired at the SR-71s in deepest hope of bringing one down. It never happened. According the Kelly Johnson,*" Over 1,000 missiles had been fired in salvos without a loss of plane or crew."* Because of pilot skill, the high-tech equipment the SR-71 carried, SAMs didn't stand a chance.

Eagle Eyes

Detachment "1" was in effect for twenty-two long years. Missions were flown all over the world, Vietnam, Laos, Thailand, North Korea, off the cost of the USSR and China. That continued into the 1980s where she flew in the Persian Gulf during the Iran –Iraq war. There was a total of two thousand four hundred and ten missions flown from the first in 1968, to the close of Detachment "1" in 1990. Spotless, the SR-71 remained untouched by enemy fire, brought home the photographic reconnaissance that was so very needed and was always ready to go when and where needed. That is one helluva career. How anyone in their right mind and there are many in Washington, D.C. that aren't could find a reason to hate such a successful program is beyond reason.

The Yom Kippur War

It wasn't long before the SR-71 would face the first of her really urgent sorties. On October 6, 1973, Israel found herself defending her homeland against the Syrians and the Egyptian armies on two fronts. Both had attacked Israel anyway they could including air, sea and land. There were a series of coordinated attacks across the Suez Canal, into the Sinai desert and the Golan Heights. This all came about as a non-resolution of the 1967 Arab-Israeli war. The Arabs wanted the Sinai returned to Egypt, and Syria wanted the Golan Heights returned to them. Even the UN Resolution 242, that was negotiated by Egyptian President Anwar Sadat, could not bring about a satisfactory peace between all. Sadat wanted a peace agreement with Israel, provided that the Israelis returned all their hard gotten gains from the war of 1967. However, Israel was not about the go back to the pre-1967 borders. Since nothing would move the Israelis closer to some sort of agreement, Sadat felt that the only way to get back the disputed territories was to go in and take it back. However, there is never a war that has "limited objectives". No matter how you might plan for a limited objective, you know it will always overgrow its initial plan. Egypt put some 80,000 troops on the construction of pontoon bridges across the Suez Canal to fight some 500 Israeli soldiers. Back in the Golan Heights, there were approximately one hundred eighty Israeli tanks that took on fourteen hundred Syrian tanks. It wasn't long before the beaten back Israelis were calling to the U.S. for help. At the time, the NRO's satellites could not cover the action on the ground within the real time perspective that was needed. That was always the problem with satellites, while good for overall checking situations from on high, they could not deliver real time or close to real time reconnaissance.

The call went out to the 9th Strategic Reconnaissance Wing at Beale AFB in California to heat up the SR-71 for duty. The SR-71 would fly from home base at Beale, across the pond and head for the British base of the Royal Air Force at Mildenhall, and then carry on to the area in question in the Mideast. This was the first time such a delicately timed, critical mission of this length was ever flown. There was a backup plan just in case, which would bring the SR-71 out of Griffiss AFB in New York, fly the mission and return to Griffiss AFB. There were nearly 12,000 miles involved here for the plans. It would require at least five aerial refuelings, which meant that tankers had to be in position and waiting for the SR-71 to arrive for a refuel and then send her on her way. While this was an aerial version of the pony express, never could it have been more dangerous. Sixteen KC-135Q tankers would carry loads of the JP-7 fuel that the SR-71 needed, and head for Spain to coordinate, along with specialized support teams to handle both the tankers and the SR-71. The mission had to be flown in total secrecy, which would be a trick in itself, considering all the logistics required to do it. However, the 9th SRW was well acquainted with security missions and could handle whatever got tossed at them.

The Yom Kippur operation was going to be an eleven-hour round trip to the Mideast. As discussed, these sorties would fly from Beale AFB to the Mideast and then return to Mildenhall in the UK. At Mildenhall, Colonel Pat Halloran who (now Major General Pat Halloran, retired) was the 9th Reconnaissance Wing commander was having difficulties with the Brits, who were having a lot of second thoughts about the missions and denied the U.S. authority to run it from the UK. The Brits were afraid they would be in a problem with an oil embargo against the UK. Two SR-71s were chosen to run the flights, which were literally historic in the fact, no one had ever attempted to fly this long and this far. Of course, the program name was *"GIANT REACH."*

By October 13, 1973, SR-71 #979 left Griffiss AFB in New York with pilot Jim Shelton and his RSO, Gary Coleman, for the first of a series of missions. After six aerial refuelings, and five hours cruising at Mach 3.0, SR-71 #979 came rolling back to Griffiss AFB with the first of the historic missions under her belt. The photo reconnaissance that was taken from the mission was said to be of excellent quality and gave the bevy of defense analysts who were waiting in the wings something to really chew on. The information included what was going on with the Syrian Army. On October 25, 1973, SR-71 #979 pulled chocks again, and was on her way with pilot Al Joersz and his RSO John Fuller for another marathon flight of 11.13 hours, non-stop to the Mideast to cover what was happening in the Sinai desert and Galilee. Then it was back to Griffiss to unload their "photo take" to hand over more information to the defense analysts. November 2, 1973, found pilot Bob Helt and his RSO Larry Elliot in SR-71 #979 again, flying the same round robin trip in 11.4 hours and back to Griffiss AFB.

The very last flight from Griffiss AFB was on November 11, 1973. SR-71 #964 was used and flown by pilot Jim Wilson and his RSO Bruce Douglass. Their round robin ended at Seymour Johnson AFB, North

Carolina, due to snow at Oneida county, Rome, New York where Griffiss AFB calls home. This was one of the main problems of having the base in New York, weather could be unpredictable. This flight lasted for 10.49 hours. It was after this incident that Colonel Halloran decided to head for a warmer nest, that being Seymour Johnson AFB, in North Carolina. The "GIANT REACH" flights performed by the SR-71 were absolutely the key to helping defuse the intensely hot situation between Israel and the Arabs. The photographs that were taken offered positive proof to both the Israelis, who trusted no one and the Arabs, who also had no fond trust of anyone. At least the hot part of the war was over, thanks to information provided by *"GIANT REACH"* Seymour Johnson AFB became the new home for the SR-71, while the backup sorties flew to maintain a very fragile peace between the two warring parties.

More Round Robins

"GIANT REACH" continued from their new nest at Seymour Johnson AFB. On December 2, 1973, SR-72 #964 was the first to fly to the Mideast from Seymour Johnson AFB, which covered the Sinai desert and returned back home in 9.56 hours. December 10, 1973, had SR-71 #979, with pilots Pat Bledsoe and RSO Reggie Blackwell flying to the Mideast and back in ten hours. Following a break, the flights resumed on January 25, 1974, with SR-71 #971 and pilot Buck Admas and RSO Bill Machorek in a Mideast round robin flight that took 10.04 hours. March 7, 1974, Pilot Ty Judkins and RSO John Morgan with their SR-71 #979, were out and back to Seymour Johnson in 9.45 hours. The last of the "Giant Reach" flights flew on April 6, 1974, with pilot Lee Ransom and RSO Tom Allocca back out to the Mideast and back into Seymour Johnson in 9.46 hours. Four of the flights that came out of Griffiss AFB, NY had an average of 11.4 hours and Seymour Johnson AFB flights had an average of 10 hours each.

One thing needs to be said about this amazing mission "*GIANT REACH.*" Consider the problems that we have in the Mid-East today. Syria and the gassing of its own populace, along with having the Russians in position there. Hezbollah and the constant attempts against Israel. The total unrest of the region is something that nightmares are made of. What would real time reconnaissance of the type that the SR-71 could provide be used for today, if the asset were available? Yes, we have drones that are being flown from Creech AFB in Indian Springs, Nevada, in areas thousands of miles away , but we are finding that it is possible to compromise those drones with some very simple, inexpensive technology that can be bought off the shelf for $26.34. Cyber-attacks are on the rise. How would that effect the reconnaissance that would be needed? These compromises of drones are happening. Would an asset like the SR- 71 be viable and most reliable?

From the Darkness into the Absurd

There is an anecdote which sums up almost exactly what happened to the SR-71 program. By the 1980's, there was a USAF officer in charge of decision making for inventory. He actually asked the question about the SR-71, *"What does it really do?"* That had to be the height of stupidity, yet that was the current status of the USAF in the 1980s. The question illustrates the misunderstanding of the meaning of aerial reconnaissance. Actual knowledge of events and circumstances and the ability to gain knowledge on demand are vital to a nation's security. Apparently, this officer had no idea about that. By the summer of 1987, it was a tough time for the SR-71 program. The program needed to get funding and that meant getting it from Congress. It was amazing how the USAF could turn itself into a mess of knots to defame a program it fought so hard to get. It was an excellent program but it cost money as most good things do. The

SR-71 always delivered the goods and the question of *"what does it do?"* looks even more irrational when viewed in the records of her missions.

The decision to release the SR-71 in 1989 was met with disbelief by many in the program. The SR-71 was successful, maybe expensive, but without a doubt . . . Successful!

One of the USAF's reasons found that the SR-71 was in competition with overhead satellite programs and that was total nonsense! The satellites, which were getting commands from the ground for positioning, had NO way to direct precisely where it should go. It would take time to get it into position and by then it was most likely too late, the point on interest had moved on or changed. There was no pilot to use human input to instinctively direct the camera to look for something precise. Too expensive? That was the next thought the USAF had. There were some satellites that cost over $1 billion, which would be ten years worth of SR-71 operations. By 1989, the USAF got its wish—the SR-71 was officially retired. There was a rumor it was a personal goal of the USAF Chief of Staff, Major General Larry Welch, who was quoted as saying,*" It had been a thorn in my side for a long time and I now had the power to get rid of it."* The official rationale had to do with cost and that the aircraft didn't provide real time capability. Could that have something to do with the fact that the general washed out of the SR-71program?

Many people thought so. While it would not be the first time that politics reared its very dangerously ugly head around programs that should have remained, it did rear its head here. There was the other fact that the B-1 Lancer and the B-2 Spirit (stealth bomber) were in the wings and needed the funding. Thanks to many of the grass-rooters that fought this decision with a campaign of phone calls, petitions, telegrams to their congressmen, the SR-71 was saved in the budget for 1988. The face that the same chief of staff was waiting in the wings to choke the program, didn't help the morale of the people who fought for the program. Congress did manage to play the figures and language so that at least six of the SR-71s did survive, along with the trainer at a cost of $160,000. This left the program with the ability to regenerate the fleet within sixty days if needed.

The Air Force refused to spend the money on the program and the aircraft were "left on the ramp" to rot. If the money had been spent to keep the aircraft in proper storage, Congress would not have had to allocate some $9 million to reactivate the aircraft later on. The SR-71 did have the ability swap out noses which could carry many different sensors, they went on the way out as well. Pieces and parts were taken by various agencies never to be seen again. NASA took three of the aircraft and what was left of the assets and managed them as they saw fit.

The push to destroy the SR-71, the program that the USAF fought so hard to pull from the CIA, would soon come back to haunt them. During the Gulf war, General Norman Schwarzkopf was looking for reconnaissance of the type only the SR-71 could provide. Experience from *Operation Desert Shield* showed there were many holes in intelligence that needed to be filled for the coming *Operation Desert Storm*. The Air Force explained that there was no way that they could possibly get the SR-71 fleet back up and running in a short time. That was a questionable answer since it was only four months since the aircraft had stopped flying prior to *Desert Shield*. Whatever the issues of reconnaissance that the Allied Coalition forces experienced during the Gulf War, it seemed the lack of the SR-71s were now partly responsible. The U-2, satellites and more conventional methods were used but they could **NOT** give the advantages that the SR-71 could afford.

Was There Another Blackbird in the Wings?

There was another question that was out there concerning the SR-71. Was there a new version being worked on? That was a huge question and there was so much speculation, innuendos, conspiracies, whatever you want to call it, even wishes. Was it true? Well, at this point in time, and it is now 2019. Lockheed is still working on the prototype for the SR-72. This was supposed to be a hypersonic propulsion system, good up to Mach 6. It was meant for intelligence and reconnaissance work. Oh, it very well exists somewhere and in some form. It is most likely being worked on, but at the critical time of 1998 . . . most likely no, there was nothing, just hopes that there would be. Lockheed once again and without the brilliance of Kelly Johnson, claim that the SR-72 is a hypersonic UAV to be used for intelligence and surveillance. The work on this model was ongoing and in 2013, the demonstrator model was contracted on for delivery in 2018. We are still waiting and the date has been pushed to 2020.

A Necessary Word from the Blackbird Handlers . . .

This section would not be complete without a word from the people that actually lived and worked with these magnificent Blackbirds. Where ever the Blackbirds served, be it Area 51, Nevada, Kadena AFB, Okinawa, Edwards AFB, California and Beale AFB, California, no matter where they landed, be it Mildenhall in the UK or Bodo, Norway, they were recognized as the magnificent aircraft that were the creation of a genius by the name of Kelly Johnson and the Lockheed Skunk Works. One man remembers his days with this program. He worked in the SR-71 Flight Test division as a USAF Quality Assurance Representative/crew chief from 1980 to 1988. Using SR- 71 #61-7955 as the flight test bird, Mike Relja saw it all, right down to the loss of one of these precious aircraft, fortunately not the pilots. SR-71 #61-7974 was lost in April

1989. Wondering if this would be the end of the program, as sometimes was the case with the USAF, the statement he got from Colonel Don Emmons, the Detachment 6 commander was, *"No, the USAF loses so many F-16s we call them lawn darts."* However, they didn't know that in 1990, their Blackbird world would be turned to ashes. As the 1990 fiscal year budget was prepared, the word was around that the program was going to be terminated. There was much to be done. Contracts to cancel, aircraft to dispose of and passing the word to the many personnel around the world they were going to be out of a job. Of course, the USAF personnel were safe, they would just be transferred to wherever the USAF felt they needed help. It was the rest of the crew that had to seriously worry where the next paycheck was coming from. Yet, there was more to it than just the paycheck. There was something more and it came from the heart and gut. It was a shock to all involved. There was always the other side of the fence that grinned with glee as the SR-71 was being shut down. That was the U-2 crowd, the jealousy was always there because the SR-71 was always the "golden bird" as opposed the U-2 who never really got the attention the Blackbirds got. Mike remembers the day of the line item veto; *"The line item veto by Bill Clinton on the short USAF reactivation really didn't affect NASA a lot. We did end up with all the remaining aircraft being transferred to us. The USAF reactivation had taken back #61-7971, away from NASA since we had kept it in a flyable condition, unlike the other three sitting at Palmdale. So, 61-7971 was the first to fly for the reactivation followed by 61-7967, they had moved 61-7968 out to Edwards to get ready to be the third aircraft, when they were shutdown. NASA turned all of the 5 remaining aircraft over to the USAF Museum through GSA (General Service Administration). #61-7980 is the only SR-71 that does not belong to the USAF anymore, since it's on NASA property books now. Again the USAF (haters) had no intention of ever letting the aircraft fly operational missions again. If fact, if you remember the lost A-10 (Warthog) that disappeared, it was actually found by the USAF SR-71, out of Edwards but kept out of the news and credit give to someone else."*

According to Relja, tears were shed by everyone involved, yet they carried on to make sure that they had an orderly closeout. It didn't take long for things to get into motion, they saw things disappearing that very next week from the aircraft that were at Palmdale, which meant, things like the spike tips. The USAF told Lockheed to put it all back, no questions asked. The latest rumor was that the general in charge wanted the aircraft send to AMARC, which was the bone yard at Davis Monthan AFB, in Arizona's desert. to be chopped up like the many "excess B-52s" that were taken off duty because of the SALT treaty. Just the thought of chopping up a beautiful aircraft like the blackbird is actually too much for this author's stomach, and I am very happy that it never came to that. You must remember that at this time, as explained in other parts of this chapter, there was a group that hated the blackbirds for their many invalid reasons and others who adored them. Relja says that he had to usher some crews from AMARC around at Palmdale to look the aircraft over, do some radiation surveys etc. In Relja's own words, *"One thing I hated about my job was escorting the museum representatives in to look over aircraft to pick, it was my feeling that they didn't care about the love, blood, sweat and tears that went into this program by so many people for so many years. They just wanted a toy they could show off and add to their museum's collection without any thought to the history of the program, (maybe I'm wrong but that's how I felt at the time)."* Relja continues; *"The SR-71 Blackbird community was very close knit, we had some people in the later years that didn't give a damn but the rest of us spent a long time working this wonderful aircraft and hated to see it go, you always think that someday there will be something better to replace you, but obviously that didn't happen just politics. Congress put its two cents into the plan and ordered the USAF to save six of the aircraft for use later on. There were three that would go to NASA and three that would be reserved. Tail numbers 61-7956, 61-7962 and 61-7967, 61-7968, 61-7971 and 61-7980 were the lucky birds to be kept up. The choice was based on the last six aircraft that had been PDM, (Program Depot Maintenance[59],) and had the most time left on them. Since NASA got the "B" model with the second raised canopy, and 61-7971 and 61-7980, the other three aircraft were stored with the A-12s at Site 2 at the Lockheed, Palmdale building."*

There was another SR-71 crew chief, Kevin Westling, who served four years with the aircraft and program. Westling remembers: *"It was an honor to work on the fastest air-breathing aircraft in the world and I cherish my memories of it."* Westling was one of the "lucky ones" who got to serve at Kadena Air Base in Okinawa for a year and a half. He remembers taking care of the SR-71. *"I've gotten titanium cuts, too numerous to mention, Titanium cuts take forever to heal."* Westling knew how precious the SR-71 was as a creature that protected this nation with its reconnaissance flights, how important his job was in caring for her and making sure she was always ready for service and her pilots would be safe. He remembers being soaked with JP-7 fuel. As we know, the SR-71 leaked fuel when first loaded on the ground and really didn't seal her tanks till after she was airborne and received a new load of fuel from a KC-135 tanker almost after takeoff. *"My boots would squish when I walked. To this day I can still remember the smell of JP-7. It can't be described, but if you have ever smelled it, you know it. I am sure I still got titanium and JP-7 in my blood."*

---

[59] PDM Program depot maintenance. When and SR-71 went through Site 2 Palmdale plant or AFP42, the USAF had a contract with Lockheed to perform maintenance items needed for that aircraft, time changes, inspections, service bulletins, tank work painting etc.

The next step was to place the rest of the aircraft out to museums, who were salivating to get their hands on a Blackbird for their collections. This included the A-12s. Relja, as well as this author, knew about how the museums were scored and where the blackbirds would end up. Some aircraft ended up at wonderful museums, others on the flight deck of an aircraft carrier that had nothing to do with the aircraft or the program. This author can say she also knows that smell of JP-7 and the titanium cuts, along with the pain of trying to restore a precious piece of American history, the A-12, that was somewhere she should not have been placed as a static display. Yes, I know and I share in a small way the feelings of these men and women. Such is the way of politics, money and prestige when it came to acquiring a Blackbird. Truth be told! Relja detested his job of taking museum execs around to show the birds. He felt it then and this author felt it later, these people, with the express few, didn't give a damn about the bird and the love and heart that went into the care of each and every one of them, A-12 included. Westling too hated the idea of the museums for their birds. Westling felt strongly about it, *"It pains me to see them just sitting in museums where anyone can see and touch them. In my time working on them, if someone tried to walk up and touch one, they would be tackled to the ground, arrested and taken away. Even taking photos was limited to air shows or special permission only."* That is how strongly these birds were protected and cared for while in service to their nation.

It is also something so difficult to express in words. You have to live it, as Relja did, as Westling did and this author did, especially in the museum phase. Relja remembers how with loss of the program, some people lost their jobs, others . . . lost the will to live. Mike Relja was one of the lucky ones and was able to, at least hold onto what he had. He says that the Blackbird program was a very close knit community. There are some stories that Relja tells that truly break the heart. One of his friends, a Lockheed technical representative who traveled the world taking care of the SR-71 was often "accused" by Lockheed of being more USAF than Lockheed since he loved the aircraft so much and not always the way Lockheed wanted him to love the aircraft. When he lost his job with Lockheed and was forced into retirement, after all the years he had caring for the program and the aircraft, he sat home wasting away, drinking himself to an early grave. It wasn't just the aircraft that ended up in an early grave, some of the people who gave their lives to it went the same way. What all this is saying comes to this: there is something very magical, special, unique and any other adjective you can throw at it about the Blackbirds. No other bird in aerial reconnaissance history ever elicited such love, concern, loyalty and on the other side, hatred and angst. The Blackbirds were something so special that just comes around once. Yes, there have been many stories about successors, and hypersonic Mach 6 super aircraft but since the bird's retirement . . . nothing has been seen . . . nothing. There has never been a successor to the Blackbirds and while the stories still are out there, it leaves one to think will there ever be one given the politics, backbiting, internal warfare that constitutes attempting to find a reconnaissance aircraft worthy of the name. One of the last and saddest things that Mike Relja had to do was to oversee that the spare parts and equipment were destroyed in 2007. Was that truly necessary? Or was it political hatred that signed that order.

The last three birds that were at NASA were having a hard time staying alive. There weren't too many commercial takers who would pay to run tests on the birds that remained there. So that too, closed down taking with it not only the souls of those who worked the programs and lived with these magnificent aircraft day in and day out, it took the souls of these magnificent aircraft that came from the hand and heart of Kelly Johnson and the Lockheed Skunk Works. Again, Mike Relja remembers his own feelings; *"So a lot of people lost jobs, some lost their life or will to live, I was lucky and got picked up by NASA and got to stay with the aircraft until the very end, including the USAF short reactivation. We have a reunion up in Reno every two years on the odd years and up till 1999, when I would be up there and people asked me what I was doing now, I would simply tell them, don't know about you guys but I'm still working on the SR-71."*

This explanation or let's say, look into the world of the program and the people that worked it is necessary. It is needed to show the dedication, heart, loyalty and strength and abiding love and respect that actually goes into a program like this. There has never been a reconnaissance program or aircraft that has ever garnered the attention or support and the people who put their hearts and talent on the line for this country. Will there ever be another like the SR-71 or perhaps better, no one knows and United States intelligence or lack of it does suffer. There is only so much a satellite can do limited by the problems of space and position along with timing. There is only so much a drone can do, slow, small and able to sit for hours but not able to do much about it except to fire a couple of missiles, should the case warrant it. There is a hole left by the SR-71 that has yet to be filled.

One More Time

Since the SR-71 literally was resurrected in 1995, orders came in from Congress to reactive the three aircraft that NASA had, and brought out a $100 million check to make it happen. The USAF was scrambling like mad and needed to have the aircraft ready in thirty days due to the problems in the Mideast and North Korea. With the revitalized program for the SR-71 there were some improvements that were brought in. There was a new Common Data Link (CDL) and this brought real time images that could be downloaded to a ground station. The addition of the Optical Bar camera which was a panoramic camera, used in most of the aircraft, that could cover a seventy mile swath in one pass. It could use wet film, and had the same type of processing as the U-2. The new TEOC (Technical Objective camera) was a look down point and shoot framing camera and also a wet process camera there were new electronic counter measures (ECM) packages. DEF A2, Def H and DEF C, were all new from 1995.

These were some of the new "toys" that the SR-71 brought back into the workplace, in pursuit of its first and most decidedly important objective, to get there on target, on time and to bring back the information without getting shot down.

NASA was also looking to utilize the SR-71. NASA was in the market for a high speed test bed for their new AEROSPIKE program. NASA had already worked its way through the XB-70 Valkyrie, the YF-12 and were now looking to use the SR-71. AEROSPIKE was built to test the scram jet engine. It wasn't a totally successful Program, but it did put the SR-71 to work. NASA worked super hard to keep the aircraft in top shape and in great flying condition but by 1999, it was all over. NASA had to give up the AEROSPIKE program and the SR-71. The aircraft were then released and sent to museums to become static displays. Only the three left at NASA were in flyable condition and one had been cannibalized to keep the other two in the air. It was truly an ignominious end to such a historic, successful and fruitful program. The SR-71 facility at Edwards AFB looked like a literal ghost town. The pilots that had trained so hard, the crews that had slaved day and night on the birds were now just retirees, like their bird. There were no military pilots left that were certified to fly the SR-71. It hurt painfully to watch and know that the United States was now taking the fastest plane in the world and turning her into a static display. There really was no good, solid explanation other than politics and personalities with jealous streaks that destroyed a program which could have gone one for many more years. It was sadder to know that the USAF had once again shot itself in the foot, and was left with a big void to fill in aerial reconnaissance. The thoughts that a drone could do the job as well had yet to be proven. Meanwhile, the United States was blind. To close the chapter on the SR-71, there is something that was written and left on a hill in Okinawa. It sums up in entirety what the Blackbirds were all about and why people risked their lives to get the reconnaissance this country needed:

"There is a plaque that was left at Kadena when the SR-71 operations there shut down for good and all. It was placed on "Habu Hill" and left there for everyone to see, thanks to Det "1" Commander Lee Shelton[35]:

It reads:

"This vantage point is dedicated to the magnificent SR-71 Blackbird known worldwide as the Habu-an Okinawan Cobra of Black Sinister Appearance, great stealth and lightning fast strike.* The first SR-71 arrived at Kadena Air base on 9 March 1968 and the last aircraft departed on 21 January 1990. Through out those twenty-two years, the Habu roamed Pacific skies unchalleneged in war and peace to insure the freedom of the United States and her allies. Habu Hill stands as a memorial to the SR-71, the special men and women who sustained its strategic reconnaissance mission and to all people who gather here and know that jet noise is truly the sound of freedom."

SR-71s at Kadena AB, Okinawa (Collection of Bob Eaton)

Sayonara Habu Detachment One,
Ninth Strategic Reconnaissance Wing 1968-1990.

Plaque at Habu Hill, Kadena AB, Okinawa
(Kevin Westling Collection)

*http://www.wvi.com/~sr71webmaster/kadena2.html USAF SR-71 Kadena Operations Website

Chapter Fourteen

The Predator drone carrying Hellfire missiles,
on a search and possible destroy mission.
(U.S. Air Force)

Drones—Eyes in the Skies and More . . .

The subject of drones is a complicated one. Drones didn't just happen on the scene after the 9/11 World Trade Center attacks. Drones were in use in WWI as both targets and attack weapons though not extensively. They were used in WWII and went straight on to Korea and Vietnam, right into today. While they were not the first tool in the reconnaissance inventory early in their history, they have become the first tool today, and are used every day in either the reconnaissance mode or the strike mode. Drones have certainly evolved from the very simple to the extremely complex, changing the course of warfare forever. Drones are not just eyes in the skies, they are also killing machines. Drones now may pick off an enemy thousands of miles away while its operator watches from a TV screen as the entire strike unfolds. Most of this is done at Creech Air Force Base, in Nevada, the home of drone warfare.

Eagle Eyes

Combat has changed. Hand to hand combat, as we all know, is a brutal and bloody thing. It brings home the incredible horror of what war truly is. Man killing man with weapons, guns, knives or just their bare hands. However, drone warfare has now excluded that part of warfare. You now only have to watch with sometimes tedium personified, at a backyard, or a truck, or a store for your enemy to appear. It can take days of watching a screen, or it can happen and unfold in minutes. The tension of sitting thousands of miles away from your prey can be stressful. Yet, ask another soldier who is on the ground, in a country like Afghanistan, fighting in the dirt and heat and he might not have much sympathy for his brother in the trailer watching the enemy from above via a Predator drone. The drone pilot job isn't exactly all that easy either. While he does his job and gets to go home to family life, he almost has to live in two different worlds . . . parallel universe . . . as one drone pilot suggested. The drone pilot of today who flies the Predator or the MQ-9 Reaper face a very different work day. A reconnaissance pilot from the 1960s or 1970s, or even the SR-71 pilots and their RSOs, flew out over enemy territory, alone, unarmed facing SAM missiles or gunfire, to get the photos or information needed. Today, the drone pilot watches and waits. Sometimes he waits . . . and waits . . . and waits . . . till his enemy appears. Remember, a drone can hang over a site for hours, even days just watching.

There have been statements by ground soldiers who heard that some "drone pilots" complain about boredom. There were even stories that appeared in some technical journals and newspapers that these drone pilots were suffering from PTSD. According to military psychologists, however, this is not true. Some pilots do suffer from stress related issues but they are more involved with schedule changes, long hours in front of computer screens which are attributed to some stress problems but hardly PTSD.

In the words of some drone pilots, they feel like there are in a split universe. While the regular reconnaissance pilot straps on his aircraft and goes off on his mission, he faces myriad issues like enemy fire, bad weather, cloud cover, many things, however it is happening to him right that second. The drone pilot in his own words feels: *"It would take some time for the reality of what happened so far away to sink in . . . for "real to become "REAL*[60]*".* Another drone pilot said that the dualities of the day to day work can really play hell with the mind, going on to state; *". . . for it's a cognitive choice that I'm at work right now. So deployment served as a wall of separation—not just physically but cognitively and one of the problems is that we kept running back into is that you need to actually create this cognitive space as a factor of will. Will there was not point at which we are ever in peacetime. We are just permanently somewhere between war and peace*[61]*."* In essence, whether reconnaissance or strike mission drone pilots are still separated from the battlefield by those thousands of miles.

In another statement by a drone pilot; *"Sometimes its hard to keep switching back and forth. It's like living in two places at the same time . . .. Parallel universes. It was enough to make a Predator pilot schizophrenic".* On this statement alone, is the evolution of the drone from a robotic flying aircraft that takes pictures to a killing machine in some situations, or a hovering pair of real time eyes in another. Drones have truly turned into a living creature of sorts, capable of spying or killing. Its persona has changed from a simple tool to one of technical superiority.

---

[60] A Theory of the Drone—Gregoire Chamayou- Macmillan Press-ISBN-978-1-59558-975-0,2013—pgs109-113
[62] A theory of the drone pg113.

Eagle Eyes

How does this relate to reconnaissance history? The drone that once aided a commander of a battle by getting information regarding the order of battle for the enemy, it is now part of the new warfare, a global warfare that the military faces today. The Obama administration was really the first to use the drone to full advantage. The Bush administration had it in some cases, but it was still early in 2001 when the United States entered Afghanistan. The Obama administration changed the image of the drone by its policy of *"kill instead of capture"* in the war in Afghanistan and Iraq. The White House and the Oval office decided this was a sound policy. It was the only way to *"protect national security by hunting down and killing terrorists worldwide."*[62] Obama received the Nobel Peace Prize and this author has yet to figure out WHY! Hence, with this change in warfare policy, the drone evolved yet again. It will continue to change as presidential administrations come and go. Hopefully at some point it will stabilize and a true position on the drone and its place in global warfare will be solidified. There is a quote[63] from a new book on the 2012 presidential campaign, called *"Double Down: Game Change 2012"* written by Mark Halperin and John Heilemann, that adds more food for thought on the use of drones in the U. S. presidency. As first explained in a book review written by Washington Post's Peter Hamby, Obama *"told aides in connection with the CIA's drone program that he is "really good*

---

[62] Killing Machines: The American Presidency in the Age of Drone Warfare not Machine(s). Lloyd C. Gardner; The New Press; ISBN;978-1-595558-918-7; 2013 pg12. John Rogers "Obama: Troop surge isn't working" New Hampshire Public Radio" July 20, 2007

[64] Jay Busbee Yahoo News "New book Obama told aides that drones make him "good at killing people". November 4, 2013

at killing people." This really can send chills up the spine of anyone, it doesn't matter what your political affiliation is.

Of course, anyone who reads this book will want to make their own decisions on it, either to justify, just go totally nuts explaining this statement away or by trying to either rationalize or say it's just bizarre political banter. However, the writers Mark Halperin and John Heilemann, did spend two years working on the subject of the Obama and Mitt Romney campaigns which is where this statement emanates from. Regardless, the statement will not go unnoticed, nor should it, as it does put Obama's statement in full view of the public and military. It also puts drones on notice that they are not just eyes in the skies, but lethal killing machines as well.

Early Drones

During WWII, the drone was not much more than a radio controlled airplane. It had its beginnings in the U.K. by, believe it or not, an actor by the name of Reginald Denny, who just happened to have a passion for radio controlled models. Denny served in the British army in WWI in the Royal Flying Corp, and after the war he moved to Hollywood to pursue a career in the new form of acting, motion pictures. While acting in movies, his hobby with radio controlled model aircraft started in the 1930s. He became so fascinated with the concept, he formed a small company with partners. He opened a series of hobby shops called: "Reginald Denny Hobby Shops" under the Reginald Denny Industries. His first model airplane shop opened on Hollywood Blvd no less, in 1934. Denny's shops managed to grow into another company called the *"Radioplane Company."* Denny's idea of using radio controlled model airplanes that could be used to train the U.S. Army's anti-aircraft gunners was a stroke of genius. By 1935, he finally produced a large-scale prototype called the RP-1 and sold it to the U. S. Army.

By 1938, Denny bought the designs of another aircraft from a gentleman by the name of Walter Righter, and called his new acquisition the *"Dennymite."* Denny showed this model to the Army as the RP-2. By 1939, with a number of new modifications the RP-3 and RP-4 were built. As 1940 came in, Denny and company finally nailed a contract from the U.S. Army for the RP-4. The Army named this the RADIOPLANE O2-2. Over fifteen thousand of the O2-2s were produced for Army use during WWII.

While Denny's drones worked as far as they were visible, Edward M. Sorensen produced the just out of sight radio controlled aircraft. This aircraft was the first to be able to distinguish from a ground terminal, what the aircraft was doing which meant, was it climbing, diving, speed and going for altitude. Sorensen's many patents moved the radio controlled aircraft out of the realm of the ground pilot's vision. The Navy wasn't far behind in experimenting with radio controlled aircraft in the 1930s. The Navy and the Curtiss Airplane Company produced the Curtiss N2C-2 drone in 1937. This drone was actually controlled from another airborne aircraft, the TG-2. The NC2-2 was an anti-aircraft training drone that was in service for the Navy in 1938.

The USAAF decided to jump on board with the NC2-2 idea in 1939. The Army Air Force used planes that were obsolete and called the "A: series anti aircraft target drones."

These "A" series were later changed to "PQ" to distinguish them from the "A" for Attack aircraft also in inventory.

The Army Air Force bought hundreds of the Culver PQ-8 target drones that were radio controlled versions of the Culver CADET. The CADET was a two-seater private plane that was added to the thousands of the CULVER PQ-14 CADET derivatives of the PQ-8. The Army Air Force used the RC aircraft that were included with Army Air Force B-17s and Navy PB4Y bombers, in the failed *Operation APHRODITE*. These were explosive laden aircraft that were remote controlled after being flown by pilots to a certain part of the flight plan. At that time, the pilots would bail out with parachute and allow the bomb laden B-17s and B-24s to go on to their targets via radio control from a close following, pilot flown B-17. On this particular flight, the explosive loaded PBY-1 Catalina aircraft and the B-24 Liberator aircraft modified for radio control blew up shortly after take off, eight miles south east of Halesworth Airfield in Suffolk, England. The bodies of both Lt. Wilford John Willy and Lt. Joseph P. Kennedy Jr. were never found. Kennedy had volunteered for the flight after making his 25-mission quota. Both were given the Navy Cross posthumously.

The Navy went on to produce another drone in *"PROJECT FOX"*. This was built in the Naval aircraft factory, in Pennsylvania. This very ambitious drone carried an RCA television camera and in the control aircraft, the TG-2, there was a TV screen installed to follow the *"FOX"*. This program ran in 1941. The Navy looked to produce another TV loaded drone that was a radio controlled program, which had one hundred and sixty two control planes and one thousand assault drones. The Navy was not satisfied and was truly beside itself wondering how to develop a large scale or a small-scale program. Money was a main issue along with the fear of letting everyone know about the plans of the concept. Assault drones were never a quantified success.

Reconnaissance Drone Evolution

Drones that came out of the 1930-40s era, were usually for target or assault work. It wasn't until the later 1940s-50s that drones started to evolve into the reconnaissance tools that we are familiar with today. It took the Cold War to do it.

After WWII, the O2-2 target drone from RADIOPLANE and Reginald Denny made its debut and a number of successful training target drones called the Basic Training Target (BTT). Some of them carried a dizzying array of nomenclature like MQM-33. MQM-36, KD2R-QUAIL etc. These target drones stayed in service till the end of the 20th Century. However, the first target drone to be converted to an aerial reconnaissance was the MQM-33.

The MQM-33 drone built by the Northrop Corporation. (Northrop)

The U. S. Army was responsible for the conversion which was done in the mid-1950s. The new name was called the RP-7 and later changed to the MQM-57 FALCONER. The U.S. military bought into a number of other drones that were close in style to the Radioplane drones.

It was late in the 1950s when the MQM-57 FALCONER was purchased by the U.S. Army, along with the Aero-jet General SD-2 OVERSEER. It was close in size to the FALCONER but much heavier in weight. The successful target drone, the Ryan FIREBEE looked to be a good platform to turn into a reconnaissance drone. The converted FIREBEE was highly successful in tests for aerial reconnaissance. The RYAN Model 147 LIGHTNING BUG Series was used by the U.S. to spy on China, North Vietnam and North Korea in the 1960s-70s. The RYAN LIGHTNING BUG was not the only long range reconnaissance drone to be developed in the 1960s. However, the AQM-34L was a remotely piloted drone that could fly low level photo reconnaissance missions. They were mostly used over North Vietnam. These drones had a speed of 645 mph and a range of 750 miles. They usually were picked up after landing in the South China Sea by the Navy, off the North Vietnamese coast.

The Teledyne-Ryan AQM-34L Firebee drone used in aerial reconnaissance over North Vietnam (Nat'l Mus. Of the USAF)

RYAN Company was prolific in creating many drone models like the RYAN 154 and the RYAN /BOEING COMPASS COPES. The *Compass/Copes* program began with the USAF in 1971. The USAF wanted to develop an upgraded reconnaissance drone that could take off and land like a manned aircraft. It would also have to be at high altitudes for very long periods of time, possibly a 24-hour day for photographic reconnaissance, communications. There were two drones involved, one was the *RYAN Compass Copes R* also called the YQM-98A, and the Boeing *YQM-94Compass Copes B* that worked the program. Ryan tried another design which the USAF picked up under contract called the YQM-98A and later the YGQM-98A, which were both prototypes. The next one that RYAN came up with was the Model 235, which was an updated Model AQM-91 FIREFLY. These drones looked like sailplanes with a twin fin tail, had a retractable landing gear, and an engine on its back. The engines used were the Garrett YF-104-GA-100 turbofan. The *Compass Copes R* resembled the Model 154 except it had straight wings. The first flight of the *Compass Cope R* was August 17, 1974. The Boeing *Compass Cope B* won the competition based on the cost or lack of it. However, the RYAN YQM-98 was the better of the two. Ryan did protest, but it was useless to fight the Boeing award. The *COMPASS COPE* program was canceled in July 1977. The sensor payloads could not be created that would satisfy the program.

The YQM COMPASS COPE (USAF)

Vietnam Reconnaissance Drones

After the U-2 went down in Soviet Russian on May 1, 1960, the concept and plans for reconnaissance drones obviously became more intense. While from themed-1950s to 1959, the U.S. was sending up satellites in the DISCOVERER program for reconnaissance, the imaging did not give enough quality for the really tight problems. It was a matter of timing over the target that could happen a day before the satellite was in proper alignment. There was also the problem of getting the small important details, like being able to discern a truck from a bus. These things were important to the photo interpreter. However, after the U-2 incident, the highly secret RPV program called *PROJECT RED WAGON* was created.

After the "Gulf of Tonkin" Resolution passed by U.S. Congress on August 10, 1964, the war with Vietnam started to really heat up. The US Air Force was quick to send their UAV squadrons to deploy to Vietnam, basically on anything big enough to carry them and that meant the Lockheed C-130 Hercules. The RYAN 147B (AQM-34) would be the first drones that would be piggy backed onto a C-130. There would be one under each wing. They were released and after the mission the drones would jettison near Taiwan to be close to an area where they could be recovered. Strategic Air Command and the USAF drones that were sent to South Vietnam, were the 4025th Strategic Reconnaissance Squadron. The 4080th Strategic Reconnaissance Squadron followed closely behind in 1964. It was later redesignated the 100th Strategic Reconnaissance Wing. Both were using the RYAN FIREBEE drones loaded onto a modified DC-130 Hercules aircraft, with two drones under each wing, making a total of four drones on one mothership. When the missions were completed these drones popped their parachutes and were recovered by helicopters that were waiting close by. Of course, the North Vietcong thought the drones would make excellent target practice and made sure they availed themselves of the use. The NVA claimed many hits but only six were ever recorded as being taken down by MiGs.

The Vietnam war raged on from August of 1964 through the Fall of Saigon in 1975, which was the last combat flight. The USAF 100th SRW launched three thousand four hundred thirty-three RYAN drones for aerial reconnaissance over North Vietnam with a loss of five hundred fifty-four to North Vietnamese MiGs and ground fire. Reconnaissance drones showed their potency during the Vietnam war. However, it would take until the 1980s for the concept to really develop. From April 1966 and until 1975, the USAF successfully launched two thousand six hundred fifty-five mid-air retrieval system (RS) caught out of two thousand seven hundred forty-five trips using the RYAN 1475 model. The RYAN AQM-34L flew the most combat sorties with one thousand six hundred fifty-one missions. Approximately two hundred eleven AQM-34Ls were lost over Vietnam. One RYAN 147SC called *"Tom Cat"* made sixty-eight combat missions in Vietnam before being lost September 24, 1974. *Tom Cat* was followed by *Budweiser* with sixty-three missions and *Ryan's Daughter* (after a popular soap opera in the States) fifty-two missions and *Baby Duck* with forty six missions.

The Ryan 147T, TE and TF (Military AQM-34P, 34Q and 34R) were the largest of the reconnaissance drones. Twenty-three AQM-34Qs were lost, thirty-four of the "R" model were lost and six AQM-34P never returned. The AQM-34L was a low-level photo reconnaissance mission over North Vietnam. The AQM-34 series comes from the BQM-34A target drones.

The AQM-34Q *COMBAT DAWN* Firebee drones were used for monitoring voice communications and photo reconnaissance along with ELINT. The AQM-34Q flew missions for COMINT or communications (voice). It was remotely flown by an operator or could be preprogrammed to fly its mission. It could pick up radio signals as far away as three hundred miles and sent them, real time, to a ground control van. Once over a safe spot, usually over water, the AQM-34Q popped its parachute with a modified helicopter waiting nearby to grab it in midair and rescue the drone. If the helicopter missed, it was retrieved from the water surface. There were four prototype versions of *COMBAT DAWN* and fifteen production models. The AQM-34Q was developed after the North

Koreans MiGs shot down a U.S. Navy Lockheed EC-121 reconnaissance aircraft in international airspace losing the thirty-one-man crew.

The M-21 (Modified A-12) and the D-21 reconnaissance drone on board (Lockheed)

The M-21 and the D-21 Drone

While drones were developing in the outside world by various companies and the military, the CIA was certainly not lax in what it was doing to help aerial reconnaissance along.

In secrecy, The CIA and Kelly Johnson came up with another concept for the A-12 Blackbird. A new drone called the D-21 and the conversion of the A-12 into the mothership to carry the new D-21. The beauty of the D-21 was its speed and altitude and of course, high quality images. The cockpit of the A-12 was redesigned and there were now two cockpits, one for the pilot and the other for the LCO or launch control operator. The project name was *"TAGBOARD."*

In 1962, the CIA hadn't shown much interest in a drone program being they had the A-12, but they were still haunted by the U-2 incident. There was always the thought of losing an aircraft. To lose an aircraft as sophisticated as the A-12 would have been a total horror. To give to the

Soviets, not to mention the pilot flying the aircraft, one of the deepest secrets in U.S. history would have been a disaster. By October 1962, Kelly Johnson got the approval to go ahead with the drone program. *TAGBOARD* was a godsend of sorts because financially they were using an aircraft that they CIA had already bought and paid for.

Johnson was designing a drone that was streamlined and light. It would be able to do the job at 90,000 ft and at a speed of Mach 3, while having the lowest radar cross section of anything that had come out of the Skunk Works. The word is *STEALTH* and that is synonymous with low radar cross section.

The D-21 weighed only 17,000 lbs. and was created from the same titanium and composite materials that created the mothership, M-21. The D-21 carried the Marquardt RJ43-MA-B4 ram jet engine, which was a remnant of the *BOMARC* missile program. The D-21 was only forty feet long and in its early stages was called the Q-12. By December 7, 1962, the D-21 was ready for testing at the place that didn't exist, Area 51.

The D-21 nomenclature stood for "daughter" when mated to the reconfigured A-12 the M-21 stood for "mother". Hence, the MD-21 handle. The drone program was to be used to overfly Soviet Russia and China.

On January 24, 1964, the D-21 was mated to the M-21, #60-6940. However, the first test launch didn't occur until two years later. March 1, 1966, there was a vast amount of technical issues that had to be solved. One serious problem was the amount of clearance the D-21's wingtips and the M-21's 15% inward canted vertical stabilizers. The Skunk Works used a frangible nose and tail covers on the D-21 to reduce drag for the entire configuration. The covers were blown off before the actual launch of the D-21.

The first attempt at a launch caused the already jettisoned inlet covers of the D-21 to break up into pieces, which struck the D-21's wing, causing massive damage. The inlet covers were never used again.

The D-21 with damage to wings (Lockheed)

There was also the question of the drag which Johnson tried to solve by starting the D-21's engine at above Mach 1, that allowed enough power to help the MD-21 configuration to fight the extra drag. Flight testing the D-21 was dangerous to say the least, it was also an arduous task. There were many trials and errors before the Lockheed crew got what they wanted, and felt the bird was safe enough to fly. However, even with the added power, drag was still a contentious issue and caused a lot of grief for Johnson. The MD-21 was a difficult configuration to work with no matter how it was looked at.

The first of the launches began in March 1966. Bill Park, chief pilot for Lockheed had the honor of the first flight. The MD-21 was flown over the Pacific Ocean to try its wings. This meant that the MD-21 left Area 51 in Nevada, flew to Albuquerque, New Mexico in what was considered a speed run, and they headed out to Pt. Mugu in California. After reaching the Pacific Ocean, the D-21 fired up her engine and the MD-21 pitched down to release the D-21. With the early test flights, the D-21 used minimal fuel to keep the weight load down. Later on, flights added fuel until the D-21 was up to full capacity. On July 16, 1966 with 100% fuel load, the D-21 launched. This allowed the D-21 enough fuel for a 1600-mile flight which included maneuvers.

Bad Times

On that July 16, 1966 flight test, the third test the D-21 flew, Bill Park was the pilot and Ray Torick was the LCO (launch control operator). The D-21 launch and flight was successful. The D-21 made eight programmed turns, taking photos of the Channel Islands, Santa Catalina, and San Clemente in California. The photos were taken at 92,000 ft and a speed of Mach 3. One thing did occur, the container with the film didn't eject due to an electrical problem. This was corrected at the next flight test.

July 30, 1966, another test flight released the D-21 at Mach 1.0. The D-21 passed through the MD-21's wake turbulence and that caused an "asymmetrical unstart" of the D-21's Marquardt engine. This caused the D-21 to roll right. The M-21 had pitched up, which pilot Bill Park tried to correct, but the D-21 went aft at Mach 3.25 and hit the MD-21 full force. The hit destroyed the MD-21's right rudder, engine and nacelle and a good portion of the right wing. The MD-21 went out of control and caused pilot and LCO, Park and Torick to eject, as the MD-21 headed for the ocean. Both Park and Torick got out safely with their pressure suits inflated and landed in the water. Park was picked up by a life raft about 150 miles out to sea. Torick, tragically came down closed to the ejection site but he removed his helmet visor while trying to swim. His pressure suit loaded with sea water and took Torick down, drowning him.

After Torick's body was recovered, according to Ben Rich's book *"Skunk Works,"* his biography on his years at Lockheed, he said that Keith Beswick, the flight director went to the local funeral home to cut the pressure suit off Torick's body, so they could prepare him for burial.

Kelly Johnson could bear no more. He was so distraught after the accident that he canceled the program and gave the USAF back their development money.

Johnson said: *"I will not risk anymore test pilots or Blackbirds. I don't have either to spare."* The D-21 was successful but would have to find another way to fly.

Captain Hook

While Johnson was bereft from the accident and loss of Ray Torick, he still had to find a solution for the D-21. It was then that Johnson thought about the B-52 as the mothership to carry the D-21. The B-52 had carried the X-15 and many of the lifting test body vehicles for NASA.

The M-21 was taken out of the equation. Secretary of Defense, Cyrus Vance approved the use of the B-52 as the new mothership for the D-21. The USAF supplied two specially equipped B-52Hs. The B-52 could handle sixteen hours of straight flight which gave the D-21 a 3,000-mile range. Since the USAF and Johnson now had the long range needed, they could now consider moving onto plans for China and Soviet Union.

In 1968, the new *"Captain Hook"* program was instituted and test flights were started. The B-52 was fitted with a new pylon to carry the D-21 under her immense wings. The D-21 was now called the D-21B. The D-21 pylon could attach easily to the B-52's existing hard points so no structural modifications were needed. There were two control officers that replaced the B-52's electronic warfare officer and a gunner. A stellar inertial guidance system was added along with an air conditioning system to keep the D-21 cool. The test flights departed from Hawaii, flew over the Pacific Ocean and photographed Christmas and Midway islands. "Captain Hook" flights suffered only two failures in just over fourteen months. By late 1969, the CIA started to recommend to President Nixon and the Committee on National Security various missions for the D-21B to fly.

The *"Captain Hook"* program was a technical success but didn't have much luck when it came to missions. The CIA recommended in its first plan to go to Lop Nor, China, which was a missile testing base. It was two thousand miles inland of the China-Mongolia border. Lop Nor was secluded in a 2,000 ft. depression about twenty miles wide on a 4,000 ft plateau, which was a primary interest for U.S. Intelligence. The Red Chinese were conducting missile testing there. John Parangosky, who was taking over for CIA chief Richard Bissell, really didn't like the idea of sending two D-21s in. However, the B-52H was prepared and left Beale AFB, carrying the two D-21B drones under her wings. When the bomber reached the launch point, it released the D-21 which overflew the target beyond range of the Chinese radar. The mission was useless.

Kelly Johnson described it; *"Damn thing came out of China but was lost. It wasn't spotted or shot down but it must have malfunctioned and crashed on us."*

The Chinese radar never picked up the drone and Johnson and his crew concluded that the guidance system was off somehow.

Eleven months later, President Nixon approved another mission over Lop Nor. The drone flew well but the film package was dropped and lost at sea. Another almost success.

On March 1971, Nixon approved another flight to Lop Nor. The drone flew well, and again the film package was lost at sea, after it was almost recovered by the ship. Another hit and miss for the program. Two weeks later, yet another flight was tracked for one hundred ninety miles into China and lost. It was a poor showing for a drone that could have well been the glory of aerial reconnaissance.

Cancellation

In 1971, the Defense Department let Johnson and the Skunk Works know that *"Captain Hook"* was canceled. In the usual mindset of the DOD, they wanted all the tooling destroyed as well. To state it bluntly, Johnson was frustrated and angry. He blamed the USAF for holding onto the drones for nine months at Beale AFB, before missions were activated. Johnson complained angrily that the drones were needlessly taken apart and serviced merely to justify the salaries of the USAF personnel. Johnson believed the Skunk Works should have been maintaining the drones all along not the USAF.

The 17 airframes were eventually moved to David Monthan AFB, "boneyard" and to AMARC (Aerospace Maintenance and Regeneration Center). The drones were later discovered by sheer accident when strong winds blew their tarps off in front of a group of tourists visiting the facility. This was by a back fence of the facility. It didn't take long for the word to get out and the USAF was forced to admit to the drones existence. The airframes were then dispersed to various museums. The rest were sent to NASA in the hopes of using them for a high speed test research program. There were also rumors around that the drones were being used for a liquid hydrogen project called "Aurora". This nomenclature was not true at all. In fact, AURORA was actually the code name for the B-2 Stealth bomber.

The D-21 drone and the MD-21 configuration could have been a boon to the aerial reconnaissance program. However, with all that happened, it just wasn't the "glory of the reconnaissance world that Kelly Johnson hoped it would be.

Eagle Eyes

The D-21B Separated from the B-52H
Mothership high above (Lockheed)

A New War and a New type of Weapon

Before we go any further into the newer drones that began in the late 1990s and are working now, we need to try to separate a very intricate question: surveillance and reconnaissance. They are NOT the same. After the 9/11 attacks, we were left with the war of Islamic Jihadists and their ambitions to rule the world with their fundamentalist concept of Islam. This brought about a new type of war. Yes, we had the typical hot war with guns, missiles and ground combat, aircraft: fighters and bombers raging through the skies of Afghanistan and Iraq. There was something new added, that was the drone that could kill. The *PREDATOR* drone was turned into a nightmare of the skies. Not only could she do the regular reconnaissance job, she could loiter, stay there watching for hours as her prey moved below, unaware of her presence, until the time she let loose with a Hellfire missile that she now carried on her fuselage. Along with her job of reconnaissance, she now did surveillance. Surveillance bring with it a whole new world of hurt for the enemy. They never knew or would know what hit them. There was no warning of a jet engine, or the low swoops of a close air support aircraft or fighter coming in for a run, no ... she sat silent for hours, sometimes for days ... waiting for her prey to show up so she could dismantle the truck, house, or whatever the place her prey was hiding. Back in the ground control center, drone pilots and operators sat for hours and days staking out whatever the location, waiting for that one shot, because that is all it would take, one shot. This is a frightening scenario when thought about in this light. It really should be, it changed the face of warfare.

The Bush administration, two months after the start of the war in Afghanistan made a statement; *"The conflict in Afghanistan has taught us more about the future of our military than a decade of blue ribbon panels and think symposiums. The Predator is a good example. Now, it is clear the military does not have enough unmanned vehicles."*

The drone was the "star" of the Obama administration and his antiterrorist doctrine of *"Kill rather than Capture"*. He wanted to replace torture and Guantanamo Bay with the targeted assassination by a Predator drone. Drone missions of this sort grew from the early Obama administration in early 2008 to March of 2009, with the CIA launching more than three dozen of these strikes on Al Qaeda and the Taliban. Between 2004 and 2012 the hunter/killer drones saw 120% increase in usage. The defense budget decreased in 2015. However, unmanned weapons grew 30%. That does say something of the state of Congress and what it was thinking.

President Barack Obama was a drone advocate. The drone which was once just eyes in the skies was now a killing machine. The Obama administration felt that is was better to kill enemy leaders than to capture and bring them in for questioning. Using drones to do the dirty work was less costly in terms of U.S. causalities. However, there were problems with this new process. First, a drone war created a "siege" mentality on Pakistanis. It is similar to what happened in Somalia back in 2005 and

2006 when similar strikes were used against Islamic jihadists. While strikes didn't single out and kill the militants who were the targets, public anger over the U.S. show of force did solidify the power of the extremists the U.S. was going after. It made the Islamic extremists popular and they became more extreme, creating a mess in the Ethiopian military intervention and an increase in regional insurrectionists and an increase in the offshore piracy.

When new CIA director Leon Panetta came into office, he felt that there was no alternative to drones, stating *" Very frankly, it's the only game in town in terms of confronting and trying to disrupt Al Qaeda leadership, especially compared to other U.S. military operations such as attacks from F-16s and others that go into these areas which do involve a tremendous amount of collateral damage."* Collateral damage as in reference to the strike of a missile from an F-16, which would have more random damage than a strike from a Hellfire missile which would be a pinpoint target with hardly any collateral damage.

In March of 2009 Obama told the nation his goal was to "...*disrupt Al Qaeda leadership."* "*Afghanistan faced an increasingly perilous situation.*"

There was Obama's assertion of the use of drones as hunter/killers, and that it was keeping Al Qaeda off base in Afghanistan. Obama left the military options open and was cautiously paving the way for a greater U.S. justification of the use of drones inside Pakistan and other countries as well. Under Obama's administration, the U.S. adopted a strategy which as described as *"The Third Offset"*, which would to capture the idea that it must *"USE", technical strength to compensate for advantages of opponents based on a "collaborative human/machine battle networks that synchronized simultaneous operations in air, space, sea and undersea, ground and cyber domains."* This strategy looked ahead to systems that would be able to support lots of data, so that human decision making was better and faster in combat. Defensive systems might work at the speed of light to respond to an attack, while offensives would be much more efficient so that the lead rockets would ensure that the best targets were hit first. In short, surveillance and reconnaissance now were working hand in hand, in one machine. . . A drone like *Predator* that could pack a missile, which could kill a precise target, with less or little collateral damage, and keep the combatants at a safe distance as well. It is a hell of a combination, one that is effective, to say the least, precise and deadly. No longer would a drone just look for targets, now it could kill them as well. For our purposes, we will look at the history of these new drones and how they developed.

The Birth of the Predator and today's drone

While the United States was busy trying to come up with the best drones for aerial reconnaissance, Abe Karem who lived in Israel and worked at the Israel Aircraft company, made the decision to emigrate to the United States where there were much better opportunities for starting up his own business. Karem had great hopes to work on his vision of an anti-radar decoy for the Israeli Air Force and at this point, he decided that he wanted to work on drones. In the late 1970s Karem felt that he could build a RPV (remote piloted vehicles) that were just the type of aircraft you could build alone in your garage, and this suited him just perfectly. While Kelly Johnson was working on the D-21, Karem was working on the *"Albatross."*

After his move and a couple of years of intense work, Karem found himself at the doors of DARPA.[64] His friend, a physicist by the name of Ira Kuhn had led him there. DARPA was created to fund ideas which

---

[64] Defense Advanced Research Projects Agency

would aid the military to stay on the cutting edge of technology. It was the perfect place for Karem to look for funds to keep going. *"We were DARPA's conduit to get to him"* Kuhm said. DARPA director, Robert Fossum, felt that Karem's *"ALBATROSS"* was a direct hit. The *ALBATROSS* was meant only to be a demonstration model, not operational. Karem had designed it to be a high wing on the fuselage, midway between the nose and tail rear end, which had a small vertical stabilizer of eighteen inches tall and just about half as wide, sporting a 15ft. wingspan. Two large, vertical twin tail fins, horizontal stabilizers extended in a inverted "V" shape. Karem used the inverted tail to keep the pusher props from hitting the ground on runway landings. The prop was powered by a two stroke, single cylinder, go kart engine. The *Albatross* could land and take off just like a regular aircraft, it had detachable landing gear and nose wheel. The drone weighed in at 105lbs empty and carried 95lbs of fuel.

By November 30, 1983, DARPA representatives and USAF engineers met at the dry lake bed of El Mirage near Adelanto, California, to watch the *ALBATROSS*, that was flying a path in a two miles aerial course, 1000 ft above them. She would continue to fly for three more hours. True to her form, the *ALBATROSS* was brought down three hours later, to a beautiful approach at 55 mph and touched down on the lakebed at 3:14PM. The total flight time 3:34hrs and with that little go kart engine the *ALBATROSS* could have stayed airborne for another forty-eight hours. Robert M. Williams, DARPA's official in charge of the *ALBATROSS* was pleased with the test results. Karem was also happy that he proved the USAF engineers wrong. The USAF claimed that the *ALBATROSS* would not work. DARPA knew a little better than that. This was just the beginning.

More Reasons for More Drones

Neal and Linden Blue were brothers, and young men that came from a Yale education who decided to travel and make their name in acquiring and selling companies. They came by their decisions honestly, as their father and mother were well known realtors and very active in the Republican party. Both brothers were adventurous and daring. They loved to travel, see the hotspots and ventured into purchasing an aircraft, and obtaining a syndication of newspapers that would buy their photos and stories as they traveled through Latin America. They managed to get themselves into some real problems down there and needed the U.S. government to bail them out, as they got messed up in Cuba, in some very poor timing. Having viewed some of the problems in Latin America, Neal Blue got the idea of GPS loaded bombs and felt that the Reagan administration would be interested in the idea for dealing with the Contras in Nicaragua. This led to the next step for the Blue Brothers. The company, *GA Technologies*, was up sale, price $50 million. This was just what the brothers were looking for. With some help from a Canadian Oil company that they owned, they purchased *GA technologies*. *GA Technologies* was actually part of *General Dynamics* Corporation. This division was supposed to develop peacetime uses of atomic energy. It built nuclear reactors for research and experimented with nuclear fusion. Under a Pentagon contract for President Reagan's *"Star Wars Initiative"* to create exotic ground and missile based weapons that could shoot down incoming ballistic missiles, in August 1986, Neal Blue told the Wall Street Journal newspaper that it had cost him a bit more than initially said, but now they were also on the path to a new project . . . unmanned aircraft. With the help of some very talented people, like Thomas Cassidy, a retired Naval rear admiral with 6000 hours of flight time under his belt, not to mention being the head of the Naval Fighter Weapons training center at Miramar better known as the "Top Gun" school, he actually had a cameo role in the movie, playing himself. Cassidy, when the USAF " appropriated" some Russian MiGs17s and 21s in a program that was running at Area 51 called *HAVE DOUGHNUT,* which was to develop new dog fighting techniques for the military, using enemy fighters was right at the center of the party at Area 51 . Cassidy knew how the military /industrial complex worked and he knew how to get things done. This was something the Blue brothers treasured. Cassidy met up with another entrepreneur who was an electrical engineer named Bill Sadler from Scottsdale, Arizona. Sadler had an engineering degree from MIT. He was also aviation entrepreneur with a great design based on the 1950's British version of an aircraft called the "Vampire." Sadler built ultra light aircraft along the concept of the British Vampire of the 1950s. Sadler liked the idea of attack drones and using his ultra light airplane to do just that, showing it could be made cheaply and in the thousands.

It didn't take long for the new aircraft to show up at the *Air/America/Space '88* show. At Booth 500 in the show pavilion, on May 13-23, 1988 at Brown Field, just outside San Diego, the new *General Atomic Company* with Sadler, Cassidy and the Blue Brothers as representatives, showed off its newest achievement, the *Predator* type drone vehicle, painted in camo and mounted on a pedestal to look sexy as it swooped at a deep turn angle. It was a hard item to miss and garnered a lot of attention from many of the show goers. *Aviation Week Magazine* was there to cover the show and praised it as the international space exhibition, bar none.

Down the road from the pavilion where the Blue Brothers were showing off their *Predator*, there was another company called *"Leading Systems"* that was showing off their best piece called *"AMBER."* *AMBER* was supported by DARPA which meant you know it had to be worth something. *AMBER* was displayed as a full-scale model, dressed in orange and white, with a slender fuselage, willowy wings and push prop with an inverted "V" tail. Abe Karem, the head of *Leading Systems* was there to talk about his beauty. Of course, he was getting lots of attention too, so much so that Neal Blue sent his sons down to talk to Karem about "*AMBER*". As they met at Karem's booth, Blue's sons, which they identified themselves using their father and uncle's names, Neal and Linden, attempted to ask many detailed questions about *AMBER*. Karem wasn't so sure he was going to give them much of an answer, since *AMBER* was a government project and Karem was getting very suspicious. Karem had asked about *PREDATOR* and also got nothing much as a response. Karem basically told the sons that "*How do I know you're not Russian spies*" and chuckled. However, Neal's son, Karsen wasn't exactly sure if Karem was kidding or not. He picked up a brochure and again looked at Karem's badge. He was going to tell his dad all about the man he had just met.

DARPA, General Atomics and More politics

The show was a big success and got a lot of attention. However, DARPA was still hedging about putting a lot of money into a defense project. Basically, DARPA was a system to advance military science, not fund defense projects. In 1984, for the first time since the end of the Vietnam war, senior leaders from the Navy and Army were interested in reconnaissance drones. So was the CIA, each for their own reasons. Even the Marine Corp, after the attack in Beirut, Lebanon, was interested in tactical aerial reconnaissance. It was becoming a big issue and DARPA started to think about what they were going to do with *AMBER*.

Karem was in his fifth year with DARPA and *AMBER* development. *Leading Systems* was growing and success from the show had the Navy looking to purchase ninety-six *AMBER* vehicles. In Early 1987, Karem asked DARPA not to turn *AMBER* over to the Navy. Due to a huge change in the view of UAVs, Karem was afraid that the *AMBER* would get buried under a snow drift of bureaucratic paperwork and be lost.

A 1988 Defense appropriation bill directed by the Pentagon to consolidate drone research and development under a new multiservice *"Unmanned Joint Air Vehicle Program Office"*. It was called **JPO**. This bill also killed the *AQUILA* which was the Army's seriously failed program. This was the first of the small battlefield drones ever built by the U.S. The program began in 1973 with DARPA called the **RPAODS** (*Remotely Piloted Aerial Observer Designator System*). The MQM-105 as it was later known, was launched from a five-ton truck. There were many problems within the system and of course, the money and political angst that went along with a program of this type. *AQUILA* was lost in the defense bill to fend off "duplication" of systems. Congress then cut the budget, for drone research and development from $1 to 3 million to 52.6 million until the Pentagon produced an improved "RPV" (remote piloted vehicle") plan.

The Navy was going to run the new **JPO** office and Karem knew he was in deep trouble. Karem and the **JPO** were always at each other's throats, if not over money then over regulations and politics. The Navy felt that Karem spent much too freely and Karem felt the Navy didn't 't appreciate him or his concept; anything he did was wrong.

General Atomic on the other hand had lots of favorable attention from the Air/Space 88' show. They were promoting *PREDATOR* as a fire and forget it system that would be a new family of weapons which would outrun the current systems.

Meanwhile, Karem found out that DARPA had decided to turn *AMBER* over to the military services and he knew that would be a fatal error. Karem spent two years trying to hold onto his company *Leading Systems* and *AMBER*. It finally came down to Karen having to sell to

Hughes Aircraft. He didn't want to but *Leading Systems* was bleeding cash and he didn't have much of a choice. In August of 1989, he signed on with Hughes to help produce a short range UAV. The merger would cost Karem everything he had, including his company.

The JPO pulled the rug out again from under Karem. A contract for the GNAT 750 was cancelled by the Kuwaitis' when they found out that Karem was an ex-Israeli citizen. The *GNAT* was a much earlier project that Karem had produced while still in Israel. That was a direct hit to Karem, but not an unexpected one.

Karem was trying his best to rescue his life's dream. He transferred *AMBER* to **JPO**. He knew they would put it into storage the minute they got hold of it, and would forget it ever existed. Karem tried to get at least one military service to use them to keep the program alive. *Leading Systems* was going down fast. He owed Hughes some $5 million and couldn't pay it. Karem couldn't pay a phone bill that was overdue for $1.81. IN October, he filed for bankruptcy and by November, **JPO** told Karem to send the six *AMBERS* to the Naval Weapons Station at China Lake to be put into storage. **JPO** terminated *AMBER* totally and that was the end of Karem's dream.

Hughes foreclosed on Karem in 1990. Plans to hire Karem as a UAV consultant at Hughes fell through. By 1991, Hughes was trying to sell assets of *Leading Systems* with Karem's help, ideally to someone with the money to cover all Karem's work. His longtime friend Ira Kuhn, hearing of all that happened, called Neal and Linden Blue of *General Atomics*.

Kuhn spoke to Linden, hoping to get him to bite and take Karem in. *"You guys have been wanting to get into the unmanned vehicle business?"* Kuhn told Linden. *"Why don't you get serious and go up and buy the remains of Leading Systems? I'll try to talk Abe into bringing the residual team down to your company and continue this thing."* The timing, for once, was perfect. Linden had already discussed with his brother the idea of upgrading the *PREDATOR into* a serious aircraft, not just a concept model. As it was right now, they were at a dead end with the project. Sadler still couldn't get the *PREDATOR* to fly without someone being in the cockpit. If *General Atomics* wanted in on the UAV business, Linden Blue felt, they needed to build a drone, made of a composite material that was light like a carbon epoxy, which could be formed into rigid parts with a very low RCS, almost invisible to radar. Linden Blue knew this existed. He had worked for *Gates Learjet* in his earlier days and had a background in just such aircraft parts. Linden told his brother that a high aspect ratio wing would be needed for a UAV and to create a drone that had huge amount of endurance and range. *General Atomics* needed what Abe Karem had already designed.

On February 14, 1991, Karem and the brothers met. While the hard trading Blue Brothers went straight to the point with Hughes, the deal was made for $1,850,000 including all intellectual properties from Karem. As of March 1993, Abe Karem was at his desk at the *General Atomics Aeronautical Systems* office in Adelanto, California. This was the company Neal and Linden put together after buying *Leading Systems*. Karem was told to get ready, he was going to El Mirage to meet with the CIA about the purchase of the *GNAT 750*, at least two of them. The new CIA director, Jim Woolsey wanted to be sure that his old friend Abe Karem was in attendance. Of course, in the late 1980s, Woolsey tried to stop the Pentagon and the Navy run **JPO** from killing Karem's *AMBER*, but it was nailed when word of Woolsey's intrusion into the **JPO** got out.

Reality Sets In

President Bill Clinton was facing the Bosnia/Herzsegovenia War. Clinton was looking to break the Serb blockade and he was stunned to find out how little his military intelligence agencies actually knew about what was going on in Sarajevo. With a severe weather cloud issue over

Bosnia, it was virtually impossible to try to track the Serbian artillery. Both the U-2 and the satellites were inadequate in getting the needed information. The still photo camera could not penetrate the clouds. The U-2 flights were limited due to the threat of a shoot down and orbiting satellites only had a few minutes over the target and got barely anything at all.

CIA's Woolsey thought about the UAVs. Woolsey's people got him an answer, especially one covert officer, which was called "Jane". "Jane" showed the photo around of the GNAT 750. Woolsey' recognized it as Karem's GNAT 750 design. Woolsey called Ira Kuhn and wanted to track Abe Karem down. Woolsey also knew the Blue Brothers. Again, it all added up to timing.

In 1993, Wolsey had seen the GNAT 750 fly, even before Karem had made it out to the dry lake bed at El Mirage. His only issue was that she was too loud. Her engine was like an old, cranky lawn mower. Woolsey was assured by *General Atomics* that it could be silenced. Karem had arrived and also told Woolsey that it could loiter for 24 hours. The limit on range was the next question. A GNAT could fly 130 to 150 miles from the ground station van but there was an antenna that had to communicate on a direct path, no buildings or mountains could be in between and no flying over the horizon. Woolsey remembered all of this.

The Birth of a UAV

The Under Secretary for Defense Acquisitions and Technology was the new procurement king, John Deutch. Woolsey started to discuss UAVs and the U-2 flights with him as soon as he took office. Deutch knew the USAF would totally melt down to hear that their U-2 and their pilots could no longer be called on for the missions when a drone could do it. By Spring of 1991, (when John Deutch took office) he called the CIA operations director, Thomas Twetter in for a talk. When Twetter got there, he found a table full of three-star generals sitting around the conference table. After a speech on the upcoming UAVs and burning the ears of the military, Deutch turned to Twetter and said, *"Tell them what you're up to in the drone program."* Twetter told the conference of three-star generals, short and sweet, how the program was low tech and the beauty of it, knowing that the military always liked and gravitated to the "high tech sexy programs."

However, the USAF and the Navy hated the concept because it crossed into very sacred territory of the pilot and his aircraft. The Marines wished that they had more money to spend on the drones and the Army was still burning from the failed *AQUILA*[65] program. Yet, when the word got out about the drones, the CIA was already buying into the GNAT750. After that, suddenly, all the services were hot to get involved.

Deutch spoke to Neal Blue at *General Atomics* and ask *"How soon can you deliver something."* Once again the Blue Brothers hit pay dirt. July 12, 1993, Deutch signed a two page memo called the *"Endurance Unmanned Aerial Vehicle UAV Program,"* which was a directive to *"expeditiously contract for an endurance UAV"* to provide" urgently critical, worldwide releasable, near real time intelligence information on mobile targets."* That was a large order!

---

[65] AQUILA Program: Lockheed developed for the Army the first small battlefield drone called the MQM-105 or EAGLE, in the 1970s to act as a target designator. The program had many problems and wasn't successful, but it did cost the Army quite a lot of money.

The Army's AQUILA drone (U.S. Army)

The second page went on to list the technical requirements. It wasn't long after the Neal Blue won the *PREDATOR* contract, and a team of CIA and *General Atomics* personnel started flying the *GNAT 750* over Bosnia. Launching from an airbase in western Albania called Gjadër, on the coast of the Adriatic Sea, the line of sight communications, to Sarajevo was 140 miles. The CIA used manned aircraft relay the signals to GNAT midair. The aircraft was called the RG-8 or *"Motor Glider"*.

Even with limitations, the *GNAT 750* gave everyone what they wanted and that meant that President Bill Clinton and the CIA were happily getting the information that they needed to help fight the war. Flying at 6000 ft. or lower, the *GNAT 750* that was covered with sensors, and it gave the operators the ability to distinguish not only artillery from decoys, but surface to air missile sites. Now they could see tanks and big gun movements. It was a totally successful operation. There was some distortion in the signals, but not enough to detract from the information coming in. After two months, the CIA halted flights but the *GNAT 750* did her job and she was definite worth all the effort that was put into the drone and the program. CIA director Woolsey was proud of the fact that CIA helped the Pentagon to get its own long endurance UAV.

The PREDATOR comes into Its Own

In January of 1994, *General Atomics* got the contract to build the first prototype of the *PREDATOR* drone. Changes had to be made which included a antenna in the nose, a longer fuselage and wingspan and really what this all meant was, new fabrication of parts, new engineering protocols and new flight control and software. Since this was going to be a whole new ballgame, the drone would need a new name. Deutch and the Pentagon were already looking to build many different kinds of drone for many different typed of jobs, i.e. higher and lower altitudes. Deutch and the Pentagon decided to call the low altitude drone *TIER I* and another at a higher altitude which would be *TIER II*. At least that's what they were telling everyone. In fact, it was a cover story. The *TIER I* actually was the purchase of the CIA's *GNAT 750s* and that was a deep, dark secret till *Aviation Week* magazine blew that one open in its September 1993 issue. Two months later *Aviation Week* again reported that one of the *GNAT 750s* had crashed by the El Mirage test site due to a software problem. CIA leased another *GNAT 750* from *General Atomics* which was the third one the CIA had gotten. In the meantime, *General Atomics* was putting together its premier drone, the prototype *TIER II* for the Pentagon. They needed a name and the name was . . . P*REDATOR*.

Some of those bureaucrats at government level weren't too happy about the choice of name, because it made the drone sound like a weapon. In truth, it would later turn out to be just that but at the start, it was a big turn off to those involved. Strange to say that there actually were those in Congress who were ready to do just that, put a GPS system on board to turn it into a flying bomb. *Tier II* was really starting to look like weapon instead of a drone, and this was sort of a defeating the purpose attitude. With the *TIER II* acting as a weapon, the USAF would get up on its hind legs and attempt to kill the project. It would be the last thing the USAF would want, because it would inflict a painful blow to their fighter pilots and bomber pilots. It would almost render them useless. The USAF could not have that.

The new *PREDATOR*, the name did stick finally, and she was made of the newest of the graphite epoxy that was now on the market. The composites were light and that was just what the drone needed. They were also strong. The engine for the new drone was a four cylinder, Rotax 912 piston engine, a simple enough affair that was used in some ultra light sport aircraft. She would look more like a glider with thin flexible wings, an inverted "V" tail, that many would consider a powered aircraft. However, those thin wings would keep the *PREDATOR* airborne for many long hours without using a huge amount of fuel. Of course, the most noticeable thing about the *PREDATOR* was that huge bulge in the front section, making her look almost like a beluga whale. The bump carried the satellite dish antenna. Right underneath that bulge, was the chin turret that held the infrared and daylight video cameras.

The ground operators would be housed in the standard vans used by some of the teams that raced in the NASCAR circuit. The van was convenient, could contain all the computer equipment and was comfortable enough to monitor the drone in all phases for many hours.

July 3, 1994, out at El mirage test site, *General Atomics* leaders and engineers sat to watch the first flight of their new baby. The contract was literally four days away from the six-month deadline that *General Atomics* was given. The man who would fly the new baby was Tim Just, who was hired way back when by Abe Karem while he still was the owner of *Leading Systems*. It was early in the morning at the desert site, while *General Atomics* and other contractors got together to watch the *PREDATOR* take her maiden flight. After seven-day weeks, and hours and hours of labor with no break since Christmas back in December, all were naturally anxious.

The maiden flight would turn out to be an anti-climax. Fortunately, the man flying the drone knew just how to handle her, to get her safely down and stopped without incurring an accident that would have destroyed so much serious work. The problem had to do with a simple issue, the aircraft was fuel starved once she tilted to take off. *General Atomics* didn't fill the fuel tanks to the top just in case of an accident, which also added to problem. The other problem was the parachute had deployed and this was a Sunday, the gentleman who handled repacking the parachute, which is a precise job, was not on duty, so there could be no other flight. With 15 ft. of altitude and fourteen seconds airborne, the *PREDATOR* actually did have a maiden flight, not much of one, but one nevertheless.

The Northrop Grumman Global Hawk Reconnaissance Drone
(Northrop Grumman)

Abe Karem was not present on this morning. Had he been, he might have had the whole thing figured out quickly. Abe Karem, the man who had the first dream of a drone, had quit *General Atomics* about a month earlier. He was never happy in the job with *General Atomics*. He didn't get along with Tom Cassidy, one of the head honchos from the start at *GA*, and the money wasn't enough to make him want to stay. All he was getting from *General Atomics* was just his salary, nothing more. Besides, the Blue Brothers were about the fly the golden goose, the goose that was the life's plan and dream of the man who left Israel to come to America to make his dream come true. Much like Jack Northrop who created the YB-49, that was an innovation which would show up much later as the B-2 Stealth bomber, Karem was heavily put upon and badly used by all.

Karem was not finished by any means. After he left *General Atomics*, he founded another company by the name of Frontier Systems, which he started in 1991 after *Leading Systems* went belly up. Karem went after the Pentagon contract for the *TIER II* drone that was now called the *TIER II PLUS*. This was a reconnaissance drone that had to have a range of 3000 miles and an altitude of 60,000 ft. Luck still wasn't with Karem, he lost out on the Pentagon contract which went to Northrop/Grumman and was called the *GLOBAL HAWK*.

Karem was down but not beaten, he continued to call in some old friends and managed to come up with a contract from DARPA on a small drone called the *A160 Hummingbird*, which was a lightweight unmanned helicopter. By 2004, Boeing bought out Karem and *Frontier Systems* and the *A-160 Hummingbird*. It took him literal years, but Karem finally had the success he had dreamed of. He didn't stop and kept going into his really later years and continued to create innovations in aircraft under his company name *"Karem Aircraft Inc."*

August 31, 1994, *General Atomics* brought the *PREDATOR* out into the daylight for the public. That was two months after her first maiden flight at El Mirage. They did the announcement with a flashy, forty-five-minute demo flight at El Mirage for the newspapers and many other in the VIP audience, including TV hosts like Tom Brokaw who did a complete show on the new drone. It didn't take much to sell *PREDATOR* to the public, they seemed to be already in love.

The RQ1/MQ1 Predator Drone
(ACC.AF.MIL)

The father of the drone—Abe Karem (Karem Aircraft Inc.)

The MQ-1B Predator

Out in the Nevada desert, nearby the place that doesn't exist called Area 51, there is a place that does exist and it's called Creech Air Force Base. At Creech AFB, they have the honor of being the *"Home of the Hunters."* Creech houses the 99th Air Base Wing, which provides installation support for over the 10,000 personnel who are assigned to nearby Nellis AFB and the Nevada Test and Training range. The other three groups assigned to the wing are the 99th Mission support, 99th Medical group and 799th Air Base Group.

The 799th Air Base group had two squadrons that are responsible for support and training, supporting Creech AFB in all its needs.

The 432nd Operations Group is responsible for the remotely piloted aircraft in the 24/7/365 days of the year, combat air patrols, Yes, that means every day, all day, all year long. It houses combat command and control, tactics development, intelligence support, weather support and standardization and evaluation of the USAF Air Combat Command, USAF Central Command and Air Force Materiel Command, Air National Guard, Air Force Reserve Command and the British Royal Air Force remotely piloted aircraft units. The 432nd Operations Group has and oversees global operations of six squadrons, 11th Attack, 15th Attack, 20th Attack, 42nd Attack, 89th Attack, 489th attack and the 432nd Operations Support Squadron.

The 432nd Maintenance Group keeps the airmen of the *MQ-1B* and the *MQ-9* aircraft, ground control stations, *Predator* Primary Satellite links and global integrated communications networks that are mission ready to support aircrew training, combat operations operational test and natural disaster support. The 432nd MG currently oversees three squadrons; 432nd Aircraft maintenance Squad, 432nd Maintenance Squad, and the 432nd Aircraft Communications Maintenance squadron.

Eagle Eyes

The 732nd Operations Group support the remotely piloted aircraft in Theaters of operations around the world, all year long. They support training, equipment forces to provide special abilities and they develop techniques and procedures for cutting edge combat support to worldwide operations using *Predators*. This group is a total force unit made up of members from both Nevada Air National Guard and Air Force Reserves. The 732nd OG oversees, the 17th Attack, 22nd ATK, 30th RD, and 44th RD and the 867th ATK Squadrons. Creech AFB is the mastermind behind the *Predators* operations worldwide.

MQ-1B Predator

The Predator as you have read in the previous paragraphs, did not start life as a hunter/killer. She did start out as a reconnaissance drone. The *MQ-1B Predator* is a multi-faceted, medium altitude, long endurance UAV that is used to collected various types of intelligence, and can be used to execute strike missions. The MQ-1B can loiter for a long time, has a wide array of sensors, many levels of communications and of course, precision weapons. *SCAR* which stands for strike coordination and reconnaissance, basically explains her competence. This *Predator* can also do intelligence, surveillance, reconnaissance, close air support, combat search and rescue, precision strike, buddy-laser and convoy/raid over watch, route clearance, target development and terminal air guidance. This bird is capable of just about any type of job in warfare and can support a battle commander's most complex plans.

The *MQ-1B* has a pilot that commands the mission, and another air crew member who handles sensors and weapons and acts a mission coordinator when needed. The ground control operates from a station with a line-of-sight data link or satellite data link for beyond line of sight operations. The *MQ-1B* carries an infrared sensor along with a color/b/w daylight TV camera, an image intensified TV camera, laser designator and illuminator. It carries full motion video from each of the imaging sensors and can be viewed from different streams or fused into one screen. The *MQ-1B* carried two laser guided missiles, the air to ground-114 Hellfire missile which is deadly accurate and capable of anti-armor, anti-personnel abilities.

This aircraft can be taken apart and shipped via the C-130 Hercules or a C-117 transport for anywhere in the world. This *Predator* needs a 5000ft x 75ft runway. The main concept of operations, remote split operations can employ a launch and recovery ground control method for takeoff and landing operations, in a forward operating location while the crew, based in the United States, can handle command and control of the rest of the mission past the line of sight links.

The *MQ-1B* still carries the Rotax 914F four-cylinder engine, has a wingspan of 55ft. and is 27 ft. in length. The *MQ-1B* is light weighing only 1,130 lbs without fuel and 2,250 lbs loaded.

The MQ-1B from the 15th Reconnaissance Group at Creech AFB (Steve Huckvale)

The MQ-9 Reaper

The MQ-9 is listed as an armed multi-mission, medium altitude, long endurance drone that is deployed against execution targets and only secondary as an intelligence collector. We do need to add this drone to the list because of the intelligence collection albeit, her mission is strike. The *MQ-9* carries the multi-spectral targeting system and the sensors needed to find its prey, in conjunction with the infrared sensors, color and b/w daylight TV cameras and an image intensified TV camera. Laser range finder/designator and laser illuminator along with a full motion video is also included. The secondary part of this drone is its reconnaissance power. The *MQ-9* can support strike aircraft and ground commanders. It does border surveillance, weapons tracking, embargo enforcement and all humanitarian /disaster relief work. It also aids in support of counter narcotics operations and peacekeeping support. Again, this can all be done 24 hours/7 day a week and beyond the line of sight. The drone operates in much the same fashion as the *MQ-1B* with a launch and recovery team for take-off and landing in the forward position, and the U.S. based team does command and control for the rest of the mission beyond line of sight links.

The USAF did propose the *MQ-9 Reaper* was in direct response to the Department of Defense directive to support initiatives of the overseas contingency operations. This is a larger and more powerful version of the *MQ-1 Predator* and was designed to handle time sensitive targets, with precision and diligence to destroy or disable those targets. The *"M"* designation is the Department of Defense for *Multi-role* and the *"Q"* stood for remotely piloted aircraft. The *9* is for the ninth in the series of these drones. It requires two operators, pilot and operator, she can carry AGM-114 Hellfire missiles, GBU-12 Paveway II and the GBU-38 Joint Direct Attack Munitions.

Global Hawk

The *Global Hawk* was built by *Northrop Grumman* as a high altitude, long endurance drone which was built to aid the military in the field with near real time intelligence, surveillance and reconnaissance over a large area. The *Global Hawk* is now twenty years old and has some 200,000 flight hours under her belt. The newest of the *Block 30 Global Hawk* drones carries both imaging and electronic signals on missions that can go on for up to thirty-two hours at a time. She also carries an *EISS* or *Enhanced Integrated Sensor Suite* and *ASIP* which is a *Airborne Signals Intelligence Payload*.

Reconnaissance imagery is gotten by the *EISS*, using an all weather synthetic aperture radar/moving target indication called *(SAR/MTI)* and high resolution electro-optical digital camera and a third generation infrared sensor. The *EISS* can permit the *Global Hawk* to examine large areas of ground, and uses exacting accuracy. This system merges the sensors with a range that extends more than half of the world, and remains on station for very long periods of time. The high resolution makes it easy to distinguish different types of vehicles, aircraft, people and other missiles in good and bad weather, day or night. The *Global Hawk* is a true reconnaissance drone with a little extra added. The *Global Hawk* does not carry weapons, has a high altitude ceiling of 60,000 ft. and can stand on station for anything from 24 to 32 hours. By mid-2011, the *Block 30 Global Hawks* replaced the *Block 10* aircraft that supported operations in Iraq, Afghanistan and Libya. She continues to serve the military today in getting near-real time reconnaissance to commanders and imaging analysts for many different military operations.

The Global Hawk stands with her Air Force crew.
(USAF)

Drones and Their Legacy

Drones are here to stay. They are now a part of the Order of Battle for the U.S. Military. Yet, there are many in the military and in general that are not too pleased with the concept of fighting a war from a van and picking off a target from miles away in complete safety. If drones were soley in use as reconnaissance and surveillance equipment, that would be one thing, but they aren't. They are used as robotic killing machines and that brings up a whole new can of worms. It is the question of humane treatment. There is also the question of humane treatment in war time. It's almost an oxymoron. There are pros and cons to the use of drones. It does need to be explored before we close the chapter on their usage and legacy.

The argument isn't simple either. Drones do protect the U.S. military serviceman from harm by conducting a mission safely in a van miles from the scene of conflict. It also sets up a target that can be taken out by a Hellfire missile and thereby restricting the loss of civilian life and damage to infrastructure. Drones are way cheaper when it comes to cost efficiency than launching a flight of F-35s or F/A18s to conduct a raid on a target. It's also cheaper in the roles of surveillance and reconnaissance considering the cost of launching a reconnaissance flight of SR-71s or waiting for a satellite to get in position for argument sake. And there is also the issue of overflight of other nations, in regards to carrying out a strike or reconnaissance mission. Foreign nations don't seem to mind as much if a drone is involved in an overflight of their nation as they would if a fighter or reconnaissance flight that would have to ask for permission. A drone strike can also limit the scale of a conflict, which is some cases is preferable to keeping a heated situation under control.

However, there is the dark side of drones. Many pundits feel that drone strikes add a certain amount of terror to a civilian community that experiences it. It's a torture not knowing when or where this drone may strike again. Consider you are a small town villager and just watched a terrorist get taken out by a drone strike. It would be terrifying for you. You would never be sure what was lurking above and when it would hit again. It does one of two things, it terrorizes you or it turns you to hate and becoming a terrorist yourself in retaliation. This is not to mention that drone strikes are really illegal in international and United States humanitarian law. The law says that a strike is only legal IF the target is a threat to a country's continued existence. Then and only then is it legal. The United Nations in both 2009 and 2015 along with some 40 members of the U.S. military demanded that drone strikes be halted because the violated basic human rights. Since drone strikes are both secretive and have no real "oversight committee", controlling them, there is no way that any citizen involved could possibly have anyone held accountable for the military action. Then there is the human factor . . . . Pilots and their crew, the ones sitting in the van miles away from the scene of action become desensitized emotionally because they remove the crews from the actual war time experience of the horrors of what a war truly is. It is just too clean and a pilot can lose sense of feeling watching himself make a kill. So, the question remains, is it right to match a drone with the mission of reconnaissance and surveillance along with the capacity to load Hellfire missiles on board and take out a target.

Since the 2001 terrorist attack on the World Trade Center, the use of drone strikes has increased as we discussed. President Barack Obama was proud of his use of drone strikes and depended on them. The death toll in from 2009 to 2014 was 2,400 and rose to 6,000 by 2015. That is a lot of killing. The USAF has been using drones like throw away stick matches over the past years. In fact, almost one on every three USAF aircraft is a UAV with over fifty countries being the recipients of the drone strikes and coverage. Many are still up in arms about the inhumane factor surrounding them. There have been many case studies done that show civilians that suffer through a drone strike suffer from PTSD and that is not hard to understand, with the majority of them being local village children. No one has really stepped up to look into the treatment of these civilians. The basic reason is harsh. Anyone who is seen helping a civilian casualty of a drone strike will sometimes find themselves on the receiving end of another drone strike, so many will not venture into helping the innocent injured. In these small villages of Pakistan, and in Afghanistan, children are kept indoors for fear of drones overhead, constantly for fear of a strike. Yet given all these factors, there is nothing being done presently to change the situation to return drones to their earlier and much more acceptable role of reconnaissance and surveillance. It seems the role of the killer drone will be around for some time, as will the use of surveillance and reconnaissance drones. This brings us to the concept of whether it is better to return to the pilot and a high speed aircraft to get the reconnaissance job done.

Chapter Fifteen

The concept of the Lockheed Martin/Skunk Works Hypersonic SR-72
(Lockheed/Popular Mechanics)

The SR-72—The New Hypersonic Eyes in the Skies—The SR-72– The New Blackbird?

Back in 1992 in an article in *Aviation Week Magazine* titled *"Secret Aircraft Encompasses Qualities of High Speed Launcher for Spacecraft*[66]*"* there is a yet another "sightings" story about an aircraft that looked something like the XB-70 Valkyrie merged with the SR-71. It was described as the "mothership" and was also responsible for the "doughnuts on a rope contrails" sightings that were rampant around this time. However, further on in the article there is a notation about the USAF officials that canceled the SR-71 program stating that *"Satellites could do the job" of strategic reconnaissance. It also notes that the USAF officials in the article failed to see the fact that satellites have fixed orbits and are basically inflexible. It also mentions that this "high*

---

[66] Aviation Week Magazine-August 24, 1992, Secret Aircraft Encompasses Qualities of High Speed Launcher for Spacecraft" William B. Scott Lancaster, CA

speed"/aircraft spacecraft system could orbit a small satellite, carrying a suite of reconnaissance sensors and communication equipment and would overcome that detraction. If the second-stage vehicle were fairly "stealthily" the satellite could be launched covertly into any orbit at the most desirable time."

This article shows that even back in 1992, the USAF sort of knew that they made a huge error in canceling out the SR-71 without something to take its place. Here we are in 2018 and we still haven't got a sufficient answer to the problem. Yes, we have the *Predator* and *Global Hawk* but there is still something missing from the equation.

For many years, there has been tons of speculation about what the Lockheed Skunk Works was going to produce as the next generation of Blackbirds. It would most likely be Mach 6, and the first hypersonic intelligence, surveillance, and reconnaissance miracle to sneak out of Lockheed Skunk Works hangar doors. Oh! for the genius of Kelly Johnson and Ben Rich! While both these men left their legacies and brilliance with the Skunk Works, is the next generation Blackbird going to be equal to their legends? So far, not much has been seen at all. The Skunk Works has been doing their best to keep it a secret and succeeding, only the smallest of details has gotten out This SR-72 could be built with twin engines, which could fly at high altitude and follow everything that the USAF must have asked for in their GOR, including the ability to carry hypersonic weapons. This is something the prior blackbirds with the exception of the YF-12 Interceptor (which was never put into production, albeit three were made for tests and one lost in a crash) which carried the AIM-47 missile. Due to the nature of the fast changing world of aeronautics and enemies, the SR-72 would have to be able to do it all and do it faster than believed possible. She would need to be stealthy, work subsonic and supersonic and be able to fill the holes that defense planners foresee because of the newer satellites, subsonic and supersonic drones/ weapons that are now in play.

There has been talk that there will be a demonstrator that will be produced possibly by 2020 and Lockheed claims that this new ISR (Intelligence surveillance and reconnaissance) Mach 6 beauty, will be affordable as well as adaptable. The Skunk Works has been working with *Aerojet/Rocketdyne* for much of the past seven years in trying to develop a method to use off the shelf turbines with a scramjet,[67] that would give the SR-72 the heart to hit Mach 6. One of the biggest problems has been to get past the Mach 3 realm. Just like the first attempts to get past Mach 1, there has been a real problem to develop just such an engine that would break through the shell of Mach 3. The biggest issue still remains the high speed turbine engine, much of which was based on the DARPA's FALCON program, circa 2008, reusable hypersonic demonstrator. The FALCON program also contained the HCV hypersonic cruise vehicle. Sadly, NASA who was a forerunner in this type of testing in hypersonics, did cancel much of their research, including the X-43C that was a combined cycle propulsion demonstrator. Another major loss to research and development in the United States aerospace industry, but that is another story. The name for this new hypersonic blackbird is supposed to be "Black Swift," at least that is what it is called right now, it could change.

Lockheed Martin and *Aerojet /Rocketdyne* are linked in trying to develop the engine to create the *Black Swift*. There have been a few things, like "hyperburner" that have been mentioned, which would start off as augmentor and then switch to a ramjet as the Mach numbers increased. Again, they are still in development. All of this is speculative as *Lock-*

---

[67] Scram jet stands for supersonic combusting ramjet. The Ramjet is the air breathing jet engine that would carry the combustion which takes place within the supersonic airflow.

heed and the Air Force are not exactly handing out "Spec" sheets on the *Black Swift*. However, the USAF does have plans on the books to have a hypersonic weapon developed by 2020 and that is fast approaching. With the hopes of seeing a flight research vehicle that is piloted, *Lockheed* says that this bird would be about the size of the F-22 Raptor, which is about 62 feet in length and that is much smaller than the original Blackbird that was about 107 feet.

As with the SR-71, speed will be her protector as well as altitude and they are working on building the *Black Swift* as a weapon carrier for a hypersonic missile, something that the SR-71 did not do. Considering that it has been twenty years since the SR-71 has been retired, it's about time for *Lockheed* to sneak something out to Area 51 or thereabouts for testing. If there is one thing that this country does need is a high speed, high altitude, real time reconnaissance platform. *Black Swift* may be that answer. At least we do hope so.

The United States Military services needs to have the fastest real time reconnaissance it can get. The nature of the enemy that the U.S. has been fighting since the 9/11 attacks, is low, desperate and despicable. We also have the problems with North Korea, Iran, Afghanistan the many different facets of problems in the Mid-East and Ukraine, not to mention Africa and many other hot spots around the world. These adversaries will try anything at any time. The United States needs that "one-upmanship" that only real time surveillance and reconnaissance can give. The United States needs to maintain that upper hand at all times if the country will remain at the height of its military superiority.

Epilogue

Man or Machine?

We have explored the development of aerial reconnaissance in the United States. The question of this book has been Man or Machine? Who better handles the urgent and important job or aerial reconnaissance? What is the answer? Is there an answer? Do we depend on drones and surveillance, reconnaissance, hunter/killer machines that allows for our personnel to be miles away from a danger zone and yet allow them to pick the one target for the day? Or do we need a man in the cockpit of a well-honed aircraft that can deliver real time reconnaissance which can be forwarded to commanders on the ground almost instantly given the new technologies, and allow them to move to another location with speed and stealth. Drones are slow, they can be patient and wait for days, hours, weeks if need be to cover one target. Think about that: one target. While a fast moving aircraft can cover many areas at a high altitude with speed and stealth, covering a large ground swath that can give the order of battle against an enemy, or relay information on troop formation and movement, a bigger picture if you will. A reconnaissance satellite can't do that, as it must wait until it is in the right position high above the earth. Does the United States see far enough into the future to realize that one target does not the end of a confrontation make? The more information, the better. The faster it is delivered, the better. Should the Military and the intelligence community of the United States bank on drones for its most important job? Or should the Military invest heartily in filling that large hole the SR-71 left?

While drones do have their place in the military/intelligence structure, so does the fast, stealthy, forward seeing reconnaissance aircraft of the future, whether that is *Black Swift* or some other aircraft we don't yet know about. Just as the venerable B-52 Stratofortress has been the backbone of the USAF bombing fleet for some sixty years and she is still viable. The same attention should have been paid the manned reconnaissance aircraft program. We have lost something here, the ability for stealthy, real time reconnaissance. The United States needs to have that third leg to rely on. Satellites and drones are just not enough, not in today's world. Where and when will we see the next level for aerial reconnaissance. It has been a long time coming. Whether it is manned or unmanned, is still a vital question. One that remains to be answered either by technology or politics. However, we are still without an updated, reliable, stealthy, high altitude, Mach 5+ capable aircraft that can bring the information home . . . now . . . when it is needed.

Let's hope to see the SR-72 *"Black Swift"* or her progeny soon . . . hopefully very soon.

Bibliography

Mayday!
Eisenhower, Khrushchev and the U-2 Affair
1988, Harper Collins, NY
Michael Beschloss

For the President's Eyes Only
Secret Intelligence and the American Presidency from Washington to Bush
1995 Harper Collins, New York
Christopher Andrew

Deep Black
Space Espionage and National Security
1986, Random House, New York
William E. Burrows

Beyond the Wild Blue
A History of the U. S. Air Force
1947-1997
1997, St. Martin's Press New York,
Walter J. Boyne

At the Highest Levels: The Inside Story of the End of the Cold War
1993, Little, Brown, Boston Mass.
Michael R. Beschloss and Strobe Talbot

Black Lightning
The Legacy of the Lockheed Blackbirds
2017, Speaking Volumes Publications, Santa Fe, New Mexico
Jeannette Remak and Joseph Ventolo Jr.

A-12 Blackbird- Declassified
2001, Motorbooks International, MI.
Jeannette Remak and Joseph Ventolo Jr

The Puzzle Palace
1983, Penguin Books, New York
James Branford

The CIA and Overhead Reconnaissance U-2 and OXCART Programs 1954-1974
Central Intelligence Agency, Langley VA

The U-2s Intended Successor Project OXCART 1956-1968
Central Intelligence Agency, Langley VA.

United States Air Force History- An Annotated Bibliography
1971, Office of the Air Force History
Mary Ann Cresswell and Carl Berger

Lockheed SR-71 Secret Missions Exposed
1993 Osprey Aerospace UK
Paul Crickmore

Lockheed Blackbird- Beyond the Secret Missions
2004 (Revised edition) Osprey Publishing, UK
Paul Crickmore

Air War over South East Asia –Vol 3
1984, Signal Squadron Publications
Lou Drendel

Lockheed Aircraft since 1913,
1987, Naval Institute Press, MD
René J. Francillon

SR-71 Revealed-The inside Story
1996, Motorbooks Intl, MI
Richard H. Graham

The Wizards of Armageddon
1983, Stanford University Press, Stanford CA
Fred Kaplan

High Cold War-Strategic Air Reconnaissance and Electronic Intelligence War
1998, Haynes Publishing Somerset, England
Robert Jackson

Wings of the CIA, Histoire and Collections
1998, Paris France
Frédéric Lert

Lockheed Martin SR-71 Researcher's Handbook Vol II
Lockheed Martin

In Retrospect, The Tragedy and Lessons of Vietnam
1995, Times Books, NY
Robert S. McNamara with Brian VanDeMark

Lockheed Martin Skunkworks,
1995, Midland Publishing, Leicester, UK
Jay Millar

The CIA and the U-2 Program 1954-1974
1998, Center for Studies in Intelligence, CIA Washington D.C.
Gregory W. Pedlow and Donald E. Welzenbach

Dark Eagles, A History of Top Secret U.S. Aircraft Programs
1995, Presidio Press, Novato, Ca
Curtis Peebles

The Agency –The Rise and Fall of the CIA 1986,
Touchstone Press, Simon and Schuster, NY
John Ranelagh

Ideas, Concepts Doctrine Volume II--Basic Thinking in the USAF
1989, Air University Press, Maxwell AFB, Al.
Robert Frank Futrell

Encyclopedia of Espionage, Intelligence and Security Volume I A-E
2004, Gale Group—Thomas Learning
K. Lee Lerner and Brenda Wilmoth, Editors

Strategic Intelligence and National Security
1992 September
U.S. Army War College
Seeing the Enemy- Army, Air Force Aerial Reconnaissance Support to U.S, Army Operations in the Mediterranean in World War II
1998, University of Nebraska, Lenoke, Nebraska
David W. Densler, Major USAF

Piercing the Fog –Intelligence and Army Air Forces Operations in World War II
1996, Air Force History and Museum Washington D.C.
John F. Kries General Editor

Aerial Interdiction Air Power and Land Battles in Three American Wars
1994, Center of Air Force History Washington D.C.
Eduard Mark

Command of Observation Aviation: A Study in Control of Tactical Air Power
1956, Air University, Maxwell AFB, Nebraska
Robert Futrell

Unmanned Vehicles in the U.S. Armed Services: A Comparative Study of Weapon System Innovations
(PhD Dissertation)
2000, June - John Hopkins University, Washington D.C.
Thomas P. Ehrhard

Unmanned Aviation: A Brief history of Unmanned Aerial Vehicles
2004, American Institute of Aeronautics and Astronautics (AIAA)
Laurence R. Newcome

Air Warfare in the Missile Age
2002, Smithsonian Institution Press, Washington D.C.
Lon O. Nordeen

Lighting Bugs and Other Reconnaissance Drones:
the "Can-Do" Story of
Ryan's "Unmanned Spy Planes"
1982, Aero Publishers, California
William Wagner

Bush at War
2002, Simon and Schuster New York
Bob Woodward

Attack of the Drones- A History of Unmanned Aerial Combat
2004, Zenith Press, MI.
Bill Yenne

CORONA America's First Satellite Program
CIA Cold War Records
1995, Center for Study of Intelligence, CIA Washington D.C.
Kevin C. Ruffner, Editor

Obama's Killer Drones
June 25, 2016
CounterPunch
Jeanne Mirer and Marjorie Cohn

Jeannette Remak

The Obama Administration's Drone-Strike Dissembling
Debunking John Brennan's claim that "the president
requires near certainty of no collateral damage"
to allow a drone-killing to go forward
The Atlantic Magazine (POLITICS)
March 14, 2016
Conor Friedersdorf

Obama's Legacy: Drone wars
The Blog- HUFF Post
March 27, 2013
Bob Burnett

Early Cold War Flights
Symposium—Volume 1- Memoirs
2003, Office of the Historian—National Reconnaissance Office
R. Cargill Hall and Clayton D. Laurie - Editors

Aerial Reconnaissance
The 10th Photo Recon Group in World War II
1981 Aero Publishers, Fallbrook CA.
Tom Ivie

INDEX

100th Strategic Reconnaissance Wing, 346
10th, 145
10th Photographic Reconnaissance Group, 92
1110th Air Support Group, 163
1110th ASG, 167, 169
155th Night Reconnaissance Squadron, 94
204th Photo-mapping, 129
343rd SRW, 140
4025 Strategic Reconnaissance Squad, 146
4025th SRS, 147
4080th Strategic Reconnaissance Wing, 146
456th TCW, 167
456th Troop Carrier Wing, 165
66th Tactical Reconnaissance Wing, 145
799th Air Base Group, 374

A

A-12 Blackbird, 7, 6, 116, 121, 236, 261, 268, 281, 305, 348, 389
A-20 Havoc, 80, 84
Abe Karem, 358, 362, 365, 366, 370, 371, 373
Air Corp Act of 1926, 39
Air Corp Act of 1930, 40
Albatross, 358, 359
Amelia Earhart, 71
America First society, 64
American Volunteer Group, 60
Andrew Goodpaster, 211
AQM-34, 346, 347
AQM-34L, 344, 347
AQM-34P, 347
AQM-34Q, 347
AQM-91, 345
Arad-234, 86
Area 51, 257, 260, 272, 275, 277, 278, 279, 280, 281, 282, 283, 286, 289, 295, 310, 313, 326, 349, 350, 361, 374, 385
Art of War, 3, 9

Atlas ICBM, 171
Atomic Energy Commission, 121, 275

B

B-18 bombers, 87
B-24 Liberator, 88, 101, 342
B-29 Superfortress, 84, 85, 88, 162
B-314 "California Clipper", 59
B-57 Canberra, 144, 145, 190
B-58 Hustler, 271
Bald Eagle, 181, 185
Bell Aircraft, 146, 184
Bill Park, 350, 351
Billy Mitchell, 34, 36, 38, 42, 50, 71
Black Knight, 146
Black Shield, 231, 291, 294
Black Swift, 384, 385, 386, 387
BLIND BAT, 303, 304
BLUE BOOK" Project, 166
Bock's Car, 122
Boeing Compass Cope B, 345

C

C-119F Boxcar, 165
CADET, 341
CAMCO, 60
Captain Hook, 352, 353, 354
Carpet, 88
Central Aircraft Manufacturing Company, 60
Central Intelligence Agency, 7, 103, 104, 106, 107, 117, 197, 389
Chennault, 57, 58, 59, 60, 61
Chiang Kai Shek, 59, 60
Civil War, 1, 4, 10, 11, 17, 18, 19, 95, 148, 169
CL-282, 181, 182, 184, 185, 190, 191, 192, 193
CL-400, 268
Claire Chennault, 57, 59
Clarence Johnson, 187

Constance Babington Smith, 96
CORONA satellite, 121, 175, 265, 284
Cuban Missile Crisis, 118, 230, 234, 241, 250
CULVER PQ-14, 341
Culver PQ-8, 341
Curtis LeMay, 182
Curtiss, 40, 59, 75, 341

D

D-21, 289, 311, 348, 349, 350, 351, 352, 353, 354, 358
DARPA, 7, 358, 359, 361, 362, 363, 372, 384
Detachment 1, 168, 303, 316, 318
DH-4 De-Haviland, 36
Discoverer, 111, 177, 251
Discoverer satellite, 177
Doolittle Raid, 89
Dornier DO 17, 5
Douglas Aircraft, 175, 262, 301, 302
Douglas DC-3 transport, 87

E

Earhart, 71
Eastman Kodak, 7, 14, 35, 46, 110, 173, 175, 178, 287
EC-121, 303, 348
ECM, 136, 147, 213, 247, 291, 292, 311, 312, 333
Edwin Land, 142, 191, 203, 236, 261, 283
Eisenhower, 6, 149, 150, 151, 171, 172, 174, 181, 183, 186, 187, 188, 191, 192, 193, 197, 198, 203, 208, 209, 210, 211, 217, 218, 219, 220, 229, 233, 238, 254, 277, 284, 293, 388
ELINT, 108, 119, 136, 139, 145, 146, 156, 157, 158, 181, 189, 221, 230, 303, 312, 347
Elliott Roosevelt, 81
Enola Gay, 122, 123
Enterprise, 17, 18, 20, 301, 306, 307

F

F-2 Banshees, 133
F-3 (A-20J Havoc), 94
F-4, 80, 82, 84, 85
F-5, 82, 84, 92, 93
F-6, 85, 90
F-9, 81, 84
Fairchild K-3 camera, 45
FALCONER, 343
FERRET, 138
Fifth Air Force, 307
First Aero Squadron, 29, 30, 31
Flying Tigers, 57, 59, 60
Focke-Wulf 190, 87
FockeWulf-FW-189, 86
Folmer–Schwing camera, 35
Francis Gary Powers, 6, 208, 212, 222, 224, 226, 227

G

General Atomics, 362, 364, 365, 366, 367, 368, 369, 370, 371, 372
General Electric J-73, 184, 198
General Henry "Hap" Arnold, 64, 70, 71
General Operational Requirement, 146, 171
GENETRIX, 148, 149, 150, 151, 152, 206
George B. McClellan, 95
George Eastman, 14
George Goddard, 34, 43, 284
GIANT REACH, 321, 322, 323
GLOBAL HAWK, 372
GNAT 750, 364, 365, 366, 368, 369
GOR#53-WC-16507, 146
GRAND SLAM, 211, 212, 213, 215
Gulf of Tonkin, 255, 301, 346
Gulf of Tonkin resolution, 255
GUSTO, 261, 264, 268, 269, 270, 274

H

Harry Truman, 105, 127
HAVE DOUGHNUT, 361
HE-111 bomber, 64
Henry L. Simpson, 52
Herbert O. Yardley, 52

Hickam, 74, 75
Howard Hughes, 82, 83
HYCON, 288

I

ICBM, 178, 188, 209, 234, 239, 240
Imagery Analysis, 111, 233

J

Jack Ledford, 247
James Baker, 114, 284
James Killian, 183, 203, 236, 284
John F. Kennedy, 234, 237, 238, 247, 282, 292
John J. Pershing, 10, 31
JOINT STARS, 102
Junkers JU-87 Stuka dive bomber, 64

K

Kaiten, 74
Karem, 358, 359, 362, 363, 364, 365, 366, 371, 372, 373
Karl Polifka, 80, 81
KC-135, 241, 291, 292, 329
Kelly Johnson, 6, 110, 169, 181, 182, 183, 184, 185, 186, 187, 191, 193, 198, 200, 206, 218, 224, 228, 239, 259, 260, 261, 265, 266, 268, 269, 275, 280, 282, 318, 326, 331, 348, 349, 352, 353, 354, 358, 383
Kennedy, 226, 238, 239, 242, 243, 244, 248, 293, 342
KEYHOLE, 6, 177
KH11, 112
KINGFISH, 270, 271
Kodachrome, 46
KODAK, 16

L

L-17, 134
L-5Gs, 134
LANDSAT, 111

Lavochkin LA-9, 125
Leo Geary, 227, 228, 257
Lindbergh, 63, 64, 65
Lou Schalk, 281, 282
Louis Jacques Daguerre, 13
Luftwaffe, 62, 64, 65, 66, 80, 86, 87, 91, 113
Lundahl, 111, 233, 249

M

M-113 flash cartridge, 131
M-21, 348, 349, 351, 352
Madame Chiang, 59
MAGIC, 69, 79, 80
Martin Aircraft Company, 145, 146, 147
Mason M. Patrick, 40
Messerschmitt ME-109G, 86
MIDAS, 173, 176
MiG 15, 108, 125, 131
Mike Relja, 7, 326, 330, 331
MOBY DICK PROJECT, 156
MOHAWK missions, 298
Montgolfier brothers, 4, 148
MOSQUITO ABLE, 134
MOSQUITO BAKER, 134
MOSQUITO HOW, 134
MOSQUITO MELLOW, 134
MOSQUITO missions, 133
MQ-1 Predator, 377
MQ-1B Predator, 374, 375
MQ-9, 337, 374, 377
MQM-105, 363, 367
MQM-33, 343
MX-1594, 157

N

Nakajima Type 97, 58
NAPRW, 82
National Intelligence Estimates, 120
National Security Act, 103, 104, 107
NC2-2, 341
NICE GIRL, 313, 314
NIE, 120
Night Reconnaissance, 94
Northrop F-15 Reporter, 82

Northwest African Photographic
   Reconnaissance Wing, 82

O

Operation CAROUSEL, 294
OPERATION GRAND SLAM, 210
Operation Husky, 82
Operation LONG GREEN, 243
Operation Overflight, 212, 215, 228
Operation TOPPER, 253
Orville, 21
OSS, 105, 106, 107
OXCART, 6, 119, 121, 256, 257, 261,
   265, 274, 275, 276, 278, 279, 281,
   282, 286, 288, 289, 293, 305, 307,
   308, 310, 311, 312, 315, 389
Ozzie Ritland, 175, 274, 275

P

P2V-5 Neptune, 144
P-38, 81, 84, 85, 88, 90, 92, 183
P-40C, 60
P4M-Mercator, 144
P-51 Mustang, 85, 90, 130
Pancho Villa, 4, 30
Patrick, 50
PBY Catalina, 100
PBY-1, 342
Pearl Harbor, 68, 69, 71, 72, 74, 77, 87,
   88, 183, 188
Perkin-Elmer, 284, 285
Pershing, 10, 31, 39, 47
Photo Interpreter, 110, 116, 117, 236
photogrammetry, 40
PIED PIPER, 172
Pratt and Whitney, 83, 146, 182, 183,
   184, 185, 191, 196, 212, 248, 252,
   256, 257, 268, 269, 273, 283
PREDATOR, 355, 362, 363, 365, 368,
   369, 370, 371, 372, 373
President Truman, 103, 105, 108, 110,
   122, 124, 157
PROJECT WHALE TALE, 259

Q

Q-12, 349

R

RA-5C Vigilante, 298, 299
Radiometric resolution, 112
RADIOPLANE, 341, 342
Radioplane Company, 340
RAINBOW 4, 69, 70
Ralph A. Ofstie, 56
RAND Corporation, 149, 157, 162, 262
Ravens, 140
RB-17, 155
RB-26, 131
RB-66, 300, 302
Reginald Denny, 340, 342
Republic X-12, 82
RF-101 Voodoo, 144, 145
RF-80, 129, 131, 132, 135
RF-84 Thunderjet, 131
RF-86A, 131
Richard Bissell, 173, 186, 193, 196, 197,
   203, 210, 211, 217, 218, 229, 236,
   265, 270, 274, 275, 353
Rudolph Abel, 223
Ryan FIREBEE, 293, 343
RYAN Model, 343

S

SAMOS, 173
Sentry Optical Reconnaissance Program,
   173
Sergeant A.V. Laws, 24
Sgt. Laws, 25, 26, 32
Sidney Cotton, 96, 98
SIGINT, 52, 69, 78, 79, 105, 146, 147,
signal intelligence, 69, 77, 105
SILVER JAVELIN, 291, 293
SKYHOOK, 148, 152, 153, 154, 155,
   156, 162, 170
SKYLARK, 290, 291, 293
Spectral resolution, 112
SR-71, 7, 1, 2, 6, 114, 119, 290, 310, 311,
   312, 313, 314, 315, 316, 317, 318,
   319, 320, 321, 322, 323, 324, 325,

326, 328, 329, 331, 332, 333, 334, 335, 337, 382, 383, 385, 386, 389, 390, 391
SR-72, 322, 326, 382, 383, 384, 387
Strategic Library Bombing Encyclopedia, 116
SUNTAN, 268

T

T-6, 129, 134
T-6 Trainer, 134
Thaddeus Lowe, 17, 19

U

U-2 Dragon Lady, 110, 115, 175, 202, 259, 266
UCAVs, 119
ULTRA, 79, 80
United States Army Signal Corp, 30
USAEC, 121
USAF's Strategic Library Bombing Encyclopedia, 116
USS PUEBLO, 119, 291, 305

V

VACANT SEAS, 71
VIDICON, 172

VMD-54, 101
VMJ-1, 133
VQ-1 Squadron, 144

W

WB-29, 123
Wheeler, 74, 75, 76
Wilbur Wright, 22
William J. Donovan, 105
Woodrow Wilson, 32, 46
Wright Brothers, 20, 21, 22
WS-117L, 171, 172, 173, 174
WS-46L, 168, 169
WS-46L balloons, 168

X

XF-11, 82
XXI Bomber Command, 88, 89

Y

Yokota, Japan, 116, 135, 139, 146, 307
Yom Kippur War, 319

Z

Zeppelin, 5

On Sale Now!

To Slip the Surly Bonds
by
Jeannette Remak

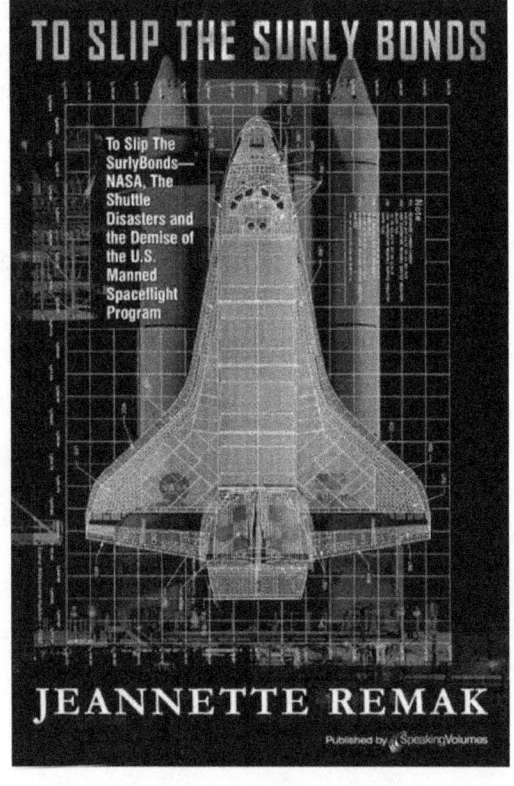

**For more information
visit:** www.SpeakingVolumes.us

On Sale Now!

Black Lightning:
The Legacy of the Lockheed Blackbirds
by
Jeannette Remak and Joseph Ventolo Jr.

**For more information
visit:** www.SpeakingVolumes.us

Sign up for free and bargain books

Join the Speaking Volumes mailing list

Text
ILOVEBOOKS
to 22828 to get started.

Message and data rates may apply.

www.ingramcontent.com/pod-product-compliance
Lightning Source LLC
Chambersburg PA
CBHW022057150426
43195CB00008B/170